THE SAYINGS OF JESUS

IN THE PSEUDO-CLEMENTINE HOMILIES

THE SAYINGS OF JESUS

IN THE PSEUDO-CLEMENTINE HOMILIES

by

Leslie Lee Kline

Published by

SOCIETY OF BIBLICAL LITERATURE

and

SCHOLARS' PRESS

DISSERTATION SERIES, NUMBER 14

1975

Distributed by

SCHOLARS' PRESS
University of Montana
Missoula, Montana   59801

THE SAYINGS OF JESUS IN THE PSEUDO-CLEMENTINE HOMILIES

by

Leslie Lee Kline
Harvard University
Cambridge, Massachusetts 02138

Ph.D., 1971   Adviser:
Harvard University   Helmut Köster

Library of Congress Catalog Card Number: 75-1645

ISBN: 0-88414-050-4

Printed in the United States of America
Printing Department
University of Montana
Missoula, Montana 59801

FOREWORD

I would like to express my special appreciation
to Professor Helmut Köster without whose inspiration
and valuable insights this thesis would have been much
less than it is. My thanks also to Professors John
Strugnell and Dieter Georgi for their encouragement
and helpful suggestions. Finally, but not least, I
want to thank my wife Louise -- who typed the original
draft of this thesis that was not at all easy to type --
for her help, patience, and much encouragement; my
daughters Lesley and Becky, for their patience and
understanding; and Camilla Ream -- who amidst a very
busy schedule typed the draft for publication in the
Society of Biblical Literature Dissertation Series --
for a job well done.

CHAPTER I

INTRODUCTION

The History of Research

The history of research into the Pseudo-Clementines as a
whole has been surveyed by Georg Strecker.[1] The focus of the
present chapter is only on those scholars who have dealt directly
with the question of gospel material or sayings of Jesus in the
Pseudo-Clementines.[2]

We begin with the work of K. A. Credner.[3] As his predeces-
sors on the subject he mentions the following:[4] J. Mill who considered the Pseudo-Clementines to be dependent upon the canonical
gospels but with expansions from the Gospel of the Ebionites[5];
A. Neander who thought the gospel underlying the Homilies (=H)
was a recension of the Gospel according to the Hebrews[6]; and
Orelli who saw in the quotations in H a use of our four gospels
but with the addition of apocryphal traditions from "the ancients"
or which he (the Homilist) himself had composed.[7] Credner himself compiled a list of the sayings of Jesus in H -- which he
noted were "older and more original" than the Recognitions (=R)
-- and compared them to the canonical gospels and citations in
the fathers. He noted two major things about the character of

---

[1]Das Judenchristentum in den Pseudoklementinen (TU 70; 1958),
pp. 1-34. (Hereafter = Judenchristentum.)

[2]A survey of the work done to 1878 is found in H. M. van
Nes, Het Nieue Testament in de Clementinen (1887), pp. 1-11.

[3]Beiträge zur Einleitung in die biblischen Schriften, I
(1832), pp. 268-436 (and esp. pp. 268-351). (Hereafter =
Beiträge.)

[4]Ibid., pp. 283-84.

[5]Novum Testamentum Graecum, ed. Kuster (1723), Prol., p. 64.

[6]Genetische Entwickelung der vornehmsten gnostischen Systeme
(1818), pp. 418-19.

[7]Selecta patr. eccles. capp. (1821), p. 22.

the sayings in H: (1) they were closely connected with the Gospel
of Matthew (and secondarily with Luke) but with frequent variations; and (2) they often were parallel with the sayings of Jesus
in Justin. This latter relationship was subsequently to become
the central nexus of the research on the question in the writers
who followed Credner. Credner's conclusion was that the same
apocryphal gospel underlay both H and Justin, a gospel which he
identified with the Gospel of Peter and the Gospel of the Ebionites (or Nazoreans) attested later by Epiphanius (Pan. 30), and
which he assumed to be the same as the Gospel of the Hebrews. He
also thought it underlay Tatian's Diatessaron. But he recognized
that it was not the same as the Preaching of Peter mentioned in
the fathers. In an appendix on the gospel quotations in R, he
primarily noted that R had less of them than H and shows a greater
tendency toward agreement with the canonical texts.[8]

Credner was apparently opposed in an article by Frank.[9]
Frank emphasized the frequent agreement of the quotations in the
Homilies with the canonical gospels. His conclusions were that
the canonical gospels (Matthew and Luke for the most part, but
also John) had been used, that H had quoted them even more
freely than Justin, and that an uncanonical gospel had also been
used but it could only have been a later reworking of Matthew and
Luke.

In his work on "the apostolic memoirs of Justin Martyr"
Karl Semisch devoted a section to the issue of the "gospel quotations" in the Pseudo-Clementines.[10] In short order he argued for
a free use of all four canonical gospels and saw little likelihood that an extracanonical gospel such as the Gospel of the
Hebrews had been used. The sayings which had no parallel in the
canonical gospels he explained as creations from the oral

---

[8] Beiträge, pp. 415-36.

[9] "Die evangelischen Citate in den clementinischen Homilien,"
Studien der evangelischen Geistlichkeit Würtembergs 19 (1847),
144-95. I have not had access to this article. It is briefly
discussed by A. Hilgenfeld, Kritische Untersuchungen über die
Evangelien Justins, der clementinischen Homilien und Marcions
(1850), p. 307 (hereafter = Krit. Untersuchungen); cf. also G.
Uhlhorn, Die Homilien und Recognitionen des Clemens Romanus
(1854), p. 113, and Nes, Het Nieue Testament, pp. 2-3.

[10] Die apostolischen Denkwürdigkeiten des Märtyrers Justinus
(1848), pp. 356-64.

tradition or free constructions of the author of H himself.

Adolf Hilgenfeld followed with two major works. In the
first he dealt with the relationship of H and R -- placing R
before H -- and with the question of their sources.[11] He viewed
R not as a unity but as a compilation of sources.[12] In the
second work he devoted most of his attention to the gospel
sources of Justin Martyr.[13] He concluded, following Credner's
lead, that Justin had made use of the Gospel of Peter, the Grundschrift of the Gospel of Mark, a reordered recension of the Gospel
of Matthew, the Gospel of Luke, perhaps the Protevangelium Jacobi,
and a peculiar passion narrative -- the Acta Pilati.[14]

In the case of the H he concluded that H had primarily used
the same Gospel of Peter that Justin had used, perhaps with a few
further developments, as well as Matthew and perhaps also Luke.
In neither the case of Justin or H had the Gospel of John been
used.[15] But Hilgenfeld was then left with the problem of R which
clearly had the form of gospel sayings that were posterior to
those in H, usually more reconciled to the canonical text. How
was this to be explained vis-à-vis his theory of the priority of
R? Hilgenfeld had to assume that R had undergone "corrections"
of its gospel texts within its own textual history and that
originally it had used gospels which were not identical with the

---

[11]Die clementinischen Recognitionen und Homilien, nach ihrem
Ursprung und Inhalt (1848), pp. 19-25. At this point the debate
was being carried on with the assumption that either H or R was
directly dependent on the other. A common Grundschrift behind
both had not been suggested. Adolf Schliemann (Die Clementinen
nebst den verwandten Schriften und der Ebionitismus [1844]) had
argued for the priority of H and Hilgenfeld for R on the basis
of which contained the earlier form or the more "Jewish" form of
certain viewpoints (such as the doctrine of the True Prophet).
The Grundschrift hypothesis of Waitz (see infra), however, made
it possible to understand how sometimes H and sometimes R might
better preserve the earlier form of certain ideas.

[12]They are: the "Kerygmen des Petrus" (R 1.27-72; cf.
R 3.75) which were originally bound with the Epistula Petri and
the Contestatio and which later underwent an anti-Basilidian
revision (mostly in R 2 and 3); the Περίοδοι Πέτρου (R 4-7), and
the Ἀναγνωρισμοὶ Κλήμεντος (R 8-10).

[13]Krit. Untersuchungen (see n. 9).

[14]Ibid., p. 304.

[15]Ibid., p. 388.

4

canonical gospels.[16]   But it was Hilgenfeld's own theory of the
priority of R that was really being called into question.

  Gerhard Uhlhorn followed by examining the gospel material in
the Pseudo-Clementines in a sort of running dialogue with Hilgenfeld's conclusions.[17]   He came out opposite Hilgenfeld in the
following results: (1) H had used the canonical Mark and John in
addition to Matthew and Luke; (2) an uncanonical gospel had been
used as Hilgenfeld believed, but it was a "Hebrew Gospel" of
secondary character, derived from the canonical gospels, not
something behind them; and (3) an examination of the sayings in
H and R argue for the priority of H to R.[18]

  Johannes Lehmann expanded on this last point in order to
bolster his case that R 1-3 and R 4-10 were from different
authors.[19]   In addition he, like Hilgenfeld, saw an Ebionite
"Kerygmen des Petrus" underlying R 1-3.

  At this point we may leave the German scene for a while and
take note, first, of Britain's William Sanday.[20]   His analysis
attempted to build a case for the use of the canonical synoptic
gospels, Matthew, Luke and even Mark, as the sources of the sayings in H. (The question of the use of the Gospel of John was
not even taken up for some unknown reason.) However the phenomenon of mixed quotations (especially from Matthew and Luke) led

---

[16]Cf. ibid., pp. 370-77.

[17]See n. 9. The relevant section is pp. 111-50.

[18]Uhlhorn noted three classes of quotations in R when
compared to H (pp. 137-50): (1) those which appeared in similar
connections in H and R, (2) those which were the same saying
but in different connections in H and R, and (3) those which
were alone: group I showed more harmonizing trend toward the
canonical text in R and variation from it in H; group II showed
that the sayings in R had almost precise canonical form; and group
III exhibited similar deviations in R from the canonical text
as H often exhibited but with the added observation that most of
these occur in R 1-3 (Peter's dialogue with Simon). The first
two were strong arguments against Hilgenfeld, and Uhlhorn felt
certain that even group III pointed toward the priority of H
over R although he did not know really what to make of this last
group. But again it is the Grundschrift (= G) hypothesis that
might explain group III: they go back to G; H has dropped them,
while R preserves them.

[19]Die Clementinischen Schriften (1869), pp. 118-41.

[20]The Gospels in the Second Century (1876), pp. 161-87.

Sanday to propose the alternative possibility that H (like Justin) had either quoted the canonical gospels very freely or had used a gospel harmony made from the synoptic gospels (and others?). In addition he noted that the noncanonical quotations may have come from such a harmony; at least he felt certain that H had drawn upon apocryphal sources, perhaps oral, but mainly written.

In 1887 a Dutch writer, H. M. van Nes, surveyed the litera- ture on the subject to date and did his own analysis of each quotation of saying.[21] His results were as follows:[22] the canonical synoptic gospels had been used, especially Matthew and Luke. But the variant wording and the mixing of texts demanded the acceptance of a special source which often showed remarkable agreements with Justin but also with Barnabas, 2 Clement, Didache, Clement of Alexandria, and Origen. This source could not be older than the synoptic gospels but must be secondary to Matthew and Luke and even Mark. Nes argued that the divergence in word- ing of Matt. 19:16-18 in H from that in the Gospel of the Hebrews precluded the latter from being that special source. His con- jecture was that it was the Gospel according to the Egyptians. He noted, however, that the question of Justin's special gospel source had not yet received a satisfactory answer. On the question of the use of the Gospel of John in H Nes suggested that either a special gospel source had been used but in a different recension from our text of it.

From Credner to Nes one may speak of an era in the history of research into the Pseudo-Clementines as a whole and into the question of the sayings of Jesus in them. It was an era that had not yet discovered that H and R went back to a common Grund- schrift but assumed that one was directly dependent on the other. Neither had it yet learned to distinguish clearly enough the sources of the Pseudo-Clementines, especially within H, along with their dates or periods and areas, and to attempt to corre- late the sayings of Jesus or the gospel material with the sources thus defined. It remained for Hans Waitz to open the way into a new era of research in this regard. From 1904-1940 Waitz

---

[21]See note 2. The Homilies are considered as the primary evidence with parallel forms in R simply noted within the con- text of discussing the H passage.

[22]Ibid., pp. 97-100.

6

contributed several major works on the Pseudo-Clementines and
reviewed his results vis-à-vis the other major works that appeared
during this period. He began with the publication of his book on
the Pseudo-Clementines in 1904.[23] It was a detailed analysis of
the sources of H and R with their dates and places of origin.
His results:[24] (1) Behind H and R lies a Grundschrift (= G)
which was composed about 220-230 in Rome. (2) Its sources were
a Kerygmata Petrou (= KP) (which was reconstructed primarily out
of R 1-3 and H 2-3, 16-20), Bardesanes' Peri Heimarmenēs,
Dialogues between Clement and Appion, and a Praxeis Petrou (= PP).
The last three of these were dated around the turn of the second
to third centuries. The KP source, however, is the most important for our purposes. Waitz saw it as the secret writing of a
Gnostic, Jewish-Christian sect of the early second century,
written c. A.D. 135 in Caesarea and containing seven books of the
"sermons of Peter" (against Paul!). It then underwent an anti-
Marcionite revision in which it was expanded to ten books during
the last quarter of the century. (3) The Homilies are a rear-
rangement and expansion of the Grundschrift, although with a
little omission, by an Arian of Syria in the post-Nicean period.
(4) The Recognitions are an independent reworking of the Grundschrift by a Eunomian of Antioch in Syria in the latter part of
the fourth century.

With this division of the sources of the Pseudo-Clementines
Waitz attempted to correlate both the OT and NT quotations in H
and R.[25] At this point it may suffice to note only his results
regarding the KP source.[26] The original KP contained quotations
which belong to synoptic-like gospels, never quoted other "NT
books," never shows an acquaintance with the Gospel of John,
bears no direct relation to the gospel quotations of Justin,
never quoted words found only in Mark or Luke, never quoted the
canonical gospels verbatim, included uncanonical sayings, and
therefore drew upon a gospel source related to the Gospel of the
Hebrews, the Ebionite Gospel, and the Gospel of Peter. The

---

[23]Die Pseudoklementinen, Homilien und Rekognitionen (TU 25,4;
1904). (Hereafter = Pseudoklementinen.)

[24]Ibid., pp. 366-75.

[25]Ibid., pp. 259-366.

[26]Ibid., pp. 361-64.

anti-Marcionite reworking of KP, according to Waitz, bore many of
the same marks with two notable additions: (1) the use of Luke
for certain and possibly also of Mark, and (2) the paralleling of
many sayings with the form found in Justin.

In a subsequent article Waitz attempted to identify this
"gospel source" of KP more closely.[27] In doing so he entered the
complex debate about Jewish Christian gospels, engaging in a
dialogue especially with the work of Alfred Schmidtke.[28] Waitz's
identification of the source was that it was the Gospel of the
Twelve Apostles or the Ebionite Gospel, to be distinguished from
the Nazorean Gospel and the Gospel of the Hebrews (against
Schmidtke's identification of the Ebionite Gospel and the Hebrew
Gospel). This Ebionite Gospel, Waitz believed, was that referred
to by Origen[29] and Jerome[30] as the Gospel of the Twelve Apostles.
It was the gospel of a group of Jewish Christians in Trans-Jordan
after A.D. 70, written in Greek, which had used a Matthean type
gospel as well as other traditions. It was variously referred to
as εὐαγγέλιον καθ᾽ Ἑβραίους or Ἐβραϊκόν, the Ebionite Gospel
(because of the application of "Ebionite" to [heretical] Jewish
Christians), and the Gospel of the Twelve Apostles (who were
claimed as its authority).

In a still later article in which Waitz reviewed the works
of W. Heintze[31] and Carl Schmidt[32] the question of the source of
the gospel quotations in the anti-Marcionite reworking of KP was

---

[27]"Das Evangelium der zwölf Apostel," ZNW 13 (1912), 338-
48; continued in ZNW 14 (1913), 38-64, 117-32. Cf. also his
article on "Ebionäerevangelium oder Evangelium der Zwölf," in
E. Hennecke (ed.), Neutestamentliche Apokryphen, 2nd ed. (1924),
pp. 39-48.

[28]Neue Fragmente und Untersuchungen zu den juden-christlichen
Evangelien (TU 37,1; 1911).

[29]Hom. in Luke 1 (Rauer 9.4-5): τὸ ἐπιγεγραμμένον τὸν
Δώδεκα εὐαγγέλιον.

[30]Dial. c. Pelag. 3.2 (MPL 23.597): "In Evangelio juxta
Hebraeos . . . secundum Apostolos, . . . "

[31]Der Klemensroman und seine griechischen Quellen
(TU 40,2; 1914).

[32]Studien zu den Pseudo-Clementinen (TU 46,1; 1926).

taken up.[33] His solution for the phenomenon of the forms of
sayings of Jesus which agree with those in Justin against the
canonical gospels is that the anti-Marcionite reworking of KP
had used as a source Justin's Syntagma adversus Marcionem (πρὸς
Μαρκίωνα).[34]

Bypassing some significant works on the Pseudo-Clementines
and their sources during this period[35] one comes to the work of
H. J. Schoeps which bears directly on our problem.[36] Schoeps
builds upon the source analysis of Waitz. But he is not convinced by Waitz's early dating of KP shortly after A.D. 135 nor
of his hypothesis of a subsequent anti-Marcionite reworking of
this source after 160. Instead Schoeps wants to think of the KP
author himself as a compiler who in the period after 160 composed his work from a number of older sources or traditions. He
identifies the following sources for KP: (1) an anti-Marcionite
source, perhaps Justin's Syntagma adv. Marc. as Waitz had suggested, (2) the lost Ὑπομνήματα of Symmachus, supposed to be a
commentary on the Ebionite Gospel, (3) an Ebionite, anti-Pauline
oriented Acta Apostolorum or fragment of a Jewish Christian
Acts of the Apostles, and (4) an old Jewish Book of Adam.[37] In
an excursus Schoeps makes his case for the second of these
sources.[38] He thinks that the quotations in KP with their

---

[33]"Die Pseudoklementinen und ihre Quellenschriften," ZNW 28
(1929), 241-72.

[34]Ibid., pp. 245-46. Actually Waitz had already suggested
this solution in his 1904 book, pp. 164-67. A critique of Waitz
will be taken up in the concluding chapter.

[35]Oscar Cullmann, Le problème littéraire et historique du
roman Pseudo-Clémentin (1930); Waitz, "Pseudoklementinische
Probleme," ZKG 50 (1931), 186-94; Eduard Schwartz, "Unzeitgemässe
Beobachtungen zu den Clementinen," ZNW 31 (1932), 155-99; Waitz,
"Neues zur Text- und Literakritik der Pseudoklementinen?" ZKG 52
(1933), 305-18; J. B. Thomas, "Les Ebionites baptistes," RHE 30
(1934), 247-96; Le mouvement baptiste en Palestine et Syrie (1935);
Bernhard Rehm, "Zur Entstehung der pseudoclementinischen Schriften," ZNW 37 (1938), 77-184 (cf. also his article "Clemens
Romans II," in RAC 3 (1957), 197-206); Waitz, "Die Lösung des
pseudo-clementinischen Problems?" ZKG 59 (1940), 304-41.

[36]Theologie und Geschichte des Judenchristentums (1949)
(hereafter = Theologie); cf. also his Aus frühchristlicher Zeit
(1950).

[37]Theologie, p. 54.

[38]IV, pp. 366-80.

Ebionite "twists" reveal little about the literary problem of
Jewish Christian gospels but contribute more to the theological
problem of Ebionite exegesis of their own gospel text. In his
attempt to identify this "commentary" source Schoeps conjectures
Symmachus as its author and suggests its identification with
Symmachus' Ὑπομνήματα mentioned by Eusebius[39] and the "commenta-
ries" of Symmachus mentioned by Jerome.[40]

Finally <u>Georg Strecker</u> has devoted a chapter of his work to
the "scripture quotations" (OT and NT) in the Pseudo-Clementines.[41] He too argues for the existence of a KP source but
dates it about 200. He sees in the gospel quotations in the
Pseudo-Clementines the use of all four canonical gospels as well
as the use of other parts of the NT. The phenomena of deviations
from the canonical text and of mixed texts is solved frequently
by asserting that the author is quoting texts from memory. The
use by H of non-canonical "texts" is recognized but with no conclusion as to their source(s).[42] But Strecker is certain that no
Jewish Christian gospel has been quoted in the Pseudo-Clementines.
He discounts any direct dependence of H on Justin.[43] Therefore
the quotations in the Pseudo-Clementines provide no real basis
for positive results regarding literary sources or layers within
the Pseudo-Clementines. But Strecker does not adequately come to
terms with the variations and especially with the recurrence of
sayings which have close parallels with those in Justin and/or
other fathers but which deviate from the canonical text(s). This
is especially important if the sayings reveal harmonistic
features.

---

[39]EH 6.17.1. (Schwartz 2,2.556): καὶ ὑπομνήματα δὲ τοῦ
Συμμάχου εἰς ἔτι ἐν οἷς δοκεῖ πρὸς τὸ κατὰ Ματθαῖον ἀποτεινόμενος
εὐαγγέλιον τὴν δεδηλωμένην αἵρεσιν κρατύνειν.

[40]De vir. ill. 54 (Richardson, TU 14,1, p. 33,3-5): Symmachus "qui in Evangelium quoque κατὰ Ματθαῖον scripsit commen-
tarios, de quo et suam dogma adfirmare conatur."

[41]Judenchristentum, pp. 117-36.

[42]Ibid., p. 136: "Ob diese auf eine gemeinsame, schriftlich
fixierte Quelle zurückgehen oder aus mehreren Vorlagen zusammen-
getragen wurden oder aber zum Teil aus der mündlichen Tradition
stammen, lässt sich nicht entscheiden."

[43]Ibid., p. 133 and n. 1.

A more convincing way to proceed has been paved by the work of Helmut Köster on the apostolic fathers[44] and that of A. J. Bellinzoni, Jr. on Justin Martyr.[45] Köster's research on the formative period of the gospel tradition (that of the apostolic fathers) found that the apostolic fathers had depended on both written and oral sources or traditions in a period in which the "four gospels" had not yet been so defined nor "canonized." His concern was to trace both the sources -- "canonical" gospels, "apocryphal" gospels or oral tradition -- as well as the form critical and "history of tradition" motives of the sayings. Bellinzoni, applying this methodology to an analysis of the sayings in Justin, rightly noted the need to distinguish narrative from sayings' material. For form criticism has taught us that there are quite different laws of transmission in the two cases.[46] He concluded that for the sayings of Jesus Justin had used more than one source and that his sources were usually written. The sources were: (1) the canonical synoptic gospels (but never Mark alone and never John at all), (2) some kind of post-synoptic harmony, and (3) traditional sources, such as liturgical texts or early Christian handbooks known in similar form to other fathers in the early church. He concludes that Justin was probably not dependent on one or more extra-canonical gospels.

In my study I propose to examine the different sayings of Jesus primarily in H,[47] only secondarily in R, comparing them with the canonical gospels, Justin, and other early fathers in order: (1) to determine their sources and tendencies in H, (2) to attempt to relate these findings to the different sources that make up H, and (3) to relate these findings to the question of

---

[44]Synoptische Überlieferung bei den Apostolischen Vätern (TU 65; 1957). (Hereafter = Syn. Überlieferung.)

[45]The Sayings of Jesus in the Writings of Justin Martyr (1967). (Hereafter = Sayings.)

[46]Cf. M. Dibelius, Die Formgeschichte des Evangeliums, 3rd ed. (1959), p. 26; R. Bultmann, Die Geschichte der synoptischen Tradition, 5th ed. (1961).

[47]H, as will be shown repeatedly, usually represents a form of the sayings closer to the Grundschrift than R and further from the canonical texts. In addition it has far more of the sayings than R. Its evidence is clearly primary while that of R is usually confirmatory, i.e., when it supports H in a reading that departs from the canonical texts.

the history of the gospel tradition in the early church.   In
short the goal of the thesis is to contribute further, concrete
evidence that will help illuminate the early history of the gospel tradition in the late second and early third centuries.

The Text

The textual tradition of the Pseudo-Clementines does not
appear to present any great difficulties. The Greek text of the
Homilies is preserved in two manuscripts, one of the eleventh or
twelfth centuries[48] (which on the whole is superior to the fol-
lowing one) and one of the fourteenth century,[49] as well as
several Greek "epitomies."[50] The critical edition is B. Rehm,
Die Pseudoklementinen I: Homilien, 2nd ed. by F. Paschke (GCS
42; 1969). In addition there is a Syriac manuscript containing
R 1.1.1-4.1.4 and H 10.1.1-14.12.4 from the year A.D. 411.[51]
The critical edition of this is W. Frankenberg, Die syrischen
Clementinen mit griechischem Paralleltext (TU 48,3; 1937). The
Latin text of the Recognitions is found in about 100 mss. from
the sixth to the fifteenth centuries. The critical edition is B.
Rehm, Die Pseudoklementinen II: Rekognitionen (GCS 51; 1965).

---

[48]Codex Parisinus gr. 930: contains H 1.1-19.14.

[49]Codex Vaticanus Ottobonianus gr. 443: complete.

[50]Cf. A. R. M. Dressel, Clementinorum Epitomae Duae, 2nd ed.
(1873).

[51]Brit. Mus. add. 12150; R 1.1.1-4.1.4 is also found in the
Syriac ms. Brit. Mus. add. 14609 (ninth century).

CHAPTER II

HARMONIZED AND CONFLATED READINGS

By "harmonized readings" I mean those that combine the readings of more than one gospel on a given text, e.g., Matthew and Luke; by "conflated readings" I mean those that combine readings from two (or more) places within the same gospel, e.g., Mt. 6.32 and 6.8. These two classifications are treated together in this chapter because they both point in the same direction: the use of a harmony or harmonized collection of sayings of Jesus in H. For it would make no difference to one combining texts whether he did so at one point from two (or more) different sources and at another point from two different places within one of the sources.

It is apparent from the outset that the explanation of the harmonized readings will play a key role in the understanding of the source(s) of the sayings of Jesus in the Pseudo-Clementine Homilies. Particular attention will be given to the occurrence of similar harmonized or conflated readings in the early fathers of the church, especially Justin Martyr who will be seen to exhibit the most striking parallels with many of the sayings in H and especially in the harmonized sayings. The first ten sayings of this chapter, in fact, have parallels in Justin. For this reason it has been deemed appropriate to list regularly in the parallel columns the texts of Justin when he has cited the same sayings of Jesus as found in H. The text cited is that of E. J. Goodspeed, Die Ältesten Apologeten (1914).

A special note needs to be made regarding the use of the designation "H" in the thesis. It will be the policy of the thesis to refer to the material in the Pseudo-Clementine Homilies most commonly as H without distinguishing between the various possible layers (such as KP, PP, G, and the Homilist himself). The problem of relating the form of sayings of Jesus in H to the various layers within H will be taken up in the Conclusion.

13

14

1. H 19.2.5b

H 19.2.5	Ju, D. 76.5	Mt. 25.30	Mt. 25.41
ὑπάγετε	ὑπάγετε	ἐκβάλετε	πορεύεσθε
			ἀπ᾽ ἐμοῦ
			κατηραμένοι
εἰς τὸ σκότος	εἰς τὸ σκότος	εἰς τὸ σκότος	εἰς τὸ πῦρ
τὸ ἐξώτερον,	τὸ ἐξώτερον,	τὸ ἐξώτερον.	τὸ αἰώνιον
5 ὃ ἡτοίμασεν	ὃ ἡτοίμασεν		⌜τὸ ἡτοιμασμένον[1]
ὁ πατὴρ	ὁ πατὴρ		
τῷ διαβόλῳ	τῷ σατανᾷ		τῷ διαβόλῳ
καὶ τοῖς ἀγγέλοις	καὶ τοῖς ἀγγέλοις		καὶ τοῖς ἀγγέλοις
10 αὐτοῦ.	αὐτοῦ.		αὐτοῦ.

[1] ὃ ἡτοίμασεν ὁ
πατήρ μου D 1
22 pc it.

Irenaeus, AH 3.33.2 (Harvey 2.126)
Abite maledicti in ignem aeternum, quem praeparavit Pater meus diabolo et angelis eius.
(Cf. also 2.6.1 [Harvey 1.268]; 4.55.1 [Harvey 2.265]; 4.66.1 [Harvey 2.302].)

Clement, Protr. 9/83.2 (Stählin 1.63)
καὶ "τὸ πῦρ" δὲ προσηπείτε, "ὃ ἡτοίμασεν ὁ κύριος τῷ διαβόλῳ καὶ τοῖς ἀγγέλοις αὐτοῦ."

Hippolytus, Antichr. 65 (Bonwetsch 1,2.45)
πορεύεσθε ἀπ᾽ ἐμοῦ οἱ κατηραμένοι εἰς τὸ πῦρ τὸ αἰώνιον ὃ ἡτοίμασεν ὁ πατήρ μου τῷ διαβόλῳ καὶ τοῖς ἀγγέλοις αὐτοῦ.

Cf. H 20.9.1
τοῦτον αὐτὸν ὕστερον μετα τῶν αὐτοῦ ἀγγέλων συν τοῖς ἁμαρτωλοῖς εἰς τὸ σκότος το κατώτερον πέμπεσθαι;

Both H and Justin agree: (1) in combining the words of Mt. 25.30a (which forms the conclusion of the Parable of the Talents) and Mt. 25.41b (which occurs in the midst of the Parable of the Last Judgment), (2) in reading ὑπάγετε which differs from either the ἐκβάλετε of Mt. 25.30 or the πορεύεσθε of Mt. 25.41, and (3) in reading ὁ ἡτοίμασεν ὁ πατήρ instead of τὸ ἡτοιμασμένον. In this last case the same reading is found also in Codex Beza and other manuscripts of Mt. 25.41 (1 22 pc it) and was known to some of the fathers (Irenaeus, Clement, and Hippolytus). This would only prove that behind H and Justin lay a manuscript of Matthew that read ὁ ἡτοίμασεν ὁ πατήρ instead of τὸ ἡτοιμασμένον.

But the combination of the same verses by H and Justin as well as the common use of ὑπάγετε require another explanation. This could be: (A) coincidence, (B) H was using Justin, (C) Justin was using H, or (D) a common source underlies both H and Justin at this point. Mere coincidence is most improbable in such precise agreements.[1] The dependence of H on Justin which was proposed by Waitz[2] is negated in this case by Justin's use of σατανᾷ instead of διαβόλῳ.[3] σατανᾷ, as Bellinzoni argued, is a secondary change made by Justin.[4] That Justin used H has not been proposed by anyone nor does it have any good reason or other evidence to commend it. A common source behind H and Justin to account for this saying is the most convincing solution. Although one cannot from this example speak of a harmony in the strict sense of combining texts from more than one gospel, this example does indicate a source used by both H and Justin which combined sayings of Jesus using at least the Gospel of Matthew.

---

[1]Strecker (Judenchristentum, p. 133), who does not consider seriously the possibility of a harmony common to Justin and H, does admit in this case that "die Parallele bei Justin . . . wird nicht auf einem Zufall beruhen."

[2]Pseudoklementinen, p. 307.

[3]Of course it could be conjectured that Justin's lost Syn. adv. Marc. (which Waitz believed to þe the Justinian work used by H) contained the saying with διαβόλῳ, and that Justin changed it to σατανᾷ in the Apology quotation. But such a conjecture, based on what is unknown, can get us nowhere nor be convincing.

[4]Sayings, pp. 115-16.

2. H 3.19.3, 12.32.1

	H 3.19.3	H 12.32.1	Ju, A. 15.9	Lk. 6.27-28	Did. 1.3	Mt. 5.44
	ἠγάπα καὶ	ἐχθροὺς	[b] καὶ ἀγαπᾶτε	ἀγαπᾶτε	[d] ὑμεῖς δὲ ἀγαπᾶτε	ἀγαπᾶτε
		ἀγαπᾶν		τοὺς ἐχθροὺς		τοὺς ἐχθροὺς
	τοὺς			ὑμῶν,		ὑμῶν
	μισοῦντας		τοὺς	καλῶς ποιεῖτε		
5	τοὺς		μισοῦντας	τοῖς	τοὺς	
	μισοῦντας		τοὺς	μισοῦσιν	μισοῦντας	
	καὶ ἔκλαιε		ὑμᾶς,	ὑμᾶς,	ὑμᾶς, [e]	
10	ἐπὶ τοὺς					
	ἀπειθοῦντας		[c] καὶ εὐλογεῖτε	εὐλογεῖτε	[a] εὐλογεῖτε	
	καὶ εὐλόγει	καὶ	τοὺς	τοὺς	τοὺς	
	τοὺς	λοιδοροῦντας	καταρωμένους	καταρωμένους	καταρωμένους	
	λοιδοροῦντας	εὐλογεῖν,				
15		ἔτι μὴν καὶ	ὑμῖν καὶ	ὑμᾶς,	ὑμῖν καὶ	καὶ
	ηὔχετο	(1. 23)	[a,d] εὔχεσθε	προσεύχεσθε	[b] προσεύχεσθε	προσεύχεσθε
	(1. 23)			⌜περὶ⌝		
	ὑπὲρ	ὑπὲρ	ὑπὲρ	ὑπὲρ	ὑπὲρ	ὑπὲρ
	ἐχθραινόντων.	ἐχθρῶν	[a] τῶν ἐχθρῶν	τῶν	τῶν ἐχθρῶν	τῶν
20			[d] τῶν ἐπηρεαζόντων	ἐπηρεαζόντων		διωκόντων
			[a] ὑμᾶς/[d] ὑμᾶς.	ὑμᾶς.	ὑμῶν, [c]	ὑμᾶς.

H 3.19.3	H 12.32.1	Ju, A. 15.9	Lk. 6.27-28	Did. 1.3	Mt. 5.44
	εὔχεσθαι.		[1] υπερ A D Θ Koine pl. latt.	[c] νηστεύετε δὲ ὑπὲρ τῶν διωκόντων ὑμᾶς· etc. [e] καὶ οὐχ ἕξετε ἐχθρόν.	

Didascalia 5.14/21 (Lagarde 90; cf. Connolly 184)
"Pray for your enemies," and "Blessed are those who weep over the destruction of those who do not believe."

ܕܨ̈ܠ ܥܠ ܒܥܠܕ̈ܒܒܝܟܘܢ܂ ܘܛܘ̈ܒܝܗܘܢ ܠܐܝܠܝܢ ܕܒܟܝܢ ܥܠ ܐܒܕܢܐ ܕܐܝܠܝܢ ܕܠܐ ܡܗܝܡܢܝܢ܂

18

This saying (or these sayings) and the one that follows both
have parallels in Justin and the Didache and are sayings taken
from the Sermon on the Mount/Plain.[1] We may consider the four
phrases as given in H in order.

1. ἠγάπα καὶ τοὺς μισοῦντας. Both Justin and the Didache
have ἀγαπᾶτε τοὺς μισοῦντας ὑμᾶς, a form which differs from both
Matthew and Luke. H attests also the use of ἀγαπεῖν joined to
τοὺς μισοῦντας. H's use of the singular imperfect and the dropping of ὑμᾶς is due to his adaptation of the phrases into exemplary acts of Jesus. Thus a common source is very possible for
all three, a source which conflated the ἀγαπᾶτε of Lk. 6.27a or
Mt. 5.44a and the τοὺς μισοῦντας ὑμᾶς of Lk. 6.27b and changed
the dative to the accusative for obvious syntactical reasons.[2]
The ἐχθροὺς ἀγαπᾶν (in direct discourse) of H 12.32.1 is most
likely a correction back toward the canonical texts of Matthew
and Luke.

2. ἔκλαιε τοὺς ἀπειθοῦντας. This phrase is unique in this
combination of sayings to H 3.19.3. Therefore it is probably H's
own addition, perhaps referring to Jesus' weeping over Jerusalem
(cf. Lk. 19.41). The fact that H has changed the sayings into
exemplary acts of Jesus would easily account for such an addition
being made in H.

3. εὐλόγει τοὺς λοιδοροῦντας. Both Justin and the Didache
have εὐλογεῖτε τοὺς καταρωμένους ὑμῖν which is the Lucan wording
with a stylistic change of ὑμῖν to ὑμᾶς.[3] A common source for
Justin and the Didache is very probable. H's adapting the

---

[1]There is no reason to think that Q is the source rather
than a post-synoptic source. For if Q is better represented by
Matthew's two petition form as Harnack thought (The Sayings of
Jesus [1908], p. 61 [hereafter = Sayings]), then the Lucan elements in the sayings disprove the direct use of Q. Even if Luke
better represents the Q form as Bultmann seems to suggest
(History of the Synoptic Tradition, 2nd ed. [1968], p. 79 [here-
after = History]), at least one could not prove a use of Q rather
than Luke. Bellinzoni (Sayings, p. 79) has argued that the
sequence οἱ τελῶναι -- οἱ ἐθνικοί in Mt. 5.46-47 (probably = Q's
words), changed to οἱ ἀμαρτωλοί (twice) in Lk. 6.32-33, and
further to οἱ πόρνοι in Justin, Apol. 15.9, indicates that
Justin's words in Apol. 15.9 are dependent on our synoptic gospels or a post-synoptic source.

[2]So also Bellinzoni, Sayings, p. 80. Cf. also Ep. ad Diog.
6.6: καὶ Χριστιανοὶ τοὺς μισοῦντας ἀγαπῶσιν.

[3]The dative after verbs of cursing is more common in Attic
Greek than the accusative (cf. B-D-F § 152).

19

sayings into acts of Jesus could explain a possible change of
καταρωμένους to λοιδοροῦντας by H since the latter could be considered a stronger word and a better description of what Jesus
suffered.[4] Thus H, although less certainly in this instance,
would still attest the same source that underlies Justin and the
Didache.

4. ηὔχετο ὑπὲρ ἐχθραινόντων. Justin reads once εὔχεσθε
ὑπὲρ τῶν ἐχθρῶν ὑμῶν and once εὔχεσθε ὑπὲρ τῶν ἐπηρεαξόντων ὑμᾶς
(cf. Luke) while the Didache has προσεύχεσθε ὑπὲρ τῶν ἐχθρῶν
ὑμῶν. But the use of the verb εὔχεσθαι in H and Justin instead
of Luke's προσεύχεσθε and of ἐχθρῶν ὑμῶν in Justin and the
Didache instead of Luke's ἐπηρεαξόντων ὑμᾶς points once again to
a source which had altered the wording of the Lucan text. If it
be granted that H's ἐχθραινόντων is his own expansion of ἐχθρῶν
(cf. H 12.32.1), then H 3.19.3. would also attest this variant
form (as would H 12.32.1).[5] The Didache's προσεύχεσθε could be
either a later "correction" or simply has own choice or preference of words for prayer. The use of ὑπέρ in all these texts instead of Luke's περί is due either to the text of Luke used by
the source[6] or to a change which the source made, perhaps under
the influence of Mt. 5.44 (προσεύχεσθε ὑπερ τῶν διωκόντων ὑμᾶς).

Thus three of the phrases in H seem to attest a common
source known also to Justin and the Didache.[7] On the basis of H
alone one could not argue for anything more than the use of a
Lucan text (Lk. 6.27-28).[8] But Did. 1.3[9] and Justin, Apol.

---

[4]Cf. 1 Pet. 2.23: ὃς (Jesus) λοιδορούμενος οὐκ ἀντελοι-
δόρει. Cf. also 1 Pet. 3.9; 1 Cor. 4.12; Ep. ad Diog. 5.15.

[5]Cf. also Clement, Strom. 7.14/84.5 (Stählin 3.60): εὔχεσθαι ὑπὲρ τῶν ἐχθρῶν; Didasc. 5.14/21 (Lagarde 90,3): ܠܐ ܐܠ؟
ܚܒ݂ܒ݂ܝ ܚܠ ("Pray for your enemies"); and P. Ox. 1224 (Gren-
feld-Hunt 10.9): κ)αὶ π(ρ)οσεύχεσθε ὑπὲρ (τῶν ἐχθ)ρῶν ὑμῶν.

[6]υπερ is read in Lk. 6.28 by A D Koine ϑ pl and latt.

[7]On the problem of Did. 1.3-2.1 (its sources, date, and
transmission) see the excellent study by Bentley Layton, HTR 61
(1968), 343-83.

[8]Or even a Matthean text which reads like the commonly
accepted Lucan text; for so reads Mt. 5.44 in D Koine W ϑ φ pl
syP. Cf. Köster, Syn. Überlieferung, p. 225.

[9]Matthean is (perhaps) προσεύχεσθε (see above), νηστεύετε
δε ὑπὲρ τῶν διωκόντων ὑμᾶς· οὐχὶ καὶ τὰ ἔθνη (Mt.: οὐχὶ καὶ οἱ
ἐθνικοί), and καὶ ἔσῃ τέλειος (cf. Mt. 5.48). Cf. Köster, Syn.
Überlieferung, pp. 220-26.

15.9[10] both exhibit Lucan and Matthean features. Therefore the
nature of the source involved is very likely a collection of
sayings based on a harmony or combination of words from both
Matthew and Luke.[11]

---

[10]Matthean is ἐγὼ δὲ ὑμῖν λέγω (= Mt. 5.44a), used to introduce the sayings. Cf. Bellinzoni, Sayings, pp. 79-80.

[11]Waitz (Pseudoklementinen, p. 288) fails to relate the
specific phrases to other early Christian witnesses. Strecker
(Judenchristentum, p. 131) explains things by an appeal to
"Gedächtniszitation." But such coincidentally similar failures
of memory in two or three different authors are nothing short of
incredible. Even if he allows "ein unkanonisches Herrnwort" to
account for "Betet für eure Feinde," he still has not dealt with
"Love those who hate you."

3. II 15.5.5

II 15.5.5	Ju. A. 16.1-2	Lk. 6.29	Mt. 5.39-41	Did. 1.4
τῷ τύπτοντι αὐτοῦ	τῷ τύπτοντί σου	τῷ τύπτοντί σε	ἀλλ᾽ ὅστις σε ῥαπίζει (1. 5)	[a]ἐάν τίς σοι δῷ ῥάπισμα
τὴν σιαγόνα	τὴν σιαγόνα	ἐπὶ τὴν σιαγόνα	εἰς τὴν ⌐δεξιὰν[1] σιαγόνα ⌐σου,[2]	εἰς τὴν δεξιὰν σιαγόνα,
παρατιθέναι καὶ τὴν ἑτέραν,	πάρεχε καὶ τὴν ἄλλην,	πάρεχε καὶ τὴν ἄλλην	στρέψον αὐτῷ καὶ τὴν ἄλλην·	στρέψον αὐτῷ καὶ τὴν ἄλλην, καὶ ἔσῃ τέλειος·
καὶ τῷ αἴροντι αὐτοῦ	καὶ τὸν αἴροντί σου	καὶ ἀπὸ τοῦ αἴροντός σου	καὶ τῷ θέλοντί σοι	[c]ἐὰν ἄρῃ [d]τις
τὸ ἱμάτιον	τὸν χιτῶνα	τὸ ἱμάτιον	κριθῆναι καὶ τὸν χιτῶνά σου λαβεῖν,	τὸ ἱμάτιόν σου,
προσδιδόναι καὶ τὸ μαφόριον,	ἢ τὸ ἱμάτιον μὴ κωλύσῃς.	καὶ τὸν χιτῶνα μὴ κωλύσῃς.	ἄφες αὐτῷ καὶ τὸ ἱμάτιον.	δὸς αὐτῷ καὶ τὸν χιτῶνα·
	2bπαντὶ δὲ			[b]ἐὰν
ἀγγαρεύοντι δὲ ⌐μίλιον[1] συναπέρχεσθαι	ἀγγαρεύοντί σε μίλιον ἀκολούθησον		καὶ ὅστις σε ⌐ἀγγαρεύσει[3] μίλιον ἕν, ὕπαγε μετ᾽ αὐτοῦ	ἀγγαρεύσῃ σέ τις μίλιον ἕν, ὕπαγε μετ᾽ αὐτοῦ

22

H 15.5.5	Ju, A. 16.1-2	Lk. 6.29	Mt. 5.39-41	Did. 1.4
δύο.	δύο.		δύο.	δύο.

[1]omit D k sys,c.

[2]omit ℵ W 33

pm a f h.

[3]εαν αγγαρευση ℵ 33 pc.

1+ ἐν OE° e.

Megethius in Adamantius, Dial. 1.15 & 18 (Bakhuyzen 32 & 38)

15ἐάν τίς σε ῥαπίσῃ εἰς τὴν σιαγόνα, παράθες αὐτῷ καὶ τὴν ἄλλην.

18ἐάν τίς σου ἄρῃ τὸ ἱμάτιον, πρόσθες αὐτῷ καὶ τὸν χιτῶνα.

Aphraates, Dem. 9.6 (Graffin 1.420)

"Whoever strikes you on your cheek, offer him the other.
Whoever compels you to go with him a mile, go with him two more.
Whoever wishes to take your inner garment (kûtînāk = χιτών), give him also your outer garment
(martûṭāk = ἱμάτιον)."

As in the previous saying(s) there are parallels in H,
Justin, and the Didache to this group of sayings. However, as
will be seen, the Didache differs from H and Justin's "agreement"
in this case.

H contains (only) Lucan features in the first two sayings
while the third saying is a Matthean saying. Justin is similar
except for the (seemingly) Matthean order of τὸν χιτῶνα and τὸ
ἱμάτιον. So the question is: Do H and Justin presuppose a common source or not? In common they agree in the following:
(1) Luke's τῷ τύπτοντι instead of Matthew's ὅστις σε ῥαπίζει,
(2) a stylistic improvement of Luke's σε ἐπὶ τὴν σιαγόνα[1] to
σου τὴν σιαγόνα,[2] (3) Luke's πάρεχε rather than Matthew's
στρέψον αὐτῷ,[3] (4) Luke's καὶ ἀπὸ τοῦ αἴροντος, which has been
stylistically improved,[4] (5) ἀγγαρεύοντι δέ instead of Matthew's
ὅστις σε ἀγγαρεύσει,[5] (6) μίλιον without ἕν,[6] (7) a verb of
"following" or "accompanying" without direct object or prepositional phrase as in Matthew. These agreements are too numerous
and too refined to be considered accidental or coincidental. A
common source is very probable.

But then the differences between H and Justin must be
accounted for. They are: (a) H's παρατιθέναι and προσδιδόναι
versus Justin's (Lucan) verbs of πάρεχε and μὴ κωλύσῃς, (b) ἑτέραν versus Justin's (Lucan or Matthean) ἄλλην, (c) τὸ ἱμάτιον

---

[1]Plummer, St. Luke (ICC), p. 185, claims that τύπτειν ἐπί
+ the accusative is not found elsewhere in ancient Greek.

[2]Since H has changed the discourse from direct to indirect
(see the context), it can be assumed that H's source read σου
also.

[3]H's choice of παρατιθέναι is another question but it surely
would presuppose Luke's πάρεχε rather than the Matthean wording.
The use of the infinitive is of course due to the indirect mode
of discourse.

[4]κωλύειν ἀπό is not as common as κωλύειν with the accusative
(cf. Plummer [n. 1] and B-D-F § 180 [1]). The difference between
H and Justin is that H has also used the dative because of his
use of προσδιδόναι.

[5]This preserves the same pattern of beginning the saying as
in the previous two.

[6]This assumes that in H the reading of P and E^V is to be
preferred to O E^O and e which add ἕν, the latter being explained
as a correction toward the text of Matthew.

καὶ τὸ μαφόριον versus Justin's τὸν χιτῶνα η το ἱμάτιον (see Matthew), (d) Justin's addition of παντί (cf. Lk. 6.30) and σε (see Matthew), and (e) συναπέρχεσθαι in H versus ἀκολούθησον in Justin. It is noticeable from the outset that H's verbs are compound verbs (lines 6, 15, and 21) and are very likely his own substitutions. Thus differences a and e do not speak against a common source. ἑτέραν for ἄλλην is also very likely H's own change, being deemed more correct as "the other (of two)" in the reference to cheeks. παντί and σε in Justin cannot help us one way or the other. For either could easily be Justin's own addition or H's own omission. The main problem then for the hypothesis of a common source is Justin's order of τὸν χιτῶνα and τὸ ἱμάτιον and H's use of τὸ μαφόριον instead of τὸν χιτῶνα. The latter is once again best explained as H's own change. The reason already suggested by Credner,[7] Hilgenfeld,[8] and Waitz[9] is that Ebionite regulations forbade one's "standing naked" before another and underlies this change of wording in H.[10] Since removing one's χιτών would have left him "naked", the χιτών was changed to μαφόριον 'head-dress' or 'veil'.

Assuming that H's source read τὸν χιτῶνα instead of τὸ μαφόριον, Justin still presents the garments in the opposite order. Does this mean that Justin follows Matthew, while H follows Luke in this regard? Not necessarily. For Justin's use of ἤ instead of καί is revealing. Bellinzoni offers the following analysis of Justin's order:

> The difference between τὸ ἱμάτιον καὶ τὸν χιτῶνα in Lk. 6:29 and τὸν χιτῶνα ἤ τὸ ἱμάτιον in Apol. 16:1 apparently arose from a misunderstanding either by Justin or his source of the meaning of Luke's text. Whereas ἱμάτιον probably belongs to the verb αἴροντός and χιτῶνα to the verb κωλύσῃς in Luke, Justin or his source apparently thought that both nouns were the objects of the verb αἴροντος. The change from καί to ἤ comes naturally from the alteration in meaning, and the inversion of the order of χιτῶνα and ἱμάτιον may be only a stylistic change made in order to mention second the outer and more valuable garment.[11]

---

[7] Beiträge, pp. 308-09.

[8] Krit. Untersuchungen, pp. 341-42.

[9] Pseudoklementinen, pp. 327-28.

[10] See H 15.7.6: γύμνον γὰρ ἑστάναι οὐκ ἐφίεται ἔνεκεν τοῦ πάντα ὀρῶντος οὐρανοῦ. Cf. the Essenes in Josephus, BJ 2.148 and 161; and in 1QS vii 12.

[11] Sayings, p. 72.

If this change was made by Justin himself, then his source
read the same as H's (= the Lucan order of τὸ ἱμάτιον καὶ τὸν
χιτῶνα). Justin's changed order would therefore be only coincidentally the same as Matthew's. This is also Bellinzoni's
conclusion:

> The fact that Mt. 5:40 lists χιτῶνα before ἱμάτιον
> does not indicate a Matthean influence in Justin's text.
> Rather the absence of any definite influence from Matthew
> leaves little doubt that this small agreement is
> coincidental.[12]

Therefore it is possible to hypothesize a common source
behind both H and Justin which would have read:

> τῷ τύπτοντί σου τὴν σιαγόνα πάρεχε καὶ τὴν ἄλλην, καὶ
> τὸν αἴροντά σου τὸ ἱμάτιον καὶ τὸν χιτῶνα μὴ κωλύσῃς.
> (Justin, Apol. 16.2a = Mt. 5.22 ?). (παντὶ?) δὲ ἀγγα-
> ρεύοντί σε μίλιον ἀκολούθησον (?) δύο.[13]

The Didache, on the other hand, is another matter. In
contrast to H and Justin, it is more Matthean than Lucan in the
first two sayings and closer to Matthew's wording than they in

---

[12]Ibid., p. 72, n. 3.

[13]Whether Aphraates knew this source or not I will not try
to solve here. His "Whoever strikes you on your cheek" is Lucan
like H and Justin. "Whoever compels you to go with him a mile,
go with him two more" agrees with H and Justin in the omission
of ἕν, but with Matthew against H and Justin in reading "go with
him." However, one cannot be sure of H and Justin's source at
this point. "Wishes to take" shows Matthean influence against H
and Justin's following Luke. The order of kûtînāk (= χιτών) and
marṭûṭāk (= ἱμάτιον) is Matthean. "Give him" is apparently
Matthean (ἄφες αὐτῷ; cf. Didache's δὸς αὐτῷ).
The Diatessaron witnesses follow Matthew in the wording of
the sayings with a few exceptions. Δε 6.4 (Leloir, Arm. 124f.:
"A celui qui frappe ta joue, tends encore l'autre côté") reveals
Lucan influence as in Aphraates, H, and Justin. (Cf. also Δε
6.11f.; 6.14; 12.2; 19.10. Cf. further Layton, HTR 61 [1968],
351, n. 27.) Δp 1.40 (Messina 67: "e chiunque voglia la tua
tunica, dà anche la camicia") is close to Aphraates' form as is
also Δl 40 (Bergsma 45: "ende die di welt dinen roc nemen. laet
hem oc den mantel"). That Aphraates used Tatian's Diatessaron
seems certain enough although he may not have been limited to it.
(Cf. F. C. Burkitt, Evangelion da-Mepharreshe [1904], 2.109-11,
180-86; further references in C. Peters, Das Diatessaron Tatians
[1939], p. 36, n. 3.) The question of the relation of Tatian's
Diatessaron to H and Justin's "source" will be taken up in the
Conclusion.
The text cited by Megethius (in Adamantius) uses the ἐάν
τίς structure as does Didache. It also combines the Matthean
with Lucan features (τὴν σιαγόνα, ἄρῃ, and the order of ἱμάτιον
and χιτῶνα). The latter saying in Megethius comes closer to
the wording of the Didache than anyone else.

in the saying.[14] Thus it appears to represent a different
harmonization than H and Justin of these sayings.[15]

But how is one to account for the closeness of wording in
the previous group of sayings that indicated a common source for
the Didache, H, and Justin but a different relationship in this
latter group in which H and Justin stand against the Didache?
One could suppose the use of two different sources for the
Didache -- one which was used by H and Justin and another which
was more Matthean in character or was the Gospel of Matthew itself. But this could also be solved by conjecturing secondary
adaptation toward Matthew in the Didache. The former group of
sayings did not undergo this process because one of the sayings
("Bless those who curse you") had no Matthean parallel; to
another the Matthean parallel (προσεύχεσθε ὑπὲρ τῶν διωκόντων
ὑμᾶς) was taken up elsewhere in Did. 1.3 in the form νηστεύετε
δὲ ὑπὲρ τῶν διωκόντων ὑμᾶς ; and the third ("Love those who hate
you") had no additional wording in Matthew from what was in Luke.
Although it is not the purpose of this study to solve the problems of the sayings in the Didache, these comments are intended
to show that one source of the sayings of Jesus in H was known
to others -- certainly to Justin and perhaps to the author of
Did. 1.3-2.1.

---

[14]Köster, Syn. Überlieferung, pp. 217-39, argues for the use
of a "Logiensammlung" which used Matthew and Luke as well as
other traditional material as the basic source behind Did. 1.3-
2.1. Cf. also Layton, HTR 61 (1968), 343-83.

[15]Cf. ibid., p. 372, where Layton observes that the source
behind Did. 1.3b-2.1 cannot be Q, the Diatessaron of Tatian, or
Justin's harmony.

4. H 17.5.2, R 3.4.6

	H 17.5.2	R 3.4.6	Ju, A. 19.7	2 Cl. 5.4	Mt. 10.28	Lk. 12.4-5
	μὴ	nolite	μὴ	μὴ	μὴ	μὴ
	φοβηθῆτε	timere	φοβεῖσθε	φοβεῖσθε	⌐φοβεῖσθε[1]	φοβηθῆτε
	ἀπὸ	eos qui	τοὺς	τοὺς	ἀπὸ	ἀπὸ
	τοῦ	occidunt	ἀναιροῦντας	ἀποκτέννοντας	τῶν	τῶν
5	ἀποκτέννοντος	corpus,	ὑμᾶς	ὑμᾶς	ἀποκτεννόντων	ἀποκτεννόντων
	τὸ σῶμα,		καὶ μετὰ ταῦτα	καὶ	τὸ σῶμα,	τὸ σῶμα
	⌐τῇ	animam			τὴν	καὶ μετὰ ταῦτα
	δὲ	autem			δὲ	
	ψυχῇ[1]	non	μὴ	μηδὲν ὑμῖν	ψυχὴν	μὴ
10	μὴ	possunt	δυναμένους	δυναμένους	μὴ	ἐχόντων
	δυναμένου				δυναμένων	περισσότερόν
	τι		τι			τι
	ποιῆσαι·	occidere,	ποιῆσαι,	ποιεῖν,	ἀποκτεῖναι·	ποιῆσαι.
			εἶπε,	ἀλλὰ		5ὑποδείξω δὲ
15						ὑμῖν τίνα
						φοβηθῆτε·
	φοβηθῆτε	timete	φοβήθητε	φοβεῖσθε	⌐φοβεῖσθε[2]	φοβήθητε
	δὲ	autem	δὲ	(1. 15)	δὲ	
					μᾶλλον	
20						
	τὸν	eum qui	τὸν	τὸν	τὸν	τὸν
			μετὰ τὸ	μετὰ τὸ		μετὰ τὸ

H 17.5.2	R 3.4.6	Ju, A. 19.7	2 Cl. 5.4	Mt. 10.28	Lk. 12.4-5
		ἀποθανεῖν	ἀποθανεῖν ὑμᾶς		ἀποκτεῖναι
δυνάμενον	potest	δυνάμενον	ἔχοντα ἐξουσίαν	δυνάμενον	ἔχοντα ἐξουσίαν
25 καὶ σῶμα	et corpus	καὶ ψυχὴν	ψυχῆς	καὶ ψυχὴν	
καὶ ψυχὴν	et animam	καὶ σῶμα	καὶ σώματος	καὶ σῶμα	
(1. 30)	perdere		τοῦ βαλεῖν	ἀπολέσαι	⌐ἐμβαλεῖν[1]
εἰς τὴν γέενναν	in gehennam.	εἰς γέεννα(ν)	εἰς γέενναν	⌐ἐν γεέννῃ.[3]	εἰς τὴν γέενναν.
τοῦ πυρὸς			πυρός.		
30 βαλεῖν.		ἐμβαλεῖν.			
ναὶ					ναὶ
λέγω ὑμῖν,					λέγω ὑμῖν,
τοῦτον					τοῦτον
φοβήθητε.					φοβήθητε.

[1]τὴν ψυχήν O.

[1]φοβήθητε
B D Θ W λ.
[2]φοβήθητε
D Koine Θ W
λ.
[3]εἰς γέενναν
D it (-k).

[1]φαλειν p⁴⁵
D W.

In the first saying studied a conflation of two Matthean
texts was involved, the second and the third (group of) sayings
primarily followed the Lucan wording of the sayings in the case
of H and Justin (and the Didache in the second saying) but with
one saying of the third group of sayings being found only in
Matthew. In the following saying which has parallels in Justin
and 2 Clement we are confronted with a truly "harmonized" saying,
i.e., one in which Matthean and Lucan elements have been inter-
mingled. These elements will be pointed out in the course of
discussing the relationship of H, Justin, and 2 Clement.

First, it may be noted that all three of these witnesses
agree in the following two "harmonistic" combinations:

I. μὴ δυναμένων (Matthew) + τι ποιῆσαι (Luke).

  1. H: μὴ δυναμένου τι ποιῆσαι.

  2. Justin: μὴ δυναμένους τι ποιῆσαι.

  3. 2 Clement: μηδὲν ὑμῖν δυναμένους ποιεῖν.

II. καὶ ψυχὴν καὶ σῶμα (Matthew) + (ἐμ)βαλεῖν εἰς τὴν
    γέενναν (Luke).

  1. H: καὶ σῶμα καὶ ψυχὴν εἰς γέενναν τοῦ πυρὸς
     βαλεῖν.

  2. Justin: καὶ ψυχὴν καὶ σῶμα εἰς γέεννα(ν) ἐμβαλεῖν.

  3. 2 Clement: ψυχῆς καὶ σώματος τοῦ βαλεῖν εἰς
     γέενναν πυρός.

This is itself suggestive of more than coincidence.

Secondly, the differences between the three authors must be
weighed against the above similarities. The differences are:

A. Agreements of Justin and 2 Clement against H:

Justin & 2 Clement	H
1. μὴ φοβεῖσθε (Mt.)	μὴ φοβηθῆτε (Lk.)
2. Accusative object (neither Mt. or Lk.)	ἀπό + genitive (Mt.)
τοὺς ἀναιροῦντας (Ju)	ἀπὸ τοῦ ἀποκτέννοντος (H)
τοὺς ἀποκτέννοντας (2 Cl)	
3. ὑμᾶς (neither Mt. or Lk.)	τὸ σῶμα (Mt. & Lk.)
4. καὶ μετὰ ταῦτα (Lk.)	τῇ δὲ ψυχῇ (cf. Mt.)
καὶ μετὰ ταῦτα (Ju)	
καὶ (2 Cl)	
5. τὸν μετὰ τὸ ἀποθανεῖν (cf. Lk.)	τόν without μετά etc. (cf. Mt.)

B. Agreements of H and 2 Clement against Justin:

<u>H & 2 Clement</u>   <u>Justin</u>

1. Use of ἀποκτεννόντων   ἀναιροῦντας
    (Mt. & Lk.)
    ἀποκτέννοντος (H)
    ἀποκτέννοντας (2 Cl)

2. βαλεῖν (cf. Lk. P^{45} D W)   ἐμβαλεῖν (Lk.)

3. πυρός (neither Mt. or Lk.)   -----

C. Agreements of H and Justin against 2 Clement:

<u>H & Justin</u>   <u>2 Clement</u>

2. The second φοβήθητε (Lk.) φοβεῖσθε (Mt.)

3. The second δυνάμενον   ἔχοντα ἐξουσίαν
    (Mt.)   (Lk.)

D. H alone ends with the Lucan ναὶ λέγω ὑμίν, τοῦτον
φοβήθητε. Certainly not all of these agreements/disagreements
are of equal weight. But what sense can be made of them? I
propose that on the basis of the two harmonistic combinations
noted above and an examination of the nature of the differences
that a single harmonized source behind all three authors is both
possible and the best explanation. Let us consider the differences listed above.

A1 (cf. C1). Actually H (with φοβηθητε twice), 2 Clement
(with φοβεῖσθε twice), and Justin (with φοβεῖσθε - φοβήθητε) all
differ on the choice of these verbs. But the simplest explanation seems to be that Justin best represents the source with
φοβεῖσθε - φοβήθητε[1] and that H and 2 Clement have each chosen
one or the other of the forms and made their other occurrence of
the verb parallel to that one.[2] The tendency toward precise
parallelism is a common one and will be noted frequently in the
case of the sayings in H.

A2-4. Justin and 2 Clement have accusative objects[3] + ὑμᾶς,
while H agrees with Matthew and Luke in reading ἀπό + the

---

[1]Which could mean a choice of Matthew's φοβεῖσθε and then
Luke's φοβήθητε or even a variant text of Matthew (the Koine
witnesses read Matthew in just this way).

[2]There should be no difficulty in considering φοβηθῆτε
(after μή) parallel to φοβήθητε in H when one omits the accent
marks as was done in the manuscripts of the early period.

[3]Justin's choice of ἀναιροῦντας is surely his own change
(so Bellinzoni, <u>Sayings</u>, p. 110) and does not attest a different
source.

genitive[4] + τὸ σῶμα. H appears to be a movement back to the
canonical texts (of both Matthew and Luke), while Justin and 2
Clement's agreement in a form divergent from the canonical form
is more likely the source's reading. A possible indication that
H may have earlier read the accusative lies in R's reading eos
qui occidunt. This is especially significant since R's general
tendency is back toward the canonical reading itself.[5] Its
divergences, therefore, are often significant.

τὸ σῶμα and τῇ δὲ ψυχῇ in H could be part of the same
tendency (both Matthew and Luke read τὸ σῶμα), but it could also
be seen as a movement toward parallelism (see καὶ σῶμα καὶ
ψυχήν in the second half of the saying).[6] Again Justin and 2
Clement appear to preserve the source more intact than H.

A5. The absence of μετὰ τὸ ἀποθανεῖν in H can prove nothing
since such phrases are easily dropped by an author who considered
them redundant or unnecessary for his purposes.[7] Argumentum e
silentio is precarious in this regard since one can never be sure
whether the source used may have read the missing word(s) or not.

B1. As already noted (n. 3) ἀναιροῦντας is most likely
Justin's own change.

B2. The difference between βαλεῖν and ἐμβαλεῖν is too
slight to make a point of it. Both attest Luke rather than
Matthew's ἀπολέσαι.

B3. The absence of πυρός from Justin requires the same
comments as in A5 above.

C1. See under A1.

---

[4]H's use of the singular instead of the plural is probably
his own change to make the formal parallelism closer to the
singular subject of the second half of the saying. But the
singular may also have been motivated in H by the fact that the
saying is spoken by "Simon Magus," perhaps intending τοῦ ἀποκτέν-
νοντος τὸ σῶμα to refer to the Demiurge. In R, on the other
hand, the saying is cited by Peter.

[5]On the whole R is mostly a return to the Matthean text in
this saying.

[6]The dative τῇ ψυχῇ is due to τι ποιῆσαι (cf. Matthew's
τὴν ψυχήν with ἀποκτεῖναι). But this indicates that τῇ ψυχῇ
in H is secondary to the combination of μὴ δυναμένου τι ποιῆσαι
--the harmonistic combination common to H, Justin, and 2 Clement!

[7]The same can be said of 2 Clement's lack of μετὰ ταῦτα
after καί in line 7.

32

C2. This is perhaps the most serious difficulty involved
in this comparison of H, Justin, and 2 Clement. Köster argued
for the original reading being ἔχοντα ἐξοθσίαν (2 Clement =
Luke) which had been changed to δυνάμενον (in Justin and H)
under the influence of the previous use of δύναμαι in the first
half of the saying.[8] Bellinzoni accepted this explanation for
Justin, but not for H.[9] The problem for the hypothesis of a
single source behind all three authors is in weighing a (coincidental) change to δυνάμενον in both H and Justin against the
changing of an original δυνάμενον to ἔχοντα ἐξουσίαν by the
author of 2 Clement. The fact that ἐξουσία never occurs elsewhere in 2 Clement argues against the latter. But that does not
force the acceptance of the former alternative. For it may
still be conjectured that ἔχοντα ἐξουσίαν in 2 Clement is itself
a secondary or later scribal change by one who remembered the
saying in its Lucan wording at that point.[10] This possibility
seems a better solution than either the coincidental change of H
and Justin at this point or of hypotheses that do not posit a
single source for H, Justin, and 2 Clement for this saying in
view of the agreements.[11]

D. See the remarks to A5.

Hence it is possible to posit a single harmonized source
for this saying in H, Justin, and 2 Clement which probably read:

---

[8]Syn. Überlieferung, p. 97.

[9]Sayings, pp. 110-11. In regard to H he commented: "I cannot believe that τὸν δυνάμενον of Ps. Clem. Hom. is not derived
from τὸν δυνάμενον of Mt. 10:28" (ibid., p. III, n. 1).

[10]One may make a similar observation here as was made in
n. 6, viz., that the common harmonistic combination (τὸν μετὰ τὸ
ἀποθανεῖν = Luke and καὶ ψυχὴν καὶ σῶμα = Matthew) is presupposed.
ψυχῆς καὶ σώματος in the genitive is due to ἔχοντα ἐξουσίαν.
But this appears secondary to the wording τὸν δυνάμενον καὶ ψυχὴν
καὶ σῶμα εἰς τὴν γέενναν βαλεῖν. For 2 Clement's wording
still lacks a direct object for βαλεῖν.

[11]It must be kept in mind that our manuscripts of these texts
are themselves late--H from two major Greek manuscripts of the
eleventh-twelfth and fourteenth centuries, Justin from two of
the fourteenth and sixteenth centuries, and 2 Clement of the
fifth (Codex A) and eleventh centuries (plus some other language
versions). This hardly permits one to be certain in the case of
single words and small phrases that we necessarily have the exact
original reading.

33

μὴ φοβεῖσθε τοὺς ἀποκτέννοντας ὑμᾶς καὶ μετὰ ταῦτα
μὴ δυναμένους τι ποιῆσαι· φοβήθητε δὲ τὸν μετὰ τὸ
ἀποθανεῖν δυνάμενον καὶ ψυχὴν καὶ σῶμα εἰς (τὴν) γέενναν
(τοῦ) πυρὸς (ἐμ)βαλεῖν.[12]

---

[12]Waitz (Pseudoklementinen, p. 283) speaks of H 17.5.2
as having a closer relationship to Justin than to the synoptic
gospels, but once again wants to explain H as resulting from the
anti-Marcionite redaction of KP which used Justin as its source.
But the above discussion makes this solution both unnecessary
and improbable. Waitz did not even consider the evidence of
2 Clement.

H 3.37.2 (ἐὰν αὐτῷ μόνῳ προσεύχῃ τῷ σῶμά σου καὶ ψυχὴν
κολάσαι καὶ σῶσαι δυναμένῳ, which Waitz also took up in connection with 17.5.2, seems to me to be too paraphrastic to contribute anything to the discussion.

Strecker (Judenchristentum, p. 135) also recognizes the
"Textmischung" of H as well as Justin and 2 Clement, but simply
remarks: "doch ist die Parallelität nicht so stark, dass ein
unkanonischer Text angenommen werden muss."

34

5. H 17.4.3***, R 2.47.3

	H 17.4.3*	R 2.47.3**	Ju, A. 63.3***	Ju, D. 100.1	Mt. 11.27	Lk. 10.22
	οὐδεὶς	nemo	οὐδεὶς	οὐδεὶς	οὐδεὶς	οὐδεὶς
	ἔγνω	novit	ἔγνω	γινώσκει	⌐ἐπιγινώσκει[1]	⌐γινώσκει[1]
						⌐τίς ἐστιν[2]
	τὸν πατέρα	filium	τὸν πατέρα	τὸν πατέρα	τὸν υἱὸν	ὁ υἱὸς
5	εἰ μὴ	nisi	εἰ μὴ	εἰ μὴ	εἰ μὴ	εἰ μὴ
	ὁ υἱός,	pater,	ὁ υἱός,	ὁ υἱός,	ὁ πατήρ,	ὁ πατὴρ
	ὡς οὐδὲ	neque	οὐδὲ	οὐδὲ	οὐδὲ	καὶ
						⌐τίς ἐστιν[2]
	τὸν υἱὸν	patrem	τὸν υἱὸν	τὸν υἱὸν	τὸν πατέρα	ὁ πατὴρ
	τις	quis			τις	
10	⌐οὖδεν[1]	novit			⌐ἐπιγινώσκει[1]	
	εἰ μὴ	nisi	εἰ μὴ	εἰ μὴ	εἰ μὴ	εἰ μὴ
	ὁ πατὴρ	filius	ὁ πατὴρ	ὁ πατὴρ	ὁ υἱὸς[2]	ὁ υἱὸς[3]
	καὶ οἷς ἂν	et cui	καὶ οἷς ἂν	καὶ οἷς ἂν	καὶ ᾧ ⌐ἐὰν[3]	καὶ ⌐Φ[4] ⌐ἐὰν[5]
	⌐βούληται[2]	voluerit	(1. 18)		βούληται	βούληται
15	ὁ υἱὸς	filius	ἀποκαλύψη	ὁ υἱὸς	ὁ υἱὸς	ὁ υἱὸς
	ἀποκαλύψαι.	revelare.	ὁ υἱός.	ἀποκαλύψη.	ἀποκαλύψαι.	ἀποκαλύψαι.

[1]εἶδεν O.
[2]βούλεται P.

Mt. 11.27: [1]novit vg; syᵖ ܣܐ.

Lk. 10.22: [1]novit a b; syᵖ ܣܐ.

H 17.4.3*	R 2.47.3**	Ju, A. 63.3***	Ju, D. 100.1	Mt. 11.27	Lk. 10.22
				[2] πατερα-υιος, υιον-πατηρ order N X. [3] αν D.	[2] omit sys. [3] π-υ, υ-π order U N bo. [4] quibus e. [5] αν B D.

*H 18.4.2 and 18.13.1 read the same, except 18.13.1 omits ὡς.

**The Syriac of R reads: ܘܠܐ ܐܢܫ ܝܕܥ ܠܐܒܐ ܐܠܐ ܒܪܐ ܘܠܐ ܠܒܪܐ ܐܠܐ ܐܒܐ ܘܠܐܝܢܐ ܕܨܒܐ ܒܪܐ ܕܢܓܠܐ܀

***Apol. 63.13 reads the same except with the final order ὁ υἱὸς ἀποκαλύψῃ.

This saying and the four that follow have parallels both in
Justin and a number of other early fathers. In fact the list of
the citations of this saying in the fathers is so extensive that
I have chosen not to try to list them. Instead the reader is
asked to consult the article by Paul Winter in which he surveys
and analyzes the history of the development of the texts of
Mt. 11.27 and Lk. 10.22 from the first to the fifth centuries,
listing all occurrences of the citation in the fathers which he
has been able to find.[1] Working backward through the forms of
the saying, he concludes that the first century form of the text
(= Q) read:

> πάντα μοι παρεδόθη ὑπὸ τοῦ πατρός,
> καὶ οὐδεὶς ἔγνω τὸν πατέρα εἰ μὴ υἱὸς
> καὶ οἷς ἂν ἀποκαλύψῃ αὐτὸν υἱός.[2]

Whether or not this will hold up, the saying does appear to have
come from the Wisdom tradition.[3]

The citations in Justin indicate a text of the mid-second
century which probably read:[4]

> οὐδεὶς ἔγνω[5] τὸν πατέρα εἰ μὴ ὁ υἱός,
> οὐδὲ τὸν υἱὸν εἰ μὴ ὁ πατὴρ
> καὶ οἷς ἂν ὁ υἱὸς ἀποκαλύψῃ.[6]

---

[1]"Matthew xi 27 and Luke x 22 from the First to the Fifth
Century, Reflections on the Development of the Text," NovT 1
(1956/57), 112-48.

[2]Ibid., pp. 147-48.

[3]See especially Jack Suggs, Wisdom, Christology, and Law in
Matthew's Gospel (1970), pp. 71-97. That it goes back to a
Palestinian origin rather than being a creation of the Hellen-
istic Church (as Bousset [Kyrios Christos, 5th ed. (ET 1970),
pp. 83ff.] had argued) is argued by Winter (op. cit., p. 147, n.
n. 1) and W. Grundmann ("Matth. xi. 27 und die Johanneischen
'Der Vater - Der Sohn' - Stellen," NTS 12 (1965/66), 42-49).

[4]I leave out the line πάντα - πατρός since it does not enter
into the citations of the saying in H. It does appear once in
Justin's citations of the sayings (in Dial. 100.1). If a common
text is involved, this only means that H did not choose to quote
the first line as Justin also did not in Apol. 63.

[5]γινώσκει in Dial. 100.1 is most likely either Justin's own
change or a later scribal correction. Cf. Bellinzoni, Sayings,
pp. 26-28, and Winter, op. cit., p. 137.

[6]Tatian may possibly be adduced as a witness to the same
text. Ephraem cites the Diatessaron in Comm. 10.15 as follows:
"Nemo noscit (ܘ ܥ) Patrem nisi Filius, neque Filium nisi Pater"
(Leloir, Syr., pp. 49, 51). ܘ ܥ could represent either ἔγνω or

Such a text was widely known to and used by the fathers. It differed from the form of Mt. 11.27 and Lk. 10.22 (as known to us from most of the manuscripts) in the following respects:

1. ἔγνω instead of (ἐπι)γινώσκει: H, R (novit), Justin (Apol.), Irenaeus (quoting the "heretics"), Clement, Tertullian (novit), Origen, (cf. Adamantius), Eusebius, and Epiphanius (Ancor. 73.1). It is Irenaeus who seems first to have made a point of the two forms and that for polemical reasons. To the "heretics" he ascribes the use of ἔγνω (=cognovit),[7] but he himself consistently uses γινώσκει (=cognoscit).[8] Explicitly he says of the form with cognoscit: "Sic et Matthaeus posuit, et Lucas similiter, et Marcus [!] idem ipsum: Johannes enim praeterit locum hunc."[9] But the form with cognovit is introduced with the words: "Hi autem qui peritiores Apostolis volunt esse, sic describunt."[9] The reason for Irenaeus' objection was that the "heretics" were using the aorist form ἔγνω as a basis to deny that men knew the Father before the coming of Christ ("et interpretantur, quasi a nullo cognitus sit verus Deus ante Domine nostri adventum: et eum Deum qui a prophetis sit annuntiatus, dicunt non esse Patrem Christi").[9] But in spite of his protest the widespread attestation of other (especially early) fathers to ἔγνω shows that a text with ἔγνω was known to and used by more than the "heretics" and that Irenaeus' objections did not prevail until later when the manuscripts and later fathers show a preference for γινώσκει (or οἶδεν).[10]

2. The order Father-Son, Son-Father: H (and the Syriac of R), Justin, probably Tatian,[11]

γινώσκει. But he clearly attests the reversed order of Father and Son.

[7]AH 1.13.2 (Harvey 1.180) = the Marcosians; 2.18.6 (Harvey 1.300) = the Valentinians; 4.11.1 (Harvey 2.158) = unnamed "heretics."

[8]AH 2.4.5 (Harvey 1.263) and 4.11.1-2 (Harvey 2.158-59).

[9]AH 4.11.1 (Harvey 2.158).

[10]So Winter, op. cit., pp. 137-39. Cf. additional bibliography on p. 137, n. 1. Cf. also the discussion over ἔγνω, γινώσκει, and οἶδε in Adamantius, Dial. 1.23 (Bakhuyzen 42, 44).

[11]See n. 6. To this evidence one may add Ephraem, Comm. 18. 16 (Leloir, Arm. 326) and Δv (Todesco 63: "et nesuno cognosse Dio Pare se non lo Fiolo, e lo Fiolo negun cognosce se no lo Pare").

38

Irenaeus,[12] Tertullian, Origen (De princ. 2.6.1),[13] Eusebius,
Adamantius, Athansius (Sermo maior de fide 28), Didymus Alex.
(De trinitate 1.26), Epiphanius, and some manuscripts of Matthew
(N X) and Luke (U N bo). Noticably absent from the list is
Clement of Alex. Winter has suggested that it was he who, perhaps struck by the incongruity of thought in saying that the
Revealer (the Son) was unknown, yet revealed the Father to
others, changed the order so as to move the line about "no one
knows the Son except the Father" further away from the last line
and thus ease somewhat the clash of these two incompatible
lines.[14] This would then explain the fact that Origen, following
on Clement's innovation, usually follows the order Son-Father,
Father-Son. But the more common form before Clement, and still
widely known and used after him, was Father-Son, Son-Father.

3. οἷς instead of ᾧ: H,[15] Justin, and Irenaeus.[16] Winter
considers the difference only an insignificant grammatical difference and does not discuss it further.[17] I also fail to see
any significance in the use of one or the other. But it may at
least help confirm that H's reading is closer to Justin's than
to later attestations of the saying.

4. ἄν instead of ἐάν: H, Justin, Irenaeus (of the
Valentinians), Clement, Origen, Eusebius, and Athanasius.
Epiphanius, on the other hand, attests the later (stylistic)
preference for ἐάν. But this is a scribal choice and cannot
really help us much.

---

[12]Irenaeus does not seem to be concerned about this order
and cites both orders in his own citations of the saying:
F-S, S-F in 2.4.5 (and some manuscripts of 4.11.2) and S-F, F-S
in 4.11.1(-2).

[13]However Origen usually cites the order S-F, F-S.

[14]Op. cit., pp. 141-43. However see the comments of Suggs,
Wisdom, pp. 72-77.

[15]Cf. the Syriac of R 2.47.3: ܐܠܡ ܠܕܘܗ.

[16]Irenaeus attests in his own citations both the singular
and the plural: cui in 4.11.1, quibus in 2.4.5, and quibuscunque
in 4.11.2.

[17]Op. cit., p. 127.

5. ἀποκαλύψῃ instead of βούληται ἀποκαλύψαι: Justin, Irenaeus,[18] Clement, Tertullian, Origen, Eusebius, Athanasius, and Epiphanius. Winter makes the suggestion that βούληται ἀποκαλύψαι is a later Greek expansion of ἀποκαλύψῃ, made for syllabic reasons when the saying was cited in liturgical worship.[19]

Turning to H one notes that H agrees with Justin in reading ἔγνω, the order Father-Son, Son-Father, οἷς, and ἄν, but differs in reading βούληται ἀποκαλύψαι and τις οἶδεν. Yet no other father attests the same combination of elements as in H. One must at least suspect the possibility of secondary "correction" in H toward a text of Matthew. The tendency of such a "correction" would appear to be the adding of words in Matthew that may have been missing from H (βούληται and τις οἶδεν) but otherwise not to change the wording of H. Alternatively the τις οἶδεν could be an addition to provide a parallel with the first line (οὐδεὶς ἔγνω) and the addition of βούληται due to its familiarity from liturgical usage (assuming the explanation of Winter above). In other words H may go back to the same text as Justin although some doubt remains in this case.

Because, as Winter has shown, both Matthew and Luke have undergone alteration from their original form(s), we cannot be sure whether to consider the saying to be based on a text of Matthew or Luke or on a harmonization of both. But because of its form, known to Justin and other fathers but differing from the (later) canonical form, I include it in this chapter.

R, on the other hand, is clearly a return to the text of Matthew, retaining <u>novit</u> (=ἔγνω) but otherwise following the later accepted text of Matthew (with Son-Father, Father-Son order, <u>cui</u> = ᴓ, and <u>voluerit</u> <u>revelare</u>). But the Syriac of R still preserves the plural (‎ܐܠܝܢ ‎ܕܠܗܘ) as in H.

---

[18]Again Irenaeus knows both ἀποκαλύψῃ (=revelaverit; 2.4.5 and 4.11.2) and βούληται ἀποκαλύψαι (=<u>voluerit revelare</u>; 4.11.1). In fact he is the earliest evidence for the latter reading.

[19]<u>Op. cit.</u>, pp. 143-44.

6. H 3.57.1b, R 5.13.2

H 3.57.1b	R 5.13.2	Ju, A. 15.13	Ju, D. 96.3	Mt. 5.45	Lk. 6.36
Γγίνεσθε[1]	estote	γίνεσθε δὲ	γίνεσθε	ὅπως γένησθε	γίνεσθε
ἀγαθοὶ καὶ	boni et	χρηστοὶ καὶ	χρηστοὶ καὶ	υἱοὶ	οἰκτίρμονες
οἰκτίρμονες	misericordes	οἰκτίρμονες	οἰκτίρμονες		καθὼς[1]
ὡς	sicut et	ὡς καὶ	ὡς καὶ	τοῦ πατρὸς	ὁ πατὴρ
ὁ πατὴρ	pater	ὁ πατὴρ	ὁ πατὴρ	ὑμῶν τοῦ	ὑμῶν[2]
ὁ ἐν	vester	ὑμῶν	ὑμῶν ὁ	ἐν[1] οὐρανοῖς,	
τοῖς οὐρανοῖς	caelestis		οὐράνιος.		
			καὶ γὰρ		
			τὸν παντο-		
			κράτορα θεὸν		
			χρηστὸν καὶ		
	misericors	χρηστός	οἰκτίρμονα		οἰκτίρμων
	est,	ἐστι καὶ	ὁρῶμεν,		ἐστίν.
	qui	οἰκτίρμων,		ὅτι[2]	
ὃς		καὶ	καὶ		
ἀνατέλλει	oriri facit	(l. 21)	(l. 21)	(l. 21)	
τὸν ἥλιον	solem	τὸν ἥλιον	τὸν ἥλιον	τὸν ἥλιον	
	suum	αὐτοῦ	αὐτοῦ	αὐτοῦ	
(l. 18)		ἀνατέλλει	ἀνατέλλοντα	ἀνατέλλει	
ἐπ' ἀγαθοῖς	super bonos	ἐπὶ ἀμαρτωλοὺς	ἐπὶ ἀχαρίστους	ἐπὶ Γπονηροὺς	
καὶ πονηροῖς	et malos	καὶ δικαίους	καὶ πονηροὺς	καὶ ἀγαθοὺς[3]	

40

H 3.57.1b	R 5.13.2	Ju, A. 15.13	Ju, D. 96.3	Mt. 5.45	Lk. 6.36
		καὶ πονηρούς.			
25 καὶ ⌜φέρει² τὸν ὑετὸν	et pluit	καὶ βρέχοντα	καὶ βρέχοντα	καὶ βρέχει	
ἐπὶ δικαίοις καὶ ἀδίκοις.	super iustos et iniustos.	ἐπὶ ὁσίους καὶ πονηρούς.	ἐπὶ ὁσίους καὶ πονηρούς.	ἐπὶ δικαίους καὶ ἀδίκους.	

¹γίνεσθαι P* O*.
²φέρε O.

Mt. 5.45:
¹+ τοις θ pm
²ὅστις 1573
pc sy; ος
lat.
³αγ. κ. πον.
lat sy sa.

Lk. 6.36:
¹+ και A D
Koine θ pm
lat.
²+ εν τοις
ουρανοις bo pt,
ο ουρανιος ℵ*²
φ pc Eth.

Mt. 5.48
Ἔσεσθε οὖν ὑμεῖς τέλειοι ²ὡς ὁ πατὴρ ὑμῶν ὁ ⌜οὐράνιος¹ τέλειός ἐστιν. [¹εν τοις ουρανοις D* Θ pm.]

Lk. 6.35b
καὶ ἔσεσθε υἱοὶ ὑψίστου, ὅτι αὐτὸς χρηστός ἐστιν ἐπὶ τοὺς ἀχαρίστους καὶ πονηρούς. (Cf. Ju.)

H 11.12.1
οὐκ ἄν οὐδὲ τὸν ἥλιον αὐτοῦ ἀνέτειλεν ἐπὶ ἀγαθοὺς καὶ πονηροὺς οὔτε τὸν ὑετὸν αὐτοῦ ἔφερεν ἐπὶ δικαίους καὶ ἀδίκους.

H 12.26.7
εὐεργετοῦντα δικαίους καὶ ἀδίκους, ὡς αὐτὸς ὁ θεὸς πᾶσιν ἐν τῷ νῦν κόσμῳ τόν τε ἥλιον καὶ τοὺς ὑετοὺς αὐτοῦ παρέχων.

H 18.2.2
τὸν δημιουργόν, παρέχοντα τὸν ἥλιον ἀγαθοῖς καὶ κακοῖς
καὶ τὸν ὑετὸν δικαίοις καὶ ἀδίκοις.

Clement, Strom. 2.19/100.4 (Stählin 2.168)
γίνεσθε ἐλεήμονες καὶ οἰκτίρμονες,
ὡς ὁ πατὴρ ὑμῶν ὁ οὐράνιος οἰκτίρμων ἐστίν.

Clement, Paed. 1.8/72.2 (Stählin 1.132)
"ὅτι αὐτὸς χρηστός ἐστιν ἐπὶ τοὺς ἀχαρίστους καὶ πονηροὺς"
καὶ προσέτι "γίνεσθε οἰκτίρμονες" λέγων,
"καθὼς ὁ πατὴρ ὑμῶν οἰκτίρμων ἐστίν,"
... φησὶν "ἐπιλάμπει τὸν ἥλιον τὸν αὑτοῦ ἐπὶ πάντας."

Naasenes in Hippolytus, Phil. 5.7.26 (Wendland 3.84-85)
τοῦτον εἶναί φησιν [the Naasene] ἀγαθὸν μόνον, καὶ περὶ
τούτου λελέχθαι τὸ ὑπὸ τοῦ σωτῆρος λεγόμενον·
"Τί με λέγεις ἀγαθόν; εἷς ἐστιν ἀγαθός,
ὁ πατήρ μου ὁ ἐν τοῖς οὐρανοῖς,
ὃς ἀνατέλλει τὸν ἥλιον αὐτοῦ ἐπὶ δικαίους καὶ ἀδίκους
καὶ βρέχει ἐπὶ ὁσίους καὶ ἁμαρτωλούς." (Cf. Ju.)

Macarius, Hom. 19.2 (MPG 34.644)
γίνεσθε ἀγαθοὶ καὶ χρηστοί,
καθὼς καὶ ὁ Πατὴρ ὑμῶν ὁ οὐράνιος οἰκτίρμων ἐστί.

Epiphanius, Pan. 33.10.5 (Holl 1.461)
ὅμοιοι γένεσθε τῷ πατρὶ ὑμῶν τῷ ἐν τοῖς οὐρανοῖς,
ὅτι ἀνατέλλει αὐτοῦ τὸν ἥλιον ἐπὶ ἀγαθοὺς καὶ πονηροὺς
καὶ βρέχει ἐπὶ δικαίους καὶ ἀδίκους.

Hilary, Tract. in Ps. 118, Let. 8.8 (MPL 9.559)
Estote boni sicut Pater vester qui est in coelis,
qui solem suum oriri facit super bonos et malos,
et pluit super justos et injustos.

Augustine, C. Adim. 7 (CSEL 25.129)
Estote benigni quemadmodum Pater vester coelistis,
qui solem suum oriri facit super bonos et malos.

Manichaeans in Augustine, C. Adim. 7 (CSEL 25.127)
Estote benigni sicut Pater vester coelestis
qui solem suum oriri facit super bonos et malos.

This saying, like numbers 2 and 3, comes from the Sermon on
the Mount/Plain and shows a preference for Lucan wording where
there is both a Matthean and a Lucan form of the saying involved.
The latter half of the saying is known only from Matthew however
(cf. to no. 3 above).

Bellinzoni has already argued that there underlies the
saying in Justin "a harmony of Lk. 6.36 and Mt. 5.45b (with
elements from Lk. 6.35 and Mt. 5.48), a harmony in wide circula-
tion in the early church and used by several of the

fathers."[1] He reconstructs the source as follows:

γίνεσθε χρηστοὶ καὶ οἰκτίρμονες,
ὡς καὶ ὁ πατὴρ ὑμῶν ὁ οὐράνιος χρηστός ἐστι καὶ οἰκτίρμων,
καὶ τὸν ἥλιον αὐτοῦ ἀνατέλλει ἐπὶ ἀγαθοὺς καὶ πονηροὺς
καὶ βρέχει ἐπὶ δικαίους καὶ ἀδίκους.[2]

We may consider the elements of this reconstruction with
primary attention on H and Justin but also with regard to the
reading of the fathers listed.

1. The wording of (primarily) Lk. 6.36 has been combined
with Mt. 5.45b: H, R, Justin, (Clement), Epiphanius, Hilary,
and Augustine.

2. The quotation begins with Luke's γίνεσθε: H, Justin,
Clement, Macarius; = estote: R, Hilary, and Augustine.

3. The use of Luke's οἰκτίρμονες (H, Justin, Clement,
probably R [misericordes], and Augustine [benigne]) is joined
with another adjective: χρηστοί (Justin), ἀγαθοί (H), or
ἐλεήμονες (Clement).[3] It is Justin who most likely reproduces
the source which seems to have added χρηστοί due to the influence
of Lk. 6.35 (ὅτι αὐτὸς χρηστός ἐστιν ἐπὶ τοὺς ἀχαρίστους καὶ
πονηρούς).[4] For this assumption best explains the variations at
this point: H[5] changed the source's χρηστοί to ἀγαθοί, Clement
to ἐλεήμονες, while Macarius retained χρηστοί but changed
οἰκτίρμονες to ἀγαθοί.

4. The double adjectives were then probably repeated
(χρηστός ἐστι καὶ οἰκτίρμων) as Justin reads. That H lacks this
conclusion to the saying need be seen only as his own omission.
The fact that R reads misericors est may indicate that the
Grundschrift had read the source as Justin reproduces it but
dropped χρηστὸς καί after it had changed the initial χρηστοί to

---

[1]Sayings, p. 13.

[2]Ibid., p. 14.

[3]Macarius has ἀγαθοὶ καὶ χρηστοί.

[4]The τέλειος - τέλειος of Mt. 5.48 was available but not
chosen. Why? Perhaps χρηστός (as other fathers preferred
ἀγαθός) was considered more appropriate for what is described in
the saying--God's kindness rather than "perfection." Whether
polemical considerations (e.g., the Gnostic use of τέλειος)
entered cannot be said.

[5]In this case this means that the Grundschrift already read
ἀγαθοὶ καὶ οἰκτίρμονες as R (boni et misericordes) shows.

44

ἀγαθοί. The same argument could be applied to Macarius (ἀγαθοὶ καὶ χρηστοί - οἰκτίρμων ἐστι) and Clement (ἐλεήμονες καὶ οἰκτίρμονες - οἰκτίρμων ἐστίν). The alternative would be for the source to have read: χρηστοὶ καὶ οἰκτίρμονες - οἰκτίρμων ἐστίν and for Justin to have added the χρηστὸς καί for the sake of parallelism. But even so, a common source is still indicated for these fathers' reading of this saying.

5. Justin reads ὡς καί in both his citations of the saying. It is unlikely that he would have added καί both times had not his source read thus.[6] This is further confirmed by the reading of R (sicut et) and Macarius (καθὼς καί). H (with only ὡς), it may be concluded, has simply dropped the seemingly unnecessary καί.

6. All of the fathers listed read in addition to the Lucan ὁ πατὴρ ὑμῶν either ὁ οὐράνιος (caelestis) or ὁ ἐν τοῖς οὐρανοῖς (qui est in caelis).[7] Clearly the source read the additional phrase. But it is difficult to determine if the source had read a text of Luke that contained it[8] or was influenced by the ὁ οὐράνιος of Mt. 5.48 or the τοῦ ἐν οὐρανοῖς of Mt. 5.45.

7. In Bellinzoni's reconstruction of the source the last half of the saying differs from the wording of Mt. 5.45b only in reversing the order of ἐπὶ πονηροὺς καὶ ἀγαθούς to ἐπὶ ἀγαθοὺς καὶ πονηρούς. This reversed order is attested by H,[9] R, Epiphanius, Hilary, and Augustine. H's placing ἀναστέλλει before τον ἥλιον is inconsequential. His use of φέρει τὸν ὑετόν instead of βρέχει is no more than his own choice of wording[10] as

_____

[6]Some manuscripts of Lk. 6.36 also add και: A D Koine ϑ pm lat.

[7]The two expressions seem to be interchangeable according to a writer's inclination or preference.
   Justin's omission of either expression in Apol. 15.13 could be his own omission or that of a later scribe under the influence of the Lucan text. But Justin shows that he knows the additional phrase (ὁ οὐράνιος) for this saying in Dial. 96.3. The additional words of Dial. 96.3 (καὶ γὰρ παντοκράτορα θεόν) are surely Justin's own addition. Cf. Bellinzoni, Sayings, p. 10 and n. 2.

[8]ο ουρανιος is added to Lk. 6.36 by ℵᵃ 13 69 and Eth; εν τοις ουρανοις by bo^pt.

[9]Cf. also H 11.12.1 and 18.2.2 (ἀγαθοῖς καὶ κακοῖς).

[10]Cf. also H 11.12.1 (τὸν ὑετὸν αὐτοῦ ἔφερεν), 12.26.7 (τοὺς ὑετοὺς αὐτοῦ), and 18.2.2 (τὸν ὑετόν).

is his change of the adjectives after ἐπί from accusatives to datives. The real difficulty is in Justin's variations to Mt. 5.45b. Here I would agree with Bellinzoni's judgment (1) that "in Apol. 15.13 Justin chose to modify his source by omitting βρέχει," and (2) that "Justin's inconsistency in quoting ἁμαρτωλοὺς καὶ δικαίους καὶ πονηρούς in Apol. 15.13 and ἀχαρίστους καὶ δικαίους and ὁσίους καὶ πονηρούς in Dial. 96.3b perhaps indicates that he both times modified a source that contained the reading found in many of these other fathers."[11]

In short there was a common harmonized source of this saying (or these sayings) which was used by H, Justin, and other fathers.[12]

---

[11]Sayings, p. 13.

[12]Waitz (Pseudoklementinen, pp. 284-86) recognized the close connection of H and Justin, but refers it to his theory of an anti-Marcionite redaction of KP. My analysis, however, indicates that H cannot be explained directly from Justin (as we know him) but rather by a common source behind both.
     Strecker (Judenchristentum, p. 131) admits the use of "einen unkanonischen Text" which contained a "Textmischung" found in numerous fathers but does not venture to say more about it or to make anything of it in his final results.

7. H 18.3.4-5

H 18.3.4-5*	Mt. 19.16-18	Lk. 18.18-19	Mk. 10.17-18	Ju, A. 16.7	Ju, D. 101.2
τῷ εἰπόντι φαρισαίῳ "Τί 5 ποιήσας ζωὴν αἰώνιαν κληρονομήσω;" ..."Τί με "Μή με λέγε ἀγαθόν. 10 ὁ γὰρ ἀγαθὸς εἷς ἐστιν, ὁ πατὴρ 15 ὁ ἐν τοῖς οὐρανοῖς..." "Εἰ δὲ θέλεις εἰς τὴν ζωὴν εἰσελθεῖν, ⌐τήρησον[1] τὰς ἐντολάς." 20 ἐξ τοῦ [5]	εἷς... "Διδάσκαλε,[1] τί ἀγαθὸν ποιήσω ἵνα σχῶ ζωὴν αἰώνιαν;" 17 ..."Τί με ἐρωτᾷς περὶ τοῦ ἀγαθοῦ; εἷς ἐστιν ὁ ἀγαθός.[2] εἰ δὲ θέλεις εἰς τὴν ζωὴν εἰσελθεῖν, ⌐τήρει[3] 18 ...λέγει τὰς ἐντολάς." (cf. 1. 22)	τις ἄρχων... "Διδ. ἀγαθέ, τί ποιήσας ζωὴν αἰώνιαν κληρονομήσω; 19 ..."Τί με..." λέγεις ἀγαθόν; οὐδεὶς ἀγαθὸς εἰ μὴ εἷς ⌐ὁ θεός.[2] τὰς ἐντολὰς οἶδας." (cf. 1. 22)	εἷς... "Διδ. ἀγαθέ, τί ποιήσω ἵνα ζωὴν αἰώνιαν κληρονομήσω; 18 ..."Τί με..." λέγεις ἀγαθόν; οὐδεὶς ἀγαθὸς εἰ μὴ εἷς ὁ θεός. τὰς ἐντολὰς οἶδας." (cf. 1. 22)	τινος... "Διδ. ἀγαθέ," "οὐδεὶς ἀγαθὸς εἰ μὴ ὁ θεός, ὁ ποιήσας τὰ πάντα."	τινος... "Διδ. ἀγαθέ," ..."Τί με λέγεις ἀγαθόν; εἷς ἐστιν ἀγαθός, ὁ πατήρ μου ὁ ἐν τοῖς οὐρανοῖς."

H 18.3.4-5*	Mt. 19.16-18	Lk. 18.18-19	Mk. 10.17-18	Ju, A. 16.7	Ju, D. 101.2
εἰπόντος·	αὐτῷ·				
"Ποίας;"	"Ποίας;"				
25 ἐπὶ τὰς					
τοῦ νόμου					
ἐπεμψεν.					

¹τηρει Ο.

Mt. column notes:
¹+ αγαθε c
Koine NΔΦ
φ 118 209 565
pm syPsa bopt.
²+ o θεος
lat syᶜ bopt;
o πατηρ e.
³τηροσον
relj; txt B
D 565.

Lk. column notes:
¹+ φαρισαιων
syᶜ.
²Omit ℵ* B*.

---

*H 18.17.4 contains lines 4-16; H 18.1.3 contains lines 9-16; H 3.57.1 and 17.4.2 contains lines 9-13.
In H 17.4.2 and 18.1.3 Simon Magus is the one who quotes the words.

Marcion in Hippolytus, Phil. 7.30.6 (Wendland 3.217)
ὡς αὐτὸς (Jesus) ὁμολογεῖ·
"Τί με λέγετε ἀγαθόν; εἷς ἐστιν ἀγαθός."

Marcion in Epiphanius, Pan. 42.11.15, Schol. 50 (Holl 2.144)
"Διδάσκαλε ἀγαθέ, τί ποιήσας ζωὴν αἰώνιαν κληρονομήσω;" ὁ δέ· "Μή με λέγε ἀγαθόν· εἷς ἐστιν ἀγαθὸς ὁ θεός." προσέθετο ἐκεῖνος "ὁ πατήρ"...

48

Ptolemy in Epiphanius, Pan. 33.7.5 (Holl 1.456)
ἕνα γὰρ μόνον εἶναι ἀγαθὸν θεόν, τὸν ἑαυτοῦ πατέρα
ὁ σωτὴρ ἡμῶν ἀπεφήνατο, ὃν αὐτὸς ἐφανέρωσεν.

Naasenes in Hippolytus, Phil. 5.7.26 (the text has been given in
the previous saying, No. 6).*

Marcosians in Epiphanius, Pan. 34.18.10-11 (Holl 2.33)
Ἔνια δὲ καὶ τῶν ἐν τῷ εὐαγγελίῳ καιμένων εἰς τοῦτον
τὸν χαρακτῆρα μεθαρμόζουσιν, ὡς...
καὶ τῷ εἰπόντι αὐτῷ "διδάσκαλε ἀγαθέ"
τὸν ἀληθῶς ἀγαθὸν θεὸν ὡμολογηκέναι εἰπόντα
"τί με λέγεις ἀγαθόν; εἷς ἐστιν ἀγαθός,
ὁ πατὴρ ἐν τοῖς οὐρανοῖς·"

Irenaeus, AH 1.13.2 (Harvey 1.178)
Τί με λέγεις ἀγαθόν; εἷς ἐστιν ἀγαθός,
ὁ Πατὴρ ἐν τοῖς οὐρανοῖς.

Clement, Paed. 1.8/72.2 (Stählin 1.132) (Cf. Paed. 1.8/74.1)
οὐδεὶς ἀγαθός, εἰ μὴ ὁ πατήρ μου ὁ ἐν τοῖς οὐρανοῖς.

Clement, Strom. 2.20/114.3,6 (Stählin 2.175) [= Valentinus]
εἷς δὲ ἐστιν ἀγαθός, ... ὁ μόνος ἀγαθὸς πατήρ, ...

Arians in Epiphanius, Pan. 69.19.1 (Holl 3.168)
Εἶτα πάλιν φησὶν ὁ μανιώδης Ἄρειος· "πῶς εἶπεν ὁ κύριος,
'Τί με λέγεις ἀγαθόν; εἷς ἐστιν ἀγαθὸς ὁ θεός,'"

Ephraem, Comm. 15.2 (Leloir, Arm., 264; cf. Syr. 140)
Bon maître, . . . Personne n'est bon, sinon un seul:
le Pere, qui est dans le ciel.

This saying which occurs several times (at least portions
of it) in H also shows common harmonistic features in common
with Justin and other fathers. The wording of the different
occurrences of the saying in H is the same in all cases listed.

H's harmonistic character is clear: (1) τί ποιήσας ζωὴν
αἰώνιαν κληρονομήσω; = Luke; (2) μή με λέγε ἀγαθόν is probably
an alteration of Luke (or Mark); (3) ὁ γὰρ ἀγαθὸς εἷς ἐστιν =
Matthew.[1] εἰ δὲ θέλεις - ποίας (which occurs only in H 3.18.4-5)

---

*Bellinzoni, Sayings, p. 19 (but cf. p. 13, n. 1), wrongly
lists this reference as Origen, Contra Haereses. The work was
handed down as Origen's until 1859 when the edition of L. Dunker
and F. G. Schneidewind restored it to Hippolytus. (Cf. Quasten,
Patrology, 2.166.)

[1]The Lucan wording τί με λέγεις ἀγαθόν; οὐδεὶς ἀγαθὸς εἰ
μὴ εἷς ὁ θεός is read for Matthew by C Koine W Δ Φ φ 118 209
565 pm syP sa boPt. But this would not explain H's (or the
fathers') mixing of Luke's wording (1 and 2 above) with Matthew's
(3 above).

is from Matthew. Now it is precisely the combining of Luke's
τί με λέγεις ἀγαθόν; with Matthew's ὁ γὰρ ἀγαθὸς εἷς ἐστιν (H,
Justin [Dial. 101.2], Irenaeus, Hippolytus [of the Naasenes], and
Epiphanius [of the Marcosians, Marcion (μή με λέγε ἀγαθόν), and
the Arians]), and the addition of ὁ πατήρ (μου) (ὁ) ἐν τοῖς
οὐρανοῖς (H, Justin [Dial. 101.2], Irenaeus, Clement, Hippolytus,
Epiphanius [of the Marcosians], and Ephraem) that both distinguish this form of the saying from the canonical texts and proves
again a common source not only for H and Justin but one known to
a number of fathers (and the "heretics").[2]

H's peculiarities may be adjudged as his own changes.

1. He has introduced the saying with τῷ εἰπόντι φαρισαίῳ.
This does not affect the saying itself but attests to a tradition
like that known to sy[c] which introduced Lk. 18.18 with "a certain
leader of the Pharisees."[3]

2. H's lack of διδάσκαλε (= Matthew) or διδάσκαλε ἀγαθέ
(= Mark and Luke) cannot tell us whether his source read the
address or not. But Justin, Epiphanius, and Ephraem read
διδάσκαλε ἀγαθέ.

3. H reads the Lucan (= Marcan) τί με λέγεις ἀγαθόν; (as
opposed to the Matthean τί με ἐρωτᾷς περὶ τοῦ ἀγαθοῦ;) in a form
that is attributed by Epiphanius to Marcion: μή με λέγε
ἀγαθόν. This may be explained for H partly by the fact that the
saying is twice (H 17.4.2 and 18.1.3) on the lips of Simon Magus
who at one level in the Pseudo-Clementines represents Marcion.[4]

---

[2]Waitz (Pseudoklementinen, p. 282) again reverts to his
hypothesis of an anti-Marcionite redaction of KP which used
Justin as a source. It should by now be apparent that in the
examples thus far H cannot be explained from Justin, and that
Waitz's failure to consider the same mixing of texts elsewhere
makes this part of his theory virtually worthless.
Strecker (Judenchristentum, p. 131) again notes the text
mixing as attested in many of the fathers and concludes: "Diese
Lesart hat sich also längere Zeit neben der kanonischen behaupten
können." Obviously! But where and how?

[3] ܠܩܘ ܠܪܝ ܘܣ (Burkitt 1.370). Was there perhaps an identification of "the rich ruler" (ἄρχων is from Lk. 18.18) and
Nicodemus in Jn. 3, an ἄρχων τῶν Ἰουδαίων?

[4]Cf., e.g., Waitz, Pseudoklementinen, pp. 102, 110-11, 164,
and passim. The use of a Marcionite form of a saying of Jesus
arises again in H 18.15.1. The other two occurrences (H 3.57.1
and 18.3.4-5) on the lips of Peter would suggest that the author
(G or H) simply continued to cite the saying as already given
(in its Marcionite form). But the Marcionite form is itself a
mixed text and probably dependent on the hypothesized harmonistic

50

4. The change of word order in H's ὁ γὰρ ἀγαθὸς εἷς ἐστιν
for the Matthean εἷς ἐστιν ὁ ἀγαθός is merely a stylistic
change.

H is therefore most likely dependent on the same harmonized
source as Justin (in <u>Dial</u>. 101.2)[5] and other fathers.

---

source. For it includes a clearly Matthean element--εἷς ἐστι
ἀγαθός. We will return to the question of an anti-Marcionite
layer in H in the concluding chapter.

[5]<u>Apol</u>. 16.7 is thought by Bellinzoni to rest on a different
source than <u>Dial</u>. 101.2 (see <u>Sayings</u>, pp. 20, 95-100, 118-21).
In the case of <u>Apol</u>. 16.7 no other text than Lk. 18.18-19 need
be presupposed. While Justin used the "harmony" earlier in
<u>Apol</u>. 16, he may have also had a copy of Luke and used it in
16.7 instead of the harmony's reading. Otherwise a later
scribal change should be conjectured for <u>Apol</u>. 16.7.

8. H 8.4.1, R 4.4.3

	H 8.4.1	R 4.4.3	Mt. 8.11	Lk. 13.29	Ju, D. 76.4	Ju, D. 120.6*
	πολλοὶ	multi	πολλοὶ	καὶ		
	ἐλεύσονται	veniet	(1. 5)	ἥξουσιν	ἥξουσιν	ἥξουσι γάρ,
	ἀπὸ ἀνατολῶν	ab oriente	ἀπὸ ἀνατολῶν	ἀπὸ ἀνατολῶν	ἀπὸ ἀνατολῶν	ἀπὸ δυσμῶν
	καὶ δυσμῶν	et occidente	καὶ δυσμῶν	καὶ δυσμῶν	καὶ δυσμῶν	καὶ ἀνατολῶν
5			ἥξουσιν			
	⌐ἄρκτου τε	⌐a¹ septentrione		⌐καὶ ἀπὸ¹ βορρᾶ		
	καὶ	et		καὶ		
	μεσημβρίας¹	meridiano		νότου		
	καὶ	et	καὶ	καὶ	καὶ	καὶ
10	ἀνακλιθήσονται	recumbent	ἀνακλιθήσονται	ἀνακλιθήσονται	ἀνακλιθήσονται	ἀνακλιθήσονται
	⌐εἰς κόλπους²	⌐in sinibus²	μετὰ		μετὰ	μετὰ
	᾿Αβραὰμ	Abraham	᾿Αβραὰμ		᾿Αβραὰμ	᾿Αβραὰμ
	καὶ ᾿Ισαὰκ	et Isaac	καὶ ᾿Ισαὰκ		καὶ ᾿Ισαὰκ	καὶ ᾿Ισαὰκ
	καὶ ᾿Ιακώβ.	et Iacob.	καὶ ᾿Ιακώβ		καὶ ᾿Ιακώβ	καὶ ᾿Ιακώβ
15			ἐν τῇ	ἐν τῇ	ἐν τῇ	ἐν τῇ
			βασιλείᾳ	βασιλείᾳ	βασιλείᾳ	βασιλείᾳ
			τῶν οὐρανῶν.	τοῦ θεοῦ.	τῶν οὐρανῶν.	τῶν οὐρανῶν.

¹καὶ βορρᾶ καὶ θαλάσσῃ E.
²μετά E.

¹et a Δᵈᵖ πg.
²in sinu Δᵈ; cum Π.

¹καὶ ℵ A D Koine Θ 𝔐 lat; απο 𝔓75 070 i; txt B al it.

*Ju, D. 140.4 reads the same, omitting the γάρ.

Lk. 13.28
. . . ὅταν ὄψησθε Ἀβραὰμ καὶ Ἰσαὰκ καὶ Ἰακὼβ
καὶ πάντας τοὺς προφήτας ἐν τῇ βασιλείᾳ τοῦ θεοῦ, . . .

Marcion in Epiphanius, Pan. 42.11.15, Schol. 41 (Holl 2.141)
Παρέκοψε πάλιν τό "ᾐξουσιν ἀπὸ ἀνατολῶν καὶ δυσμῶν
καὶ ἀνακλιθήσονται ἐν τῇ βασιλείᾳ."

Irenaeus, AH 4.15 (Harvey 2.165)   [Austro
Quoniam venient ab Oriente et Occidente, ab Aquilone et
et recumbent cum Abraham et Isaac et Jacob in regno
caelorum.

Origen, Frag. cat. evv. 158 (Klostermann 12.158)
τὸ δὲ ἀνακλιθήσονται ἐν κόλπῳ Ἀβραὰμ κ. τ. ε.
τὸ ἀνακλιθήσονται ἐν κόλποις Ἀβραὰμ κ. τ. ε.

Eusebius, De eccl. theol. 1.20.17 (Klostermann 4.83)
ὥσπερ δὴ ἡμῖν ἐπήγγελται ὁ σωτὴρ
εἰς κόλπους Ἀβραὰμ καὶ Ἰσαὰκ καὶ Ἰακὼβ διαναπαύσασθαι,...

Epiphanius, Pan. 23.6.3 (Holl 1.255)
ὡς λέγει "ἐλεύσονται ἐν κόλποις Ἀβραὰμ καὶ Ἰσαὰκ καὶ
Ἰακὼβ ἐν τῇ βασιλείᾳ τῶν οὐρανῶν
καὶ ἀναπαύσονται ἀπο ἀνατολῶν και δυσμῶν" κ. τ. ε.

Ephraem, Opp. I 171C = 333EF (latter omits καὶ Ἰακώβ)
ᾐξουσιν ἀπὸ ἀνατολῶν καὶ δυσμῶν καὶ βορρᾷ καὶ θαλάσσης
καὶ ἀνακλιθήσονται μετὰ Ἀβραὰμ καὶ Ἰσαὰκ καὶ Ἰακὼβ
ἐν τῇ βασιλείᾳ τῶν οὐρανῶν.

Bellinzoni has argued that Justin's three citations in the
Dialogue are from a single source which began with the Lucan
wording (ᾐξουσιν ἀπὸ ἀνατολῶν καὶ δυσμῶν) but otherwise is
Matthean (see the absence of "north and south," the presence of
μετὰ Ἀβραὰμ καὶ Ἰσαὰκ καὶ Ἰακώβ, and τῶν οὐρανῶν rather than
Luke's τοῦ θεοῦ).[1] Hence it was a harmonistic text with preference for the Matthean wording in this instance.

The Grundschrift (behind H and R) began with Matthew's
πολλοί. It is problematic whether the influence of Lk. 13.29 is
present at all. For the position of the verb (ἐλεύσονται)[2]

---

[1]Sayings, pp. 29-30.

[2]Epiphanius also attests the use of ἐλεύσονται instead of
ᾐξουσιν but this cannot itself prove anything. ἐλεύσονται is
easily exchanged for ᾐξουσιν, especially in this case so as to
make it a parallel form to ἀνακλιθήσονται.

before ἀπὸ ἀνατολῶν as Luke's ἥξουσιν before ἀπὸ ἀνατολῶν
instead of after the prepositional phrase (as in Matthew) could
be a stylistic change by G (making the verb position parallel to
ἀνακλιθήσονται) and only coincidentally in the same position as
Luke's ἥξουσιν. The addition of ἄρκτου τε καὶ μεσημβρίας[3]
is a choice of different wording from that in Luke (βορρᾶ καὶ
νότου) and is too natural an addition to "east and west" to
assume the influence of Lk. 13.29. Unfortunately for our
purposes G has omitted the ending of the saying.

But even if Lk. 13.29 is not present, the influence of Lk.
16.23 seems to be present in the words εἰς κόλπους ᾿Αβραάμ.
This addition is also attested by Origen, Eusebius, and
Epiphanius. The fact that Epiphanius adds the verb ἀναπαύσονται and Eusebius διαναπαύσασθαι would further suggest the
influence of Lk. 16.23 in the form read by D ϑ it: εν τοις
κολποις αυτου (Abraham) αναπαυομενον.

Thus we seem to have two different forms of this saying:

1. One which began with Luke and continued to the end
with Matthew as represented by Justin and probably also
Irenaeus and Ephraem.[4]

2. One which combined Mt. 8.11 with the phrase from
Lk. 16.23.

This of course raises the problem of a harmonized saying
of which H and Justin seem to have followed different sources.
This immediately leads to the question of different sources for
a saying of Jesus in H than in Justin. The fact that H consists
of various layers of material and redactions immediately suggests one possible solution: this saying belongs to another
layer or redaction of H than those which indicate a common
source with Justin. But it will be best to take up this subject
in consideration of all the sayings involved rather than one in
isolation (see the Conclusion).

---

[3]The Epitomes of H read καὶ βορρᾶ καὶ θαλάσσης. Ephraem
uses the same expression. But I confess I do not understand
this use of θαλάσσης for "south". Ephraem resided mainly in
Edessa.

[4]The addition of "east and west" in Irenaeus and Ephraem
could be their own additions or secondary influence of the Lucan
text. For it is doubtful that Justin would have omitted the
phrase three times if his source had read it.

9. H 3.55.3

H 3.55.3	Ju, A. 15.15	Mt. 6.32b	Mt. 6.8b
οἶδεν γὰρ	οἶδεν γὰρ	οἶδεν γὰρ	οἶδεν γὰρ ⌜ὁ θεος⌝[1]
ὁ πατὴρ ⌜ὑμῶν[1]	ὁ πατὴρ ὑμῶν	ὁ πατὴρ ὑμῶν	ὁ πατὴρ ὑμῶν
ὁ οὐράνιος	ὁ οὐράνιος	ὁ οὐράνιος	
5 ὅτι χρῄζετε	(1. 7)	ὅτι χρῄζετε	ὦν χρείαν ἔχετε
τούτων ἁπάντων	ὅτι τούτων	τούτων ἁπάντων.	
	χρείαν ἔχετε.		
πρὶν			πρὸ
αὐτὸν			(1. 11)
10 ⌜ἀξιώσετε.[2]			τοῦ ὑμᾶς αἰτῆσαι
			αὐτόν.

---

[1]Omit O.

[2]ἀξιώσητε P.

[1]Omit ℵ* D Koine W θ pl latt bo.

Cf. Lk. 12.30
ὑμῶν δὲ ὁ πατὴρ οἶδεν ὅτι χρῄζετε τούτων.

H follows Mt. 6.32b exactly in the first half of the saying and then adds what appears to be the ending of Mt. 6.8b but in a different construction (πρίν + indicative [or subjunctive in P]).[1] This could mean either that his source combined Mt. 6.32 and 6.8 or that H quoted Mt. 6.32 and (from memory ?) added the phrase from Mt. 6.8.[2]

Justin cites Mt. 6.32b. But does his omission of ἁπάντων and the use of χρείαν ἔχετε indicate the influence of Mt. 6.8?[3]

---

[1]In classical and Attic Greek πρίν is usually followed by the infinitive after positive clauses but the indicative usually follows negatives and the subjunctive or optative only follows negatives. Cf. B-D-F § 395.

[2]H seems to prefer the word ἀξιοῦν; cf. Ep. Pet. 1.2; 3.1; H 2.19.2; 17.5.4.

[3]Bellinzoni, Sayings, p. 17, speaks only of the use of Mt. 6.32 by Justin but does not attempt to explain his use of χρείαν ἔχετε. The sayings that occur in Apol. 15.14 and 15 are rather complicated but do show harmonizing features from Matthew and Luke (see ibid., pp. 14-17).

If so, one could say that both H and Justin attest a mixing of
Mt. 6.32 and 6.8 although in different ways. If not, then it
could be that H and Justin both reflect the use of Mt. 6.32 and
H (independently) of 6.8 while Justin has made a change in the
final wording of 6.32.

In short this saying lacks clear enough clues either to
support or deny a common source for H and Justin.[4]

---

[4]Waitz (Pseudoklementinen, pp. 305-06) wanted to see H and
Justin as related to each other at this point but failed to deal
with the problems involved. Strecker (Judenchristentum, p. 127)
also sees both H and Justin as mixing Mt. 6.32 and 6.8 but without being really parallel to each other.

10. H 11.35.6

H 11.35.6	Ju, A. 16.13	Ju, D. 35.3	Mt. 7.15-16	Mt. 24.5
πολλοὶ	πολλοὶ γὰρ	πολλοὶ	προσέχετε ἀπὸ	πολλοὶ γὰρ
ἐλεύσονται	ἥξουσιν	ἐλεύσονται	τῶν ψευδοπροφητῶν	ἐλεύσονται
5 πρός	ἐπὶ τῷ	ἐπὶ τῷ	οἵτινες	ἐπὶ τῷ
με	ὀνόματί μου	ὀνόματί μου	ἔρχονται	ὀνόματί μου
	ἔξωθεν μὲν	ἔξωθεν	πρὸς	λέγοντες ...
ἐν Γἐνδύματι¹	ἐνδεδυμένοι	ἐνδεδυμένοι	ὑμᾶς	
	δέρματα	δέρματα	ἐν ἐνδύμασι	
10 προβάτων	προβάτων	προβάτων	προβάτων	
ἔσωθεν δὲ	ἔσωθεν δὲ	ἔσωθεν δὲ	ἔσωθεν δὲ	
εἰσι	ὄντες	εἰσι	εἰσιν	
λύκοι	λύκοι	λύκοι	λύκοι	
ἅρπαγες·	ἅρπαγες·	ἅρπαγες·	ἅρπαγες.	
15 ἀπὸ	ἐκ		16 ἀπὸ	
τῶν καρπῶν	τῶν ἔργων		τῶν καρπῶν	
αὐτῶν	αὐτῶν		αὐτῶν	
ἐπιγνώσεσθε	ἐπιγνώσεσθε		ἐπιγνώσεσθε	
αὐτούς.	αὐτούς.		αὐτούς.	

¹ἐνδύμασι Ο.

57

Syriac of H 11.35.6
"Many will come to you in sheep skins (lit. clothing);
inside they are ravenous wolves. By their fruits you will
recognize them."

ܐ‌ܠܐ‌ܝ‌ܟ‌ܘܢ ܘܐ‌ܕ‌ܒ‌ܗ, ܚ‌ܠ‌ܚ‌ܚ‌ܡ‌ܐ ܘܐ‌ܬ‌ܒ‌ܐ ܣ‌ܝ‌ܩ‌ܐ (ܕ‌ܗܘ‌ ܐ‌ܠ‌ܐ

Didascalia 6.13/25 (Lagarde 105,8-13; cf. Connolly 210)
"Men will come to you clothed in the garments (skins) of
sheep. Inside they are ravenous wolves. But by their
fruits you will know them."

(Cf. Const. Ap. 6.13.3 [Funk 335].)

In the case of Justin Bellinzoni has argued that Mt. 24.5
(or Mk. 13.6 or Lk. 21.8) (πολλοὶ γὰρ ἐλεύσονται ἐπὶ τῷ ὀνόματί
μου) has been combined with Mt. 7.15[1] and that a single harmony
underlies both citations in Justin.[2] The change in Apol. 16.13
from καρπῶν to ἔργων is probably Justin's own change.[3]

But H is closer to the reading in the Didascalia and both
to Mt. 7.15,16a than to Justin.[4] In fact it is not at all clear
whether H's πολλοὶ ἐλεύσονται and the Didascalia's "Men will
come" is due to the influence of Mt. 24.5 or merely represents
an introduction to the saying that did not want to define the
"bad guys" as ψευδοπροφῆται. Both H and the Didascalia lack the
ἐπὶ τῷ ὀνόματί μου of Mt. 24.5 which is found in Justin. Also
Justin's source probably already read ἔξωθεν (1.6) and
ἐνδεδυμένοι δέρματα, both of which are lacking in H and the
Didascalia. Thus we seem to have another case in which H is
probably not dependent on the same source as Justin. Alternatively, a use of Justin's source (accounting for πολλοὶ
ἐλεύσονται) and the Gospel of Matthew or secondary correction
back to Matthew might be possible. But the evidence of the
Didascalia argues against the latter. The nature of a possible

[1]In fact, as Bellinzoni shows, Apol. 16.13 combines Mt.
24.5; 7.15,16,19.

[2]Sayings, pp. 44-47.

[3]Ibid., p. 46 and n. 3.

[4]Waitz (Pseudoklementinen, p. 314) and Strecker (Judenchristentum, pp. 134-35) both disclaim the possibility of a
direct relationship of H and Justin in this case.

58

common source for H and the Didascalia which already had the
shortened introduction I leave open.[5]

The other peculiarities in H (με and ἐνδύματι) are either
his own or later scribal errors.[6]

---

[5]Strecker (ibid.) leaves open the possibility of an
uncanonical text.

[6]The πρός με of H makes no sense at all to me and is offset by the Syriac of H (ܠܟ 'to you').

11. H 3.51.2-3, Ep. Pet. 2.5

H 3.51.2	Mt. 5.17		
οὐκ	μὴ νομίσητε		
	ὅτι		
ἦλθον	ἦλθον		
καταλῦσαι	καταλῦσαι		
5 τὸν νόμον.	τὸν νόμον		
	ἢ τοὺς προφήτας·		
	οὐκ ἦλθον		
	καταλῦσαι		
	ἀλλὰ πληρῶσαι.		

H 3.51.3 = Ep. Pet. 2.5	Mt. 5.18	Mt. 24.35	Mk. 13.31
10	ἀμὴν γὰρ		
	λέγω ὑμῖν,		
	ἕως ἂν		
	παρέλθῃ		
ὁ οὐρανὸς	ὁ οὐρανὸς	ὁ οὐρανὸς	ὁ οὐρανὸς
15 καὶ ἡ γῆ	καὶ ἡ γῆ,	καὶ ἡ γῆ	καὶ ἡ γῆ
⌜παρελεύσονται,[1]	(1. 14)	⌜παρελεύσεται,[1]	παρελεύσονται,
ἰῶτα[2] ἓν	ἰῶτα ἓν	οἱ δὲ	οἱ δὲ
ἢ μία κεραία	ἢ μία κεραία	λόγοι μου	λόγοι μου
οὐ μὴ	οὐ μὴ	οὐ μὴ	οὐ ⌜μὴ[1]
20 παρέλθῃ	παρέλθῃ	παρέλθωσιν.[2]	παρελεύσονται.
ἀ ἀπὸ τοῦ νόμου.	ἀπὸ τοῦ νόμου,		
(Cf. Ep. Pet.	ἕως ἂν		
2.6)	πάντα γένηται.		

---

[1]παραλεύσεται O*.
[2]+ δέ in 3.51.3 o
(P has > over
ἰῶτα).

[1]παρελευσονται [1]Omit B D*.
ℵcorr Koine WΔΘ
λ φ pm.
[2]Omit verse ℵ*.

    This saying and those which follow in this chapter simply lack other witnesses among the fathers to their readings. Therefore while they further demonstrate conflated and harmonized readings in H, they tell us nothing of a possible source known to others.

The first saying is from Mt. 5.17a;[1] the second begins with wording found in Mt. 24.35 = Mk. 13.31[2] and ends with the wording of Mt. 5.18b. The omissions in H (Mt. 5.17b, 5.18a, and ἕως ἂν πάντα γένηται of Mt. 5.18b) have the effect of making the saying in H into a simple, unconditional statement about the abiding validity of the law.[3]

The fact that the conflation occurs both in 3.51.3 and Ep. Pet. 2.5 indicates that the conflated text was prior to the individual use of it in each case. This would place its usage already in the source KP of which the Epistle of Peter was the introduction[4] and would indicate that KP already cited conflated texts based on the Gospel of Matthew.

---

[1]There is no reason to think of a pre-Matthean source for H. The dropping of ἢ τοὺς προφήτας is understandable enough in light of the low estimation placed on the prophetic books in H (= KP). Cf. Strecker, Judenchristentum, pp. 175-79.

[2]παρελεύσονται could indicate the influence of Mark but could also be a correction to agree with "heaven and earth" or represent a text of Matthew that read the plural form (so ℵ corr Koine W Δ Θ λ φ pm).

[3]Cf. νόμον αἰώνιον in H 8.10.3.

[4]Cf. Strecker, Judenchristentum, pp. 137-45.

12. H 3.53.2

H 3.53.2	Mt. 13.17	Lk. 10.24
(1. 14)	ἀμὴν	
(1. 14)	γὰρ λέγω ὑμῖν ὅτι	λέγω γὰρ ὑμῖν ὅτι
πολλοὶ προφῆται	πολλοὶ προφῆται	πολλοὶ προφῆται
καὶ βασιλεῖς	⌜καὶ δίκαιοι¹	⌜και βασιλεῖς¹
5 ἐπεθύμησαν	⌜ἐπεθύμησαν²	ἠθέλησαν
ἰδεῖν,	ἰδεῖν	ἰδεῖν
ἃ ὑμεῖς	ἃ	ἃ ὑμεῖς
βλέπετε,	βλέπετε	βλέπετε
(1. 15)	καὶ οὐκ εἶδαν,	καὶ οὐκ εἶδαν,
10 καὶ ἀκοῦσαι,	καὶ ἀκοῦσαι	⌜και ἀκοῦσαι
ἃ ὑμεῖς	ἃ	ἃ
ἀκούετε,	ἀκούετε	ἀκούετε
(1. 16)	καὶ οὐκ ἤκουσαν.	καὶ οὐκ ἤκουσαν.²
καὶ ἀμὴν λέγω ὑμῖν,	(11. 1-2)	
15 οὔτε εἶδον	(1. 9)	
οὔτε ἤκουσαν.	(1. 13)	

---

¹Omit B*.   ¹Omit D it.

²ηδυνηθησαν ιδειν   ²Omit a i l.
  D.

Marcion in Tertullian, Adv. Marc. 4.25 (CSEL 47.506)
   beati oculi, qui vident quae videtis:
   dico enim vobis, quia prophetae non viderunt quae
   videtis, . . .

This saying in H shows clear signs of a harmony:
(1) βασιλεῖς = Luke, (2) ἐπεθύμησαν = Matthew, (3) ἃ ὑμεῖς
(1. 7.) = Luke, and (4) ἀμὴν λέγω ὑμῖν probably = Matthew.[1]
Otherwise the peculiarities in H appear to be his own stylistic

---

[1]I would argue that there is no good reason to suppose a
use of Q instead of Matthew and Luke by H. Although βασιλεῖς
and ἐπεθύμησαν probably stood in Q, ἀμήν is more likely Matthew's
addition than Luke's omission. For in six times that Luke
follows Mark with an ἀμὴν λέγω (Mk. 9.1 = Lk. 9.27, Mk. 10.15 =
Lk. 18.17, Mk. 10.29 = Lk. 18.29, Mk. 12.43 = Lk. 21.3, Mk.
13.30 = Lk. 21.32, Mk. 14.30 = Lk. 22.34), only once (lk. 22.34)
does he omit the ἀμήν and that for enhancing the conversational
character of the scene. In the other 5 instances he retains the
ἀμήν or changes it to ἀληθῶς (in Lk. 9.27 and 21.3). Matthew on
the other hand shows a fond preference for ἀμην λέγω ὑμῖν (or
σοι).

62

changes: (1) the change of word order (see lines 14-16), perhaps for "dramatic" effect, and (2) the addition of the second ὑμεῖς in order to complete the parallelism. But we lack parallels to a harmonized form of this saying in other fathers.[2] Still there is no reason that it could not belong to the examples which pointed to a common harmony of sayings for Justin and others.[3]

Secondly, the ὑμεῖς after ἃ is probably a Lucan addition to Q (so Harnack, The Sayings of Jesus [1908], pp. 25-26, 135). Hence H is post-synoptic, a conclusion that agrees with the character of the other harmonistic sayings in H.

[2] The Diatessaron witnesses in the reading of προφῆται καὶ δίκαιοι (Matthew) versus προφῆται καὶ βασιλεῖς (Luke), follows (1) Matthew: a, f, p, t; (2) Luke: v; or (3) combine the two: l (Bergsma 93: "Vele coninge ende profeten ende heileger") and s (Bergsma 92: "Vele coningen ende profeten ende gerechter"). But this adding of Matthew and Luke is not quite the same as a harmonized text as in H.

[3] Both Waitz (Pseudoklementinen, p. 298) and Strecker (Judenchristentum, p. 127) recognized the presence of both Matthean and Lucan elements here but neither proposed the most obvious solution--the use of a harmony! Waitz proposed either a back and forth usage of Matthew and Luke by the author himself or an independent form of the saying (?). Strecker (Judenchristentum, p. 129) solves the problem of "mixed texts" by affirming that they are quoted from memory.

13. H 3.60.2-3

H 3.60.2-3*	Mt. 24.46,45,48-51	Lk. 12.43,42,45-46
μακάριος	[46]μακάριος	[43]μακάριος
ὁ ἄνθρωπος ἐκεῖνος	ὁ δοῦλος ἐκεῖνος...	ὁ δοῦλος ἐκεῖνος...
ὃν καταστήσει	[45]...ὃν κατέστησεν	[42]...ὃν καταστήσει
ὁ κύριος αὐτοῦ	ὁ κύριος[1]	ὁ κύριος
5 ἐπὶ τῆς θεραπείας	ἐπὶ τῆς ⌐οἰκετείας[2]	ἐπὶ τῆς θεραπείας
τῶν συνδούλων αὐτοῦ	αὐτοῦ	αὐτοῦ
τοῦ διδόναι αὐτοῖς	τοῦ δοῦναι αὐτοῖς	τοῦ διδόναι
τὰς τροφὰς	τὴν τροφὴν	ἐν καιρῷ
ἐν καιρῷ αὐτῶν,	ἐν καιρῷ;	[τὸ] σιτομέτριον;
10 μὴ ἐννοούμενον	[48]ἐὰν δὲ εἴπῃ	[45]ἐὰν δὲ εἴπῃ
καὶ λέγοντα	ὁ κακὸς δοῦλος	ὁ δοῦλος ἐκεῖνος
	ἐκεῖνος	
ἐν τῇ καρδίᾳ ⌐αὐτοῦ[1]	ἐν τῇ καρδίᾳ αὐτοῦ·	ἐν τῇ καρδίᾳ αὐτοῦ·
χρονίζει	χρονίζει	χρονίζει
ὁ κύριός μου	μου ὁ κύριος,	ὁ κύριός μου
15 ἐλθεῖν.		ἔρχεσθαι,
[3]καὶ ἄρξηται	[49]καὶ ἄρξηται	καὶ ἄρξηται
τύπτειν	τύπτειν	τύπτειν
τοὺς συνδούλους	τοὺς συνδούλους	τοὺς παῖδας
⌐αὐτοῦ[1]	αὐτοῦ	
		καὶ τὰς παιδίσκας,
20 ἐσθίων καὶ ⌐πίνων[2]	⌐ἐσθίῃ δὲ καὶ πίνῃ[3]	ἐσθίειν τε καὶ πίνειν
μετά ⌐τε[3] πορνῶν	μετὰ	
καὶ μεθυόντων.	τῶν μεθυόντων,	καὶ μεθύσκεσθαι,
καὶ ἥξει	[50]ἥξει	[46]ἥξει
ὁ κύριος	ὁ κύριος	ὁ κύριος
25 τοῦ δούλου ἐκείνου	τοῦ δούλου ἐκείνου	τοῦ δούλου ἐκείνου
ἐν ὥρᾳ, ᾗ	ἐν ἡμέρᾳ ᾗ	ἐν ἡμέρᾳ ᾗ
οὐ προσδοκᾷ,	οὐ προσδοκᾷ	οὐ προσδοκᾷ
καὶ ἐν ἡμέρᾳ, ᾗ	καὶ ἐν ὥρᾳ ᾗ	καὶ ἐν ὥρᾳ ᾗ
οὐ γινώσκει,	οὐ γινώσκει,	οὐ γινώσκει,
30 καὶ διχοτομήσει	[51]καὶ διχοτομήσει	καὶ διχοτομήσει
αὐτόν,	αὐτόν,	αὐτόν,
καὶ τὸ ⌐ἀπιστοῦν[4]	καὶ τὸ	καὶ τὸ
αὐτοῦ μέρος	μέρος αὐτοῦ	μέρος αὐτοῦ
μετὰ τῶν ὑποκριτῶν	μετὰ τῶν ὑποκριτῶν	μετὰ τῶν ἀπίστων
35 θήσει.	θήσει.	θήσει.

64

| H 3.60.2-3* | Mt. 24.46,45,48-51 | Lk. 12.43,42,45-46 |

[1]Rehm prints αὐτοῦ.

[2]πίννων P*.

[3]Omit P*.

[4]ἄπιστον P*.

[1]+ αυτου Koine W Δ
Θ φ pm lat sy^{S,P} sa bo.

[2]θεραπειας D Koine
λ al c.

[3]εσθιειν δε και πινειν
G (W) 565 700 al.

*H 3.64.1 repeats lines 1-6.

The sayings in H are a clear harmonization of Mt. 24.45-51
and Lk. 12.42-46. Distinctively Matthean are: (1) αὐτοῖς (1. 7),
(2) τὰς τροφάς (1. 8; based on Matthew's τὴν τροφήν), (3) τοὺς
συνδούλους αὐτοῦ (1. 18), (4) μετὰ . . . μεθυόντων (11. 21-22),
(5) μετὰ τῶν ὑποκριτῶν (1. 34), and (6) probably αὐτοῦ (1. 4)
as read by some manuscripts of Matthew (Koine W Δ Θ φ pm lat
sy^{s,P}sa bo). Clearly Lucan are: (1) ὃν καταστήσει (1. 3),
(2) ἐπὶ τῆς θεραπείας (1. 5) (although a Matthean text as in D
is possible), (3) τοῦ διδόναι (1. 7), (4) ἐλθεῖν (1. 15; Luke
has ἔρχεσθαι, but Matthew no equivalent), and (5) ἀπιστοῦν
(1. 32), probably reflecting Luke's ἀπίστων (1. 34). The
remainder are either common to Matthew and Luke or are changes
in H's source or made by H. These later include the following
(in addition to slight changes noted above):

1. Substitution of ἄνθρωπος for δοῦλος (1. 2).

2. Addition of τῶν συνδούλων (1. 6).

3. Addition of αὐτῶν (1. 9).

4. Change of Mt. 24.48 = Lk. 12.45 from a threat to a
description of that which is not (μή) characteristic of this
"blessed" man and the addition of ἐννοούμενον and change from
εἶπῃ to λέγοντα.

5. Change to participle (1. 21).

6. Addition of τε πορνῶν (1. 21).

7. Addition of καί (1. 23).

8. Reversed order of lines 26 and 28.

But it is obvious from this survey that the changes are
minor and either stylistic or simple deductions from or logical
additions to the context itself.

14. H 3.61.1

H 3.61.1	Mt. 25.26-27,30	Lk. 19.22-23
δοῦλε πονηρὲ	πονηρὲ δοῦλε	πονηρὲ δοῦλε.
καὶ ὀκνηρέ,	καὶ ὀκνηρέ,	
	ᾔδεις ὅτι . . .	ᾔδεις ὅτι . . .
ἔδει σε	27ἔδει σε οὖν	23καὶ διὰ τί οὐκ
5	βαλεῖν	ἔδωκάς
τὸ ἀργύριόν μου	⌜τὰ ἀργύριά¹ μου	⌜μου τὸ ἀργύριον¹
προβαλεῖν	(1. 5)	
ἐπὶ τῶν τραπεζιτῶν,	τοῖς τραπεζίταις,	ἐπὶ τράπεζαν;
καὶ ἐγὼ ἂν ἐλθὼν	καὶ ἐλθὼν ἐγὼ	κἀγὼ ἐλθὼν
10	(1. 13)	σὺν τόκῳ
ἔπραξα	ἐκομισάμην ἂν	ἂν ⌜αὐτὸ ἔπραξα.²
τὸ ἐμόν·	τὸ ἐμὸν	
	σὺν τόκῳ.	(1. 10)
ἐκβάλετε	(1. 16)	
15 τὸν ἀχρεῖον δοῦλον	30καὶ τὸν ἀχρεῖον δοῦλον	
	ἐκβάλετε	
εἰς τὸ σκότος	εἰς τὸ σκότος	
τὸ ἐξώτερον.	τὸ ἐξώτερον·	

---

¹το αργυριον A C D
Koine λ φ pl.

¹231 D Koine W^corr
Γ Δ λ φ pl.
²21 D Koine W Γ Δ
λ φ pl.

Again a harmonization of Matthew and Luke appears involved. Matthean are δοῦλε πονηρὲ καὶ ὀκνηρέ, ἔδει σε (προ)βαλεῖν, "the money-changers or bankers" (in the plural), τὸ ἐμόν, ἐκβάλετε - ἐξώτερον. ἔπραξα is from Luke. τὸ ἀργύριόν μου may be Lucan or the reading of the Matthean text that was used.[1] καὶ ἐγὼ ἂν ἐλθὼν has equivalents in both Matthew and Luke.

Otherwise H has omitted Mt. 25.26b = Lk. 19.22b and σὺν τόκῳ[2] as well as made his own stylistic changes--change of word

---

[1]το αργυριον is read in Mt. 25.27 by A C D Koine λ φ pl.

[2]Perhaps this latter was considered offensive in view of the OT command against lending "at interest" (cf. Ex. 22.25; Lev. 25.36f.; Deut. 23.19f. etc.).

66

order, addition of προ- to βαλεῖν, and ἐπί to "the bankers."
This saying could also belong to (may I now call it) "the
harmonized source."

15. H 3.54.2

H 3.54.2	Mt. 19.8,4	Mk. 10.5-6
Μωυσῆς	Μωυσῆς	
κατὰ τὴν	πρὸς τὴν	πρὸς τὴν
σκληροκαρδίαν ὑμῶν	σκληροκαρδίαν ὑμῶν	σκληροκαρδίαν ὑμῶν
ἐπέτρεψεν ὑμῖν·	ἐπέτρεψεν ὑμῖν	ἔγραψεν ὑμῖν
5	ἀπολῦσαι	
	τὰς γυναῖκας ὑμῶν·	τὴν ἐντολὴν ταύτην.
ἀπ᾽ ἀρχῆς γὰρ	ἀπ᾽ ἀρχῆς δὲ	⌐6ἀπὸ δὲ ἀρχῆς
		⌐κτίσεως¹
οὕτως οὐκ ἐγένετο.	⌐οὐ γέγονεν¹ οὕτως.	
10 ὁ γὰρ κτίσας	⌐4ὁ ⌐κτίσας²	
ἀπ᾽ ἀρχῆς	⌐ἀπ᾽ ἀρχῆς³	
τὸν ἄνθρωπον		
ἄρσεν καὶ θῆλυ	ἄρσεν καὶ θῆλυ	ἄρσεν καὶ θῆλυ
ἐποίησεν αὐτόν.	ἐποίησεν ⌐αὐτούς.⁴	ἐποίησεν ⌐αὐτούς.²

¹οὐκ εγενετο D.
²ποιησας ℵ C D
Koine W φ pl lat sy.
³Omit ff¹ ff² syˢ.
⁴Omit a ff¹ syˢ·ᶜ.

¹Omit D pc b ff² q sy.
²Omit D W pc it.

   The order of the saying is Marcan but the wording is Matthean
(Μωυσῆς, ἐπέτρεψεν, οὕτως-ἀρχῆς). The variations in wording from
Matthew are changes that presuppose no other source than Matthew:
(1) κατὰ for πρὸς, γάρ for δέ, οὕτως in a different word order,
and the addition of γάρ (1. 10) are all stylistic changes; (2)
the omission of ἀπολῦσαι τὰς γυναῖκας ὑμῶν could be either to
adapt it to another context in H (see infra) or appeared that way
already in his source but for reasons which cannot now be dis-
cerned; (3) οὐκ ἐγένετο is also the reading of D and may reflect
the text read or a stylistic change already present in his source,
and (4) τὸν ἄνθρωπον + αὐτόν for αὐτούς must certainly be a
dogmatic change to conform to the theory that Adam was androgy-
nos.¹ A similar reading occurs in 2 Clem. 14.2: λέγει γὰρ ἡ

   ¹This was a Jewish tradition that probably arose under
Greek influence. Cf. Strack-Billerbeck 4.405-06. Rabbinic
sources even took over the term from Greek (ἀνδρόγυνος) in the
form סונינ‍ירדנא. Later, Gnostic groups made use of the

γραφή: ῾Εποίησεν ὁ θεὸς <u>τὸν ἄνθρωπον</u> ἄρσεν καὶ θῆλυ.[2] Beyond
this there is lacking other evidence for H's reading.[3]

H introduces this saying with the words πλὴν ταληθῆ τοῦ
νόμου εἰδὼς Σαδδουκαίοις πυνθανομένοις καθ᾽ ὃν λόγον Μωυσῆς ἑπτὰ
συνεχώρησεν γαμεῖν, ἔφη. Is this confusion of stories due to a
simple failure of memory as Strecker suggests?[4] Perhaps. But
one must consider other possibilities as well. Such would be the
use of a source such as a sayings' collection or harmony of sayings which lacked the synoptic gospels' contexts. Whether
ἀπολῦσαι τὰς γυναῖκας ὑμῶν would in that case have been lacking
in H's source and caused the confusion or was intentionally
omitted by H to adapt it to a different context cannot be easily
determined.

This saying raises the subject of Marcan influence. Up to
now we have seen only (clearly) Matthean and Lucan texts involved
in the harmonizations. Even here there is lacking any particu-
larly Marcan <u>wording</u>. The order in H can be explained as that
of Mk. 10.5-6 with the Matthean wording filled in. But it could
also be a coincidental agreement with Marcan order. That is to
say H's order of phrases is self-understandable: (1) the way
things used to be (lines 1-4), (2) but that is not truly what
God intended (lines 7 - 9), and (3) the reason or clinching argument (lines 10-14). In the latter case no Marcan influence need
be presupposed.

---

idea. Cf. A. Bohlig, <u>Mysterion und Wahrheit</u>, pp. 90-91.

[2]Cf. also the Bohairic version of Gen. 1.27 which omits the
LXX ἐποίησεν αὐτούς so as to read, "And God made man; in the
image of God he made him male and female."

[3]Unless the witness of Δ p could be counted which against
the other witnesses of Δ (which all follow the Matthean order and
wording) follows the Marcan order and wording (Messina 211: "A
causa della durezza del vostro cuore Mose comando cio a voi. Da
principio Dio creo insieme maschio e femina"). Less certain is
whether Δ t 101 (Todesco 278: "Non evete voi letto, che colui
che fece <u>l'uomo</u> [my emphasis] dal cominciamento, maschio e
femina li <u>fece?</u>") preserves the remnant of a reading like H's
τὸν ἄνθρωπον.

[4]<u>Judenchristentum</u>, p. 127. Waitz' attempt (<u>Pseudoklemen-
tinen</u>, pp. 298-99) to see in H's reading a text which <u>lay behind</u>
Matthew and Mark can hardly be a serious consideration since
Mark's wording is prior to Matthew's but H is based on <u>Matthew's</u>
<u>wording</u>.

69

16. H 11.33.1-2, R 6.14.2-3

H 11.33.1	R 6.14.2	Mt. 12.42	Lk. 11.31
βασίλισσα	Regina	βασίλισσα	βασίλισσα
νότου	austri	νότου	νότου
ἐγερθήσεται	surget	ἐγερθήσεται	ἐγερθήσεται
	in iudicio	ἐν τῇ κρίσει	[ἐν τῇ κρίσει][1]
5 μετὰ	cum	μετὰ	μετὰ
			τῶν ἀνδρῶν
τῆς γενεᾶς	generatione	τῆς γενεᾶς	τῆς γενεᾶς
ταύτης	hac	ταύτης	ταύτης
καὶ κατακρινεῖ	et condemnabit	καὶ κατακρινεῖ	καὶ κατακρινεῖ
10 αὐτήν,	eam,	αὐτήν·	αὐτούς·
⌐ὅτι¬[1]	quia	ὅτι	ὅτι
ἦλθεν	venit	ἦλθεν	ἦλθεν
ἀπὸ		ἐκ	ἐκ
τῶν περάτων	finibus	τῶν περάτων	τῶν περάτων
15 τῆς γῆς	terrae	τῆς γῆς	τῆς γῆς
ἀκοῦσαι	audire	ἀκοῦσαι	ἀκοῦσαι
τὴν σοφίαν	sapientiam	τὴν σοφίαν	τὴν σοφίαν
Σολομῶνος·	Salomonis,	Σολομῶνος,	Σολομῶνος,
καὶ ἰδοὺ	et ecce	καὶ ἰδοὺ	καὶ ἰδοὺ
20 πλεῖον	plus quam	πλεῖον	πλεῖον
Σολομῶνος	Salomon	Σολομῶνος	Σολομῶνος
ὧδε,	hic	ὧδε.	ὧδε·
καὶ οὐ	et non		
πιστεύετε.	audiunt.		

[1]Omit O.

[1]Omit P[45] D.

Syr. of H 11.33.1

"The Queen of the South will arise against this generation and condemn it; because she came from the ends of the earth to hear the wisdom of Salomon, and behold one greater than Salomon is here, and you do not believe."

ܐܡܠܟܐ ܕܬܝܡܢܐ ܬܩܘܡ ܠܘܩܒܠ ܫܪܒܬܐ ܗܕܐ ܘܬܚܝܒܝܗ ܆ ܕܗܝ ܐܬܬ ܡܢ ܣܘܦܝܗ̇ ܕܐܪܥܐ ܠܡܫܡܥ ܚܟܡܬܗ ܕܫܠܝܡܘܢ ܆ ܘܗܐ ܕܝܬܝܪ ܡܢ ܫܠܝܡܘܢ ܗܪܟܐ ܘܠܐ ܡܗܝܡܢܝܢ ܐܢܬܘܢ.

H 11.33.2	R 6.14.3	Mt. 12.41	Lk. 11.32
Ἄνδρες	Viri	ἄνδρες	⌐ἄνδρες
Νινευῖται	Ninivitae	Νινευῖται	Νινευῖται
ἐγερθήσονται	surgent	ἀναστήσονται	ἀναστήσονται
	in iudicio	ἐν τῇ κρίσει	ἐν τῇ κρίσει
5 μετὰ	cum	μετὰ	μετὰ
τῆς γενεᾶς	generatione	τῆς γενεᾶς	τῆς γενεᾶς
ταύτης _σιν_	hac	ταύτης _σιν_	ταύτης _σιν_
καὶ κατακρινοῦ-	et condemnabit	καὶ κατακρινοῦ-	καὶ κατακρινοῦ-
αὐτήν,	eam,	αὐτήν·	αὐτήν·
10 ὅτι	quia	ὅτι	ὅτι
ἀκούσαντες			
μετενόησαν	paenitentiam	μετενόησαν	μετενόησαν
	egerunt		
εἰς	in	εἰς	εἰς
15 τὸ κήρυγμα	praedicatione	τὸ κήρυγμα	τὸ κήρυγμα
᾽Ιωνᾶ·	Ionae,	᾽Ιωνᾶ,	᾽Ιωνᾶ,
καὶ ἰδοὺ	et ecce	καὶ ἰδοὺ	καὶ ἰδοὺ
πλεῖον	plus quam	πλεῖον	πλεῖον
	Iona	᾽Ιωνᾶ	᾽Ιωνᾶ
20 ὧδε,	hic.	ὧδε.	ὧδε.[1]
καὶ οὐδεὶς			
πιστεύει.			

[1]Omit verse D.

Syr. of H 11.33.2
"The men of Nineveh will arise against this generation and condemn it; because they repented at the preaching of Jonah, and behold one greater than Jonah is here, and no one believes."

The order of the sayings is Lucan (with the Queen of the South saying first and then the Men of Nineveh saying) but the wording is either common to Matthew and Luke or is Matthean. The one place where the wording can be tested is in the Queen of the South saying where H agrees with Matthew's μετὰ τῆς γενεᾶς and αὐτήν against Luke's μετὰ τῶν ἀνδρῶν τῆς γενεᾶς and αὐτούς. However the omission of ἐν τῇ κρίσει in both sayings could reflect the use of a Lucan text since there is no apparent reason for its omission by H.[1]

Otherwise the peculiar features of H are the following:

1. ἀπό for ἐκ in 1. 13 of H 11.33.1 is a stylistic change.

2. ἐγερθήσονται for both Matthew's and Luke's ἀναστήσονται in H 11.33.2 is due to the preference for close parallelism (see ἐγερθήσεται in H 11.33.1).

3. The addition of καὶ οὐ πιστεύετε and καὶ οὐδεὶς πιστεύει at the end of the sayings is an appended comment that was already present in G.[2]

4. The addition of ἀκούσαντες in 1. 11 of H 11.33.2 is probably a late addition to H since it is lacking in both the Syriac of H and in R.

5. The absence of Ἰωνᾶ the second time in H 11.33.2 appears to be a scribal omission since the Syriac of H has it as does R.

The combination of Matthean wording and Lucan order also occurs in Δp.[3] Thus the use of harmony seems indicated for H, especially if the omission of ἐν τῇ κρίσει indicates the influence of a Lucan text (see n. 1). These two sayings could well belong also to the harmonized source.

R, on the other hand, has characteristically moved back toward the canonical text by adding in iudicio[4] and by dropping one of the appended comments--that at the end of H 11.33.2 = R 6.14.3.

---

[1] ἐν τῇ κρίσει is omitted in Lk. 11.31 by P[45] and D; all of Lk. 11.32 is omitted by D.

[2] This is confirmed by R 6.14.2: et non audiunt.

[3] 2.19 (Messina 127): "La regina dello Jemen sorgerà nel giorno del guidizio contro questa generazione e la svergognerà, . . . Gli uomini di Ninive . . ."
Unfortunately Ephraem does not give enough of these sayings to discern his readings. He mentions "the men of Nineveh" in Comm. 11.2 (Leloir, Syr. 53; Arm. 196) and uses what would appear to be Matthean wording in 11.4 ("and the Queen of the South will condemn it," Leloir, Syr. 55; Arm. 197). Otherwise the diatessaron witnesses either have Lucan wording and order (a) or Matthean wording and order (1, s, t [the sayings are missing altogether from v]). Fulda has a conflated reading in Matthean order (see Ranke 61).

[4] Unless the dropping of ἐν τῇ κρίσει took place in H after the writing of G.

17. H 3.30.3-3.31.1, R 2.30.2-5

H 3.30.3-3.31.1	Mt. 10.13-15	Mk. 6.11	Lk. 9.5	Lk. 10.6,11-12
ἐὰν ᾖ	13 καὶ ἐὰν μὲν ᾖ			6 καὶ ἐὰν ἐκεῖ[1] ᾖ
τις	ἡ οἰκία			
ἐν ὑμῖν				υἱὸς
εἰρήνης	ἀξία,			εἰρήνης,
5 τέκνον,				
διὰ τῆς				
διδασκαλίας				
ἡμῶν				
καταλάβῃ	ἐλθάτω			ἐπαναπαήσεται
10 αὐτὸν	(1.12)			ἐπ' αὐτὸν
ἡ εἰρήνη,	ἡ εἰρήνη ὑμῶν			ἡ εἰρήνη ὑμῶν·
	ἐπ' αὐτήν· . .			
εἰ δὲ ταύτην	14 καὶ ὃς ἂν	11 καὶ Γὃς ἂν τόπος	5 καὶ ὅσοι ἂν	αἱ δὲ μή γε,.. .
λαβεῖν	μὴ δέξηται	μὴ δέξηται[1]	μὴ δέχωνται	
15 ὑμῶν τις	ὑμᾶς μηδὲ	ὑμᾶς μηδὲ	ὑμᾶς,	
μὴ θέλοι,	ἀκούσῃ τοὺς	ἀκούσωσιν		
	λόγους ὑμῶν,	ὑμῶν,		
τότε ἡμεῖς Γ	ἐξερχόμενοι	ἐκπορευόμενοι	ἐξερχόμενοι	
	ἔξω Γτῆς οἰκίας	ἐκεῖθεν	ἀπὸ τῆς πόλεως	
20	ἢ[1] τῆς πόλεως		ἐκείνης	
	ἐκείνης		(1. 34)	
ἀποτιναξάμενοι	ἐκτινάξατε	ἐκτινάξατε		(1. 34)

72

H 3.30.3-3.31.1	Mt. 10.13-15	Mk. 6.11	Lk. 9.5	Lk. 10.6,11-12
εἰς μαρτυρίαν			(1. 35)	(1. 32)
25 τῶν ποδῶν	(1. 32)	(1. 32)	(1. 32)	
ἡμῶν	(1. 33)	(1. 33)	(1. 33)	11 καὶ τὸν κονιορτὸν
τὸν	τὸν κονιορτὸν	τὸν χοῦν	τὸν κονιορτὸν	τὸν κολληθέντα
		Γτον ὑποκάτω²		Γἡμῖν²
30 ἐκ τῶν ὁδῶν				ἐκ τῆς πόλεως
				ὑμῶν
	τῶν ποδῶν	τῶν ποδῶν	ἀπὸ τῶν ποδῶν	εἰς τοὺς πόδας
	ὑμῶν.	ὑμῶν	ὑμῶν	ἀπομασσόμεθα
35			ἀποτινάσσετε	
		εἰς μαρτύριον	εἰς μαρτύριον	ὑμῖν...
		αὐτοῖς.	ἐπ' αὐτούς.	
κονιορτόν,				
ὅν διὰ τοὺς				
Γκαμάτους¹				
40 Γβαστάξαντες²				
ἠνέγκαμεν				
πρὸς ὑμᾶς				
ὅπως σωθῆτε,				
εἰς ἑτέρων				
45 ἀπίωμεν				
οἰκίας καὶ				
(cf. 1. 19)				

74

H 3.30.3-3.31.1	Mt. 10.13-15	Mk. 6.11	Lk. 9.5	Lk. 10.6,11-12
πόλεις.	(cf. 1. 20)			12λέγω ὑμῖν ὅτι
31.1 ¹καὶ ἀληθῶς	15ἀμὴν			
ὑμῖν λέγομεν,	λέγω ὑμῖν			(1. 56)
50 ἀνεκτότερον	ἀνεκτότερον			(1. 57)
ἔσται	ἔσται			Σοδόμοις
Γγῆ³ Σοδόμων	γῇ Σοδόμων			
καὶ Γομόρρας	καὶ Γομόρρας²			ἐν τῇ ἡμέρᾳ
ἐν ἡμέρᾳ	ἐν ἡμέρᾳ			ἐκείνῃ
55 κρίσεως	κρίσεως			ἀνεκτότερον
				ἔσται
ἢ τῷ τῆς	ἢ τῇ πόλει			ἢ τῇ πόλει
60 Γἀπειθείας⁴	ἐκείνῃ.			ἐκείνῃ.³
τόπῳ				
ἐνδιατελεῖν.				

¹κάμπους O.	¹Omit D arm.	¹οσοι αν μη		¹21 Hesychian
²βαστάσαντες O.	²Γομορρας	δεχωνται		A D Koine W
³τῇ O.	C D Θ λ pm	Koine (Θ) pm		λ φ pl.
⁴ἀληθείας O.	it.	latt.		²υμιν א* Dᶜᵒʳʳ
		²Omit 𝔓⁴⁵ 33 pc		Θ al.
		lat syˢ.		³βασιλεια του
				θεου D a b e.

R. 2.30.2-5

2 quamcumque
civitatem
vel domum
introierimus
5
3 dicamus:
"Pax
huic domui;
et siquidem,"
10 inquit,
"fuerit ibi
filius pacis,
veniet
super ⌜eum¹
15 pas vestra,
si vero
non fuerit,
pas vestra
ad vos
20 revertetur";
4 exeuntes
autem
⌜de domo
vel de civitate

Mt. 10.11,13-15

11 εἰς ἣν δ' ἂν
πόλιν
⌜ἢ κώμην¹
εἰσέλθητε, ...

13 . . ἐλθάτω
ἡ εἰρήνη ὑμῶν
ἐπ' αὐτήν·
ἐὰν δὲ
μὴ ᾖ ἀξία,
ἡ εἰρήνη ὑμῶν
πρὸς ὑμᾶς
ἐπιστραφήτω.
14 . . .ἐξερχόμενοι

ἔξω τῆς οἰκίας
ἢ τῆς πόλεως

Mk. 6.10-11

10 . . .ὅπου ἐὰν
εἰσέλθητε
εἰς οἰκίαν, . . .

11 . . .ἐκπορευόμενοι
ἐκεῖθεν

Lk. 9.4-5

4 καὶ εἰς ἣν ἂν
οἰκίαν
εἰσέλθητε, . . .

5 . . .ἐξερχόμενοι
ἀπὸ
τῆς πόλεως

Lk. 10.5,10-12

5 εἰς ἣν δ' ἂν*

εἰσέλθητε
οἰκίαν,
⌜πρῶτον¹ λέγετε·
εἰρήνη
τῷ οἴκῳ τούτῳ
6 καὶ ἐὰν

⌜ἔκει ᾖ²
υἱὸς εἰρήνης,
ἐπαναπαήσεται
ἐπ' αὐτὸν
ἡ εἰρήνη ὑμῶν·
εἰ δὲ
μή γε,

ἐφ' ὑμᾶς
ἀνακάμψει.
10 . . .ἐξελθόντες

εἰς τὰς πλατείας
αὐτῆς

R 2.30.2-5	Mt. 10.11,13-15	Mk. 6.10-11	Lk. 9.4-5	Lk. 10.5,10-12
25 illa,²	ἐκείνης		ἐκείνης	εἴπατε·
ᵣut etiam	ἐκτινάξατε	ἐκτινάξατε		11 καὶ
pulverem	τὸν κονιορτὸν	τὸν χοῦν	τὸν κονιορτὸν	τὸν κονιορτὸν
qui adhaeserit		τὸν ὑποκάτω		τὸν κολληθέντα
				ἡμῖν ἐκ τῆς
30				πόλεως ὑμῶν
pedibus	τῶν ποδῶν	τῶν ποδῶν	ἀπὸ τῶν ποδῶν	εἰς τοὺς πόδας
nostris,	ὑμῶν.	ὑμῶν	ὑμῶν	ἀπομασσόμεθα
excutiamus		εἰς μαρτύριον	ἀποτινάσσετε εἰς μαρτύριον	
		αὐτοῖς.	ἐπ' αὐτούς.	ὑμῖν· . . .
35 super eos. ³	15 . . .ἀνεκτότερον			(1. 43)
⁵tolerabilius	ἔσται			(1. 44)
autem erit	γῇ Σοδόμων			12 . . .Σοδόμοις
terrae Sodomorum	καὶ Γομόρρων			
et Gomorraeorum	ἐν ἡμέρᾳ			ἐν τῇ ἡμέρᾳ
40 in die	κρίσεως			ἐκείνῃ
iudicii				ἀνεκτότερον
				ἔσται
quam illi	ἢ τῇ πόλει			ἢ τῇ πόλει
45 civitati	ἐκείνῃ.			ἐκείνῃ.
vel domui.				

R 2.30.2-5 Mt. 10.11,13-15 Mk. 6.10-11 Lk. 9.4-5 Lk. 10.5,10-12

¹eos Sy (ܠ ¹Omit λ it.
ܠܘܢ).

²inde Sy (ܦ
ܕܠ).

³excutite
pulverem de
pedibus
vestris
(= Mt. 10.14)
Sy (ܠܘ ܘܦ
ܪܓܠܝܟܘܢ).

*Cf. v. 10: εἰς
ἣν δ' ἂν πόλιν
εἰσέλθητε.

¹Omit D^{corr}579
r¹.

²21 Hesychian
A D Koine W
λ φ pl.

The citation in H is a free citation with its own changes
and wording. In the first half of the saying (lines 1-37) only
Luke need be presupposed, but this means both Lk. 9 and Lk. 10:

1. εἰρήνης τέκνον (lines 4-5): cf. υἱὸς εἰρήνης (1k. 10.6
(Lk. 10.6).

2. καταλάβῃ αὐτὸν ἡ εἰρήνη (lines 9-11): cf. ἐπαναπαήσεται ἐπ' αὐτὸν ἡ εἰρήνη ὑμῶν (Lk. 10.6, cf. Mt. 10.13).

3. ἀποτιναξάμενοι εἰς μαρτυρίαν τῶν ποδῶν ἡμῶν τὸν ἐκ τῶν
ὁδῶν κονιορτόν (lines 22-37): cf. τὸν κονιορτὸν ἀπὸ τῶν ποδῶν
ὑμῶν ἀποτιωάσσετε εἰς μαρτύριον ἐπ' αὐτούς (Lk. 9.5).

The parallels in Matthew and Mark to H are all in Lk. 9 or
10 and no peculiar features of Matthew or Mark occur in the first
half of the saying in H.

In the latter half of the saying (lines 38-62) lines 48-
62 follow Mt. 10.15 very closely except for the final words while
Lk. 10.12 is further away. H also attests a text (with Γομόρρας
instead of Γομόρρων) like that read by C D Θ λit. Lines 46-47
(οἰκίας καὶ πόλεις) may reflect the influence of Mt. 10.14.
Hence H represents a text which, while not a strict harmony, has
combined Lk. 10.6 to 9.5 and Mt. 10.15 (and perhaps v. 14) in
its own rewriting or paraphrase of the whole.

R however has returned much more closely to the wording of
the canonical texts:

1. quamcumque - revertetur (lines 1-20) follows the
reading of Lk. 10.5-6 with some possible influence from Mt. 10.11
(civitatem = πόλιν) and Mt. 10.13 (see veniet = ἐλθάτω of Matthew
rather than ἐπαναπαήσεται of Luke?; non fuerit = Matthew's μὴ
ᾖ?; addition of second pax vestra due to Matthew's doubling of
ἡ εἰρήνη ὑμῶν?).

78

2. exeuntes - eos (lines 21-35) shows a use of Mt. 10 (?),
Lk. 9 and Lk. 10.

a. exeuntes autem de domo vel de civitate illa (lines
21-25) appears to be Mt. 10.14 although it could also be explained as Lk. 9.5 with domo vel added because of the previous
use of domum in 1. 3. The fact that the Syriac of R reads only
ܡܢ ܬܡܢ 'from there' may further indicate that R's reading at
this point is a secondary correction to the canonical text (of
Mt. 10.14 and Lk. 9.5).

b. pulverem qui adhaeserit pedibus nostri executiamus
super eos (lines 27-35) follows the wording of Lk. 10.11. But
the Syriac (ܦܨܘ ܚܠܐ ܕܒܪܓܠܝܟܘܢ 'shake the dust from your feet')
follows Mt. 10.14.

3. tolerabilius - domui (lines 36-47), as in H, follows
Mt. 10.15 rather than Lk. 10.12.

What is clear from R is that it has eliminated the peculiar
wording of H so as to return almost entirely to wording from the
canonical texts--using both Matthew and Luke, This does not mean
that R has itself used a harmony of the gospels. Rather the use
of Lk. 10.6 at the beginning and Mt. 10.15 at the end was already
present in H (=G). R simply followed the wording of the text
involved with some additions or changes from a parallel text
(in Mt. 10 or Lk. 9). No use of Mark is discernable for R.

But whether H presupposes a harmonized source is uncertain.
As noted before the readings in H combine different texts rather
than harmonize the wording from two different texts at the same
place. But it seems strange that it should have jumped from one
text to another when his purposes could have been served by a
single account (Mt. 10, Lk. 9, or Lk. 10) unless his source
already had combined the texts. Still the paraphrastic character
of this quotation seems to distinguish it from the previous
sayings. It will be necessary to return to the relationship of
the sayings to each other and to the sources of H in the conclusion to this chapter.

18. H 2.19

[1]Ἰοῦστά τις ἐν ἡμῖν ἐστιν <u>Συροφοινίκισσα</u>, τὸ
γένος ⌐<u>Χανανῖτις</u>,⌐[1] ἧς <u>τὸ θυγάτριον</u> ὑπὸ χαλεπῆς νόσου
συνείχετο, ἣ καὶ τῷ κυρίῳ ἡμῶν προσῆλθεν βοῶσα καὶ
ἱκετεύουσα, ὅπως αὐτῆς <u>τὸ θυγάτριον</u> θεραπεύσῃ. [2]ὁ δὲ
5 καὶ ὑφ' ἡμῶν ἀξιωθεὶς εἶπεν· <u>Οὐκ ἔξεστιν</u> ἰᾶσθαι
τὰ ἔθνη ἐοικότα κυσὶν διὰ τὸ ⌐<u>διαφόροις</u>[2] ⌐χρᾶσθαι⌐[3]
τροφαῖς καὶ πράξεσιν, ἀποδεδομένης τῆς κατὰ τὴν
βασιλείον τραπέζης τοῖς υἱοῖς Ἰσραήλ. [3]ἡ δὲ τοῦτο
ἀκούσασα, καὶ <u>τῆς</u> αὐτῆς <u>τραπέζης</u> ὡς κύων <u>ψιχίων</u>
10 <u>ἀποπιπτόντων</u> συνμεταλαμβάνειν ⟨δεομένη⟩,[4] μεταθεμένη ὅπερ ἦν, ⌐τὸ[5] ὁμοίως διαιτᾶσθαι τοῖς τῆς
βασιλείας υἱοῖς τῆς εἰς τὴν θυγατέρα, ὡς ἠξίωσεν,
ἔτυχεν ἰάσεως. [4]οὐ γὰρ ἂν ἐθνικὴν οὖσαν καὶ ἐπὶ
⌐τῇ αὐτῇ πολιτείᾳ⌐[6] μένουσαν ὁ τὴν ἀρχὴν διὰ τὸ μὴ
15 ἐξεῖναι θεραπεύειν ὡς ⌐ἐθνικὴν⌐[7] μείνασαν . . . ,
⌐ἐθεράπευεν.⌐[8]

---

[1]χαναανίτις O.
[2]PO; ἀδιαφόροις Duncker in Wieseler.
[3]χρῆσθαι O.
[4]Davies; ⟨βουλομένη⟩ Lagarde.
[5]PO; τῷ Cotelier.
[6]τὴν αὐτὴν πολιτείαν O.
[7]O; + ἐθνικήν P.
[8]ἐθεράπευσεν O.
_____ = words in Mt. 15.21-28.
_ _ _ = words in Mk. 7.24-20.

    This is a very free retelling of the story of the Healing
of the Daughter of the Syrophoenician or Canaanite woman (Mt.
15.21-28 and Mk. 7.24-30) with several changes unique to H.
    That the version in H presupposes <u>Matthew</u> is proved by τὸ
γένος <u>Χανανῖτις</u> (see γυνὴ Χαναναία in Mt. 15.22), by reference to
ψιχίων ἀποπιπτόντων (see ἀπὸ τῶν ψιχίων τῶν πιπτόντων in Mt.
15.27), and perhaps also by οὐκ ἔξεστιν which is the reading of
Mt. 15.26 in D it sy[s,c]. That <u>Mark</u> is also presupposed is proved
by the use of Συροφοινίκισσα (Mk. 7.26) and τὸ θυγάτριον
(Mk. 7.25).

Other elements of the story have undoubtedly also come from Matthew or Mark but are expressed in different wording in H. Compare the following:

1. The daughter was sick although the demon possession of Matthew and Mark has been changed to ὑπὸ χαλεπῆς νόσου συνείχετο.

2. The mother came to "the Lord" (cf. κύριε in Mk. 7.28 and Mt. 15.22,25,27), beseeching his help (cf. Mk. 7.26 and more strongly Mt. 15.22).

3. The disciples interceding in her behalf (H 2.19.2a) probably reflects Mt. 15.23. But in Matthew they are annoyed and want Jesus to send her away while in H they intercede in her behalf.

4. Jesus refuses to heal her at first (cf. Mk. 7.27 and Mt. 15.24,26).

5. The woman makes an appeal by referring to the dogs who eat the crumbs from the table (cf. Mk. 7.28 and Mt. 15.27).

6. Jesus heals her daughter (cf. Mk. 7.29-30 and Mt. 15.28).

On the other hand a number of peculiar features characterize the retelling of the story in H, the major effect of which is to emphasize the "uncleanness" of the Gentiles and the necessity to convert from that way of life. This is seen in the following:

A. Jesus says, οὐκ ἔξεστιν ἰᾶσθαι τὰ ἔθνη (with the reference to "dogs" now made explicit) ἐοικότα κυσίν. Two reasons are given:

1) the "uncleanness" of the Gentiles: διὰ τὸ διαφόροις χρᾶσθαι τροφαῖς καὶ πράξεσιν; and

2) the "election" of Israel: ἀποδεδομένης τῆς κατὰ τὴν βασίλειον τραπέζης τοῖς υἱοῖς ᾽Ισραήλ.

B. The woman's daughter is healed <u>only after</u> she changes her ways to live with the sons of the kingdom (μεταθεμένη ὅπερ ἦν, etc.).

C. The final sentence explains that it would have been wrong to heal her daughter if the woman had continued to live as a Gentile.

In its character as a free retelling of the story it is somewhat like the preceding sayings which expanded on and changed the words of the commission to the twelve and the seventy(-two). But this example differs from the previous one in that <u>narrative</u> material is involved and the account is even freer. Whether they come from the same layer in the Pseudo-Clementines will be considered in the conclusion. One cannot tell whether this story in H presupposes a gospel harmony or was the author's own use of both Matthew and Mark.

Conclusion

The foregoing chapter has dealt with those readings which reveal harmonized features, usually of Matthew and Luke or two inner Matthean texts. That "harmonizing" was a going concern in the early church is now evident from many indications. Already one can see in the works of Matthew and Luke a kind of "harmony" (of Mark and Q). Some of the papyrus fragments of gospel material are well-known for containing features combined from various gospels.[1] 2 Clement, as Köster earlier pointed out, has some clearly harmonistic features,[2] as does the Didache.[3] In the case of Justin some scholars of the nineteenth century already saw the use of a gospel harmony.[4] This has been made certain by the work of Bellinzoni.[5] According to Jerome, Theophilus of Antioch composed a harmony of the gospels.[6] A fragment of his work has apparently been found.[7] Therefore Tatian was neither the first nor by any means the only one to harmonize gospel texts although his work was perhaps the first to harmonize all of the gospel material (discourse and narrative) and had the most lasting

---

[1]Cf. especially P. Egerton 2 (H-S 1.94-97).

[2]2 Clem. 4.2,5; 5.4; 9.11; cf. Köster, Syn. Überlieferung, ad loc.

[3]In Did. 1.3-2.1; cf. ibid., pp. 217-41.

[4]Cf. W. Sanday, The Gospels in the Second Century, 1876, pp. 90-106, 136-37; and M. von Engelhardt, Das Christentum Justins des Märtyrers, 1878, pp. 335-45. Cf. also (a work which I have not had access to) E. Lippelt, Quae fuerint Justini Martyris Apomnomoneumata, 1901, esp. p. 35.

[5]Sayings. Cf. also H. F. D. Sparks in JTS, 2nd Series, 14 (1963), 462-66.

[6]Ep. 121.6.15 ad Algasiam (CSEL 56.24,24-25,1): "Theophilus, Antiochenae ecclesiae septimus post Petrum apostolum episcopus, qui quattuor euangelistorum in unum opus dicta conpingens ingenii sui nobis monumenta dimisit, etc."

[7]B. de Gaiffier, "Une citation de l'Harmonie Evangélique de Théophile d'Antioche dans le 'Liber Sancti Jacobi,'" in Mél. M. Andrieu, 1956, pp. 173-79.

influence. At the same time harmonized texts are found in many
of the early fathers--especially Clement of Alexandria, Origen,
and in the Didascalia. It is clear that the textual tradition
itself, especially that of Matthew and Luke, has been under the
influence of harmonization.

My study of the harmonized and conflated sayings in H has
shown that H has used a harmonized source of sayings of Jesus
that was used also by Justin and known to other fathers. This
conclusion agrees with Waitz's conclusion in seeing a direct
relationship between H and Justin in many of the sayings but does
not require his hypothesis of an anti-Marcionite redaction of KP
which used Justin's (now lost) Syn. adv. Marc. as a source.

The problem which remains is that of attempting to group
the sayings together and relate them to the difficult source
problem. This question will be taken up more fully in the concluding chapter. Here I will deal with the sayings of the
preceding chapter.

Nos. 1-7 were seen to share a common harmonized source with
Justin.[8] Waitz agreed in the case of nos. 1 and 4-7, attributing
them to the anti-Marcionite (= A-M) redaction. No. 2 (i.e., H
3.19.3 but not 12.32.1) he attributed to KP and no. 3 to H. But
I think he did not recognize their closeness to Justin. This
means, if my analysis is justified, that Waitz's attribution of
various sayings to the sources he identifies must be questioned.[9]

Nos. 8-10 were problematic in their relation with Justin,
i.e., Justin had parallels but with rather different wording.
Waitz would agree in the case of nos. 8 and 10 which he attributed
to the Praxeis Petrou source (= PP). No. 9, however, he referred
to A-M on the strength of H and Justin's combining the same texts
(Mt. 6.32b and 6.8b) but without accounting for the different
wording. No. 8, if it ever shared a common source with Justin,
has certainly either been reworked according to another reading
(known also to Origen, Eusebius, and Epiphanius) or Justin's text
has been brought into later conformity with the canonical texts.
Otherwise H 8.4.1 is from a different layer in H than those above,
a layer which would also indicate some harmonized readings. No. 9

---

[8]Also known to other fathers.

[9]A critique of Waitz in this respect will be taken up in the
concluding chapter.

is striking for the combination of the same texts in H and Justin
and perhaps should be included in the common source even if one
cannot fully account for the difference in wording. No. 10 has
two factors in favor of a common source: (1) the opening words
πολλοὶ ἐλεύσονται, common to H and Justin (and see the Didascalia), and (2) the fact that H 16.21.4 (= Saying No. 53 discussed
in Chapter 5) may reflect the same collection of anti-heretical
sayings that Justin has collected in Dial. 35. This saying
(no. 10 in H) also occurs in Justin in Dial. 35 in that grouping.
Against this conclusion is the fact that H does not follow Justin
in his peculiar readings that depart from the text of Mt. 7.15.
But this could mean secondary reworking of H toward the Matthean
text.[10]

Nos. 11-18 are all harmonized or conflated sayings that
simply lack other parallels or witnesses. Hence their attribution to the same layer of H as those above must depend on inner
grounds of their characteristics and on other criteria of source
analysis.[11] On the former it may be said that nos. 11-16 appear
to fit well with the sayings above in harmonizing sayings of
Jesus from Matthew and Luke (except no. 15 which may involve
Marcan order--see infra). In regard to the latter, nos. 11, 12,
15 come from the same grouping of sayings (H 3.50-57) as nos. 6
and 9; no. 16 (H 11.33.1f.) is in close proximity to no. 10
(H 11.35.6). But nos. 14 and 15 are attributed by Waitz to PP
and by Strecker to a special ordination source.[12] I am unable to
solve this source problem and leave nos. 14 and 15 open in regard
to whether they belong with the other harmonized sayings or not.

Nos. 17 and 18 differ from the rest in the fact that they
are very free renditions of the canonical versions. I think that
there is little doubt that they are post-synoptic (against
Waitz). Waitz attributed no. 17 to KP and no. 18 to PP. If these
two went back to the same harmonized source as (most of) the other
others above, it would still mean that the author has done his
own free paraphrasing and additions to it. Otherwise they must

---

[10]It was noted that H 11.35.6 involves a probable corruption
(πρός με) anyway.

[11]Waitz attributed nos. 11, 12, and 15 to KP, 13 and 14 to
PP, and 16 to G.

[12]Judenchristentum, pp. 97-116.

be considered from a different layer in H.

The harmonized source (by which I mean that common to H and Justin) can be seen thus far to be a collection of sayings[13] based on Matthew and Luke. Mark may also be involved if: (1) it could be concluded that no. 11 indicated Marcan influence (παρελεύσονται) and that in no. 15 Marcan order was influential, and (2) if these two belong to the source. But in itself this evidence for Mark is slight. Bellinzoni does argue for Marcan influence in the quotations in Justin.[14] I will return to this question in the next chapter.

---

[13]This also speaks against no. 18 which includes a narrative account.

[14]Sayings, passim and p. 140.

CHAPTER III

SAYINGS BASED ON A SINGLE CANONICAL GOSPEL TEXT

The following chapter discusses sayings which come from a single place in one canonical gospel. Examples from all four canonical gospels are found in H.

A. MATTHEW

19. H 3.55.1, 19.2.4c

H 3.55.1	H 19.2.4c	Ju, A. 16.5	Mt. 5.37	Jm. 5.12
ἔστω	ἔστω	ἔστω δὲ	ἔστω δε	ἤτω δὲ
			ὁ λόγος	
ὑμῶν	ὑμῶν	ὑμῶν	ὑμῶν	ὑμῶν
τὸ ναὶ ναί,	τὸ ναὶ ναὶ	τὸ ναὶ ναὶ	⌐ναὶ ναί,	τὸ ναὶ ναὶ
5 τὸ οὖ οὖ·	καὶ τὸ οὖ οὖ·	καὶ τὸ οὖ οὖ·	οὖ οὖ[1]·	καὶ τὸ οὖ οὖ·
τὸ γὰρ	τὸ δὲ	τὸ δὲ	τὸ δὲ	ἵνα μὴ
περισσὸν	περισσὸν	περισσὸν	περισσὸν	ὑπὸ κρίσιν
τούτων	τούτων	τούτων	τούτων	πέσητε.
ἐκ τοῦ	ἐκ τοῦ	ἐκ τοῦ	ἐκ τοῦ	
10 πονηροῦ	πονηροῦ	πονηροῦ.	πονηροῦ	
ἐστιν.	ἐστιν.		ἐστιν.	

[1]το ναι ναι
και το ου ου ϑ.

Clement, Strom. 5.14/99.1 = 7.11/67.5 (Stählin 2.391; 3.48)
ἔστω ὑμῶν τὸ ναὶ ναὶ καὶ τὸ οὖ οὖ.

Eusebius, Dem. evang. 3.3/103a (Heikel 6.109)
ἔστω γὰρ ὑμῶν τὸ ναὶ ναί, τὸ οὖ οὖ.
(Cf. Comm. in Ps. 14.4 [MPG 23.152].)

Const. Ap. 5.12.6 (Funk 1.269)
εἶναι δὲ τὸ ναὶ ναὶ καὶ τὸ οὖ οὖ
τοῖς πιστοῖς παρεγγυᾷ,
καὶ τὸ τούτων περισσὸν τοῦ πονηροῦ εἶναι λέγει.

Gregory Nys., Hom. in Cant. 13 (MPG 44.1040)
ἔστω δὲ ὑμῶν ὁ λόγος τὸ ναὶ ναὶ καὶ τὸ οὖ οὖ·
τὸ δὲ περισσότερον τούτων ἐκ τοῦ διαβόλου ἐστίν.

Epiphanius, Pan. 19.6.21 (Holl 1.223)
καὶ πάλιν ἐν τῷ εὐαγγελίῳ λέγοντος
"μη ὀμνύναι μήτε τὸν οὐρανον μήτε τὴν γῆν
μήτε ἕτερόν τινα ὅρκον,
ἀλλὰ ἤτω ὑμῶν τὸ ναὶ ναὶ καὶ τὸ οὖ οὖ·
τὸ περισσότερον γὰρ τούτων ἐκ τοῦ πονηροῦ ὑπάρχει."

Cyril Alex., De ador. et ver. 6 (MPG 68.472)
ἔστω ὑμῶν τὸ ναὶ ναὶ καὶ τὸ οὖ οὖ·
τὸ δὲ περισσὸν τούτων ἐκ τοῦ διαβόλου ἐστίν.

In his discussion of this saying in Justin Bellinzoni concluded that there existed a parenetic saying about swearing that
was based on Mt. 5.34-37 harmonized either with Jm. 5.12 or the
parenetic teaching that lies behind Jm. 5.12 and that this saying
was known to several patristic writers after Justin.[1] It is the
use of ἔστω and the warning sentence τὸ δὲ περισσὸν τούτων ἐκ
τοῦ πονηροῦ ἐστιν that proves the use of Matthew[2] but the omission
of ὁ λόγος and the addition of τό before ναὶ ναί and καὶ τό
before οὖ οὔ that points to James or his tradition.

What is important for our purposes is that H and Justin
agree (excepting Justin's lack of the final ἐστιν) in this combination as do (essentially) Epiphanius (ἤτω instead of ἔστω,
περισσότερον for περισσόν, and ὑπάρχει for ἐστιν), the Apostolic
Constitutions, and Cyril (διαβόλου for πονηροῦ; cf. Gregory).
This should help emphasize the fact that some of the texts in H
drawing on Matthew may belong to the same source as that which
contains harmonized and conflated sayings common to H and Justin
and also known to other fathers.[3]

---

[1]Sayings, p. 67. M. Dibelius (Der Brief des Jakobus, 11th
ed. [1964], p. 197, n. 1) also advocates that Justin's citation
has drawn both on Matthew and the tradition represented in James.
But he notes that since Justin does not otherwise seem to know
the Ep. of James, "so wird seine Kenntnis der nichtevangelischen
Form anderswoher stammen."

[2]Dibelius (ibid., p. 298) makes a convincing case that the
saying in James is not a weakened version of Matthew but is
prior to it.

[3]Waitz (Pseudoklementinen, p. 281) naturally attributes it
to his anti-Marcionite source. Strecker (Judenchristentum, p.
134) speaks of the possibility of an uncanonical text but thinks
that Jm. 5.12 and the fathers represent only stylistic improvements of the Matthean text. But then he fails to consider how
it is that they share a common or similar text.

H 3.56.3	Mt. 5.34-35a	Jm. 5.12
	ἐγὼ δὲ λέγω ὑμῖν	
μὴ ὀμόσητε	μὴ ὀμόσαι	μὴ ὀμνύετε,
	ὅλως·	
	μήτε	μήτε
5 τὸν οὐρανόν,	ἐν τῷ οὐρανῷ,	τὸν οὐρανον
ὅτι θρόνος	ὅτι θρόνος	
⌐θεοῦ ἐστιν,[1]	ἐστιν τοῦ θεοῦ·	
μήτε τὴν γῆν,	35μήτε ἐν τῇ γῇ,	μήτε τὴν γῆν
ὅτι ὑποπόδιον	ὅτι ὑποπόδιόν	
10 τῶν ποδῶν αὐτοῦ	(1. 12)	
ἐστιν.	ἐστιν	
(1. 10)	τῶν ποδῶν αὐτοῦ·	
		μήτε ἄλλον
		τινὰ ὅρκον·

---

[1]ἐστὶ θεοῦ O.

Justin, Apol. 16.5
    μὴ ὀμόσητε ὅλως· ἔστω etc. (see under the previous saying).

In this case H presupposes only Matthew. The changes from
the text of Matthew can be adjudged as H's own:
    1. The omission of ὅλως and μήτε better adapts it to the
context in H 3.56. The saying is being used to answer the charge
that God dwells in a temple (τοῖς δὲ αὐτὸν διαβεβαιουμένοις ἐν
ναῷ εἶναι ἔφη). The omission of ὅλως and μήτε serves to move
immediately to the part about heaven being God's throne which is
the part of the saying that concerns the author in his counter
to the charge made.
    2. θεοῦ ἐστιν for ἐστιν τοῦ θεοῦ is an insignificant change
of style. It may be noted that ἐστιν is placed at the end of the
phrases in both the previous saying and in this one (twice), thus
enhancing the parallelism.
    3. The datives after the verb of swearing are changed to
the more classical style of accusatives.
    4. The final ἐστιν (see no. 2 above).
    But is H related to Justin in this case? The fact that the
previous saying from the same sayings on swearing in Mt. 5.34-37

did indicate a common source for H and Justin and that this one occurs in close proximity to the previous one in H (one chapter apart) must raise this possibility. Together H and Justin (<u>Apol</u>. 16.5) agree in the wording μὴ ὀμόσητε--undoubtedly based on Matthew's aorist tense (ἐγὼ λέγω ὑμῖν μὴ <u>ὀμόσαι</u>) but differing from James' present tense (μὴ ὀμνύετε). But there are two difficulties in seeing a common source for H and Justin.

A. Justin reads Matthew's ὅλως while H omits it. But as noted above this could well be H's own omission to adapt the saying to his context.

B. Justin proceeds from μὴ ὀμόσητε ὅλως to the saying ἔστω δὲ ὑμῶν τὸ ναὶ ναί, etc. while H follows the continuation in Mt. 5.34. But such a "jump" by Justin cannot prove that his source did not contain the intervening words of Matthew. Only that it did not serve Justin's purpose to quote them in <u>Apol</u>. 16.5. Hence this saying in H would seem best attributed to the same source as the previous one, the source known also to Justin.[1]

---

[1] Again Waitz (<u>Pseudoklementinen</u>, p. 306) attributes the saying in H to the anti-Marcionite source. Strecker (<u>Judenchristentum</u>, p. 122) does not see H and Justin as directly related.

21. H 8.6.4, 18.15.1, R 4.5.5.

H 8.6.4	R 4.5.5	Mt. 11.25	Lk. 10.21
⌐ἐξομολογοῦμαί[1]	confiteor	ἐξομολογοῦμαί	ἐξομολογοῦμαί
σοι	tibi	σοι	σοι
πάτερ	pater,	πάτερ,	πάτερ,
	domine	κύριε	κύριε
5 τοῦ οὐρανοῦ	caeli	τοῦ οὐρανοῦ	τοῦ οὐρανοῦ
καὶ τῆς γῆς,	et terrae,	καὶ τῆς γῆς,	⌐καὶ τῆς γῆς,[1]
ὅτι	quia	ὅτι	ὅτι
⌐ἔκρυψας[2]	occultasti	ἔκρυψας	ἀπέκρυψας
ταῦτα	haec	ταῦτα	ταῦτα
10 ἀπὸ σοφῶν[3]	a sapientibus	ἀπὸ σοφῶν	ἀπὸ σοφῶν
πρεσβυτέρων	et prudentibus	⌐καὶ συνετῶν[1]	καὶ συνετῶν
καὶ ἀπεκάλυψας	et revelasti	καὶ ἀπεκάλυψας	καὶ ἀπεκάλυψας
αὐτὰ	ea	αὐτὰ	αὐτὰ
νηπίοις	parvulis.	νηπίοις.	νηπίοις.
15 θηλάζουσιν.			

---

[1]ἐξομολογοῦμεν   [1]και δυνατων 1; [1]Omit P[45].
O.   omit sy[s],[c].
[2]ἀπέκρυψας O.
[3]+ καί O.

H 17.5.5
    ἔτι δὲ καὶ ἐξομολογεῖται τῷ κυρίῳ οὐρανοῦ καὶ γῆς.

Irenaeus, AH 1.13.2 (Harvey 1.180)
    ἐξομολογήσομαί σοι πάτερ, κύριε τῶν οὐρανῶν καὶ τῆς γῆς,
    ὅτι ἀπέκρυψας ἀπὸ σοφῶν καὶ συνετῶν,
    καὶ ἀπεκάλυψας αὐτὰ νηπίοις.

Clement, Paed. 1.6/32.2 (Stählin 1.109)
    ἐξομολογοῦμαί σοι πάτερ, (φησίν), ὁ θεὸς τοῦ οὐρανοῦ καὶ
     τῆς γῆς,
    ὅτι ἀπέκρυψας ταῦτα ἀπὸ σοφῶν καὶ συνετῶν
    καὶ ἀπεκάλυψας αὐτὰ νηπίοις.

H 18.15.1	Ter., AM 4.25*	Epiph., Pan. 42.11.15**
	gratias enim, inquit, ago	"εὐχαριστῶ
ἐξομολογοῦμαί	et confiteor,	
σοι		σοι
5 κύριε	domine	κύριε
τοῦ οὐρανοῦ	caeli,	τοῦ οὐρανοῦ."
καὶ τῆς γῆς,		(cf. lines 17-18)
ὅτι	quod ea,	
⌐ἅπερ¹ ἦν	quae erant	
10 κρυπτὰ	abscondita	
σοφοῖς,	sapientibus et prudentibus,	
ἀπεκάλυψας	revelaveris	
αὐτὰ		
15 νηπίοις	parvulis.	
θηλάζουσιν.		

οὐκ εἶχε δὲ
"καὶ τῆς γῆς"
οὔτε "πάτερ" εἶχεν.

---

¹ἅτινα in 18.15,3,6.

*Quoting Marcion (CSEL 47.503).

**Quoting Marcion (Holl 2.132).

First, it is necessary to take up the relationship between H 8.6.4 and 18.15.1. That one is derived in part from the other is suggested by the addition of θηλάζουσιν to νηπίοις in both,[1] an expression found in the LXX,[2] but not used in this saying in the fathers or the manuscripts of Matthew or Luke. The saying in H 18.15.1 is placed on the lips of Simon Magus and is surely

---

[1] But cf. n. 9.

[2] Joel 2.16; Lam. 2.20; cf. Ps. 8.3. Strecker (Judenchristen-tum, p. 133) suggests that the citation of Ps. 8.3 in Mt. 21.16 has perhaps suggested the use of θηλάζουσιν to the author.

intended to be the Marcionite version[3] with its omission of
πάτερ[4] and the change of ἔκρυψας ταῦτα to ἅπερ (or ἅτινα) ἦν
κρυπτά.[5] However H 18.15.1 lacks εὐχαριστῶ, attested for
Marcion's text,[6] fails to drop καὶ τῆς γῆς as Marcion's text
did,[7] but does drop καὶ συνετῶν which Marcion's text did not.[8]
Since these three things can all be explained from H 8.6.4, it
appears that H 18.15.1 (and subsequently 17.5.5?) has been formed
from H 8.6.4 but with some knowledge of the Marcionite reading.[9]

Turning then to H 8.6.4, only Matthew is presupposed according to the reading of P (ἔκρυψας) but Luke according to O
(ἀπέκρυψας). P is usually more trustworthy than O. That Irenaeus and Clement both read ἀπέκρυψας (= Luke) could help explain
O's change--toward the more commonly read Lucan text. The fact
that Matthew and Luke are otherwise identical makes it impossible
to know if a harmonized text was involved. But the presence of a
Lucan form of a saying (Lk. 6.46) occurs in the next chapter
(H 8.7.4) in the same context shows that the author or his source
knew both Matthew and Luke.

Otherwise H's differences from the canonical texts are
peculiar to H: (1) the dropping of κύριε for which I find no
obvious reason; (2) the adding of θηλάζουσιν as already noted,

---

[3]Cf. the whole chapter H 18.15.

[4]Thus the text of Marcion according to Tertullian (domine
caeli) and Epiphanius (κύριε τοῦ οὐρανοῦ).

[5]So Marcion according to Tertullian (ea quae erant
abscondita).

[6]Cf. Tertullian: gratias ago et confiteor; and Epiphanius:
εὐχαριστῶ σοι.

[7]So says Epiphanius (οὐκ εἶχε δὲ "καὶ τῆς γῆς").

[8]Tertullian has sapientibus et prudentibus.

[9]Waitz (Pseudoklementinen, pp. 283ff.) however sees H 18.15.1
as being only the Marcionite text; θηλάζουσιν is attributed as a
later addition to "der Redaktor der Homilien." He notes that
νηπίοις occurs twice more in the chapter without the addition of
θηλάζουσιν (18.15.3 and 6). But even if θηλάζουσιν is thus
explained, one is still left with the problem of ἐξομολογοῦμαι
without εὐχαριστῶ, the presence of καὶ τῆς γῆς, and the dropping
of καὶ συνετῶν for the Marcionite text. One could explain all
of this as also secondary changes by a later redactor (the
Homilist?) under the influence of H 8.6.4. In any case the
observations about H 8.6.4 would still be valid.

perhaps in order to heighten the contrast with σοφῶν πρεσβυτέρων; and (3) the change from σοφῶν καὶ συνετῶν to σοφῶν πρεσβυτέρων. This change seems to have been made in adapting the saying to its context in H 8.6 where it is affirmed that salvation
comes both to faithful Jews who follow Moses and to those who
have believed Jesus. σοφῶν πρεσβυτέρων thus refers to the Jews
who know God's ways from Moses without needing the teaching of
Jesus while νηπίοις θηλάζουσιν would refer to the ignorant
Gentiles who needed the teachings of God from Jesus. Hence the
line that follows the saying in H 8.6.5: οὕτως ὁ θεὸς τοῖς μὲν
ἔκρυψεν διδάσκαλον ὡς προεγνωκόσιν ἃ δεῖ πράττειν, τοῖς δὲ
ἀπεκάλυψεν ὡς ἀγνοοῦσιν ἃ χρὴ ποιεῖν

R has characteristically returned to the canonical text(s)
in adding pater, changing back to et prudentibus and dropping
θηλάζουσιν.

22. H 18.17.3

H 18.17.3	Mt. 7.13-14
εἰσέλθετε	εἰσέλθατε
διὰ τῆς στενῆς	διὰ τῆς στενῆς
	πύλης . . .
	¹⁴ὅτι στενὴ
5	⌐ἡ πύλη¹
καὶ τεθλιμμένης	καὶ τεθλιμμένη
ὁδοῦ,	ἡ ὁδὸς
δι᾽ ἧς εἰσελεύσεσθε	ἡ ἀπάγουσα
εἰς τὴν ζωήν.	εἰς τὴν ζωὴν
10	καὶ ὀλίγοι εἰσὶν
	οἱ εὑρίσκοντες αὐτήν.

---

¹Omit 544 pc a h k m.

H 7.7.2
ἡ μὲν οὖν τῶν ἀπολλυμένων ὁδὸς πλατεῖα μὲν καὶ ὁμαλωτάτη,
ἀπολλύουσα δὲ ἄνευ τοῦ πόνου,
ἡ δὲ τῶν σωζομένων στενὴ μὲν καὶ τραχεῖα.

H 3.18.3
γνῶσις, ᾗ μόνη τὴν πύλην τῆς ζωῆς ἀνοῖξαι δύναται,
δι᾽ ἧς μόνης εἰς τὴν αἰώνιαν ζωὴν εἰσελθεῖν ἐστιν.

H 3.52.2 (= Saying No. 57)
ἐγώ εἰμι ἡ πύλη τῆς ζωῆς·
ὁ δι᾽ ἐμοῦ εἰσερχόμενος εἰσέρχεται εἰς τὴν ζωήν.

Clement, Strom. 4.2/5.3 (Stählin 2.250)
στενὴ γὰρ τῷ ὄντι καὶ τεθλιμμένη ἡ ὁδὸς κυρίου.

Clement, Strom. 6.1/2.3 (Stählin 2.423)
διὰ στενῆς καὶ τεθλιμμένης τῆς κυριακῆς ὄντως ὁδοῦ.

H 18.17.3 is simply a shortened version of Mt. 7.13 and 14.
H speaks of "the Way" (eliminating "the Gate") and changes the
wording of "the way which leads to life" to "the way through
which you enter into life." The evidence of Clement of
Alexandria indicates the use of a shortened version of the saying in "Two Ways" or hortatory material.¹ But beyond that one
cannot identify the source(s).

---

¹Cf. Did. 1.1 and Barn. 18.1; cf. also Herm. mand. 6.2.

H 7.7.2, not cited as a saying of Jesus, also speaks of
ὁ ὁδός and seems to paraphrase only Mt. 7.13-14.

H 3.52.2 which speaks of ἡ πύλη τῆς ζωῆς will be taken up
in the chapter on Agrapha (Saying No. 57).

23. H 3.15.2ab

H 3.15.2a	Mt. 24.2	Mk. 13.2	Lk. 21.6
			ταῦτα ἃ
	⌐οὐ[1]		
ὁρᾶτε	βλέπετε	βλέπεις	θεωρεῖτε,
τὰς οἰκοδομὰς		(lines 6-7)	
5 ταύτας;	ταῦτα	ταύτας	
		τὰς μεγάλας	
	πάντα;	οἰκοδομάς;	
ἀμὴν	ἀμὴν		ἐλεύσονται
ὑμῖν	λέγω		ἡμέραι
10 ⌐λέγω,[1]	ὑμῖν		ἐν αἷς
λίθος	(1. 16)	(1. 16)	(1. 16)
ἐπὶ λίθον	(1. 17)	(1. 17)	(1. 17)
οὐ μὴ	οὐ μὴ	οὐ μὴ	οὐκ
ἀφεθῇ	ἀφεθῇ	ἀφεθῇ	ἀφεθήσεται
15 ὧδε,	ὧδε		
(1. 11)	λίθος	λίθος	λίθος
(1. 12)	ἐπὶ λίθον	ἐπὶ λίθον	ἐπὶ λίθῳ
ὃς	ὃς	ὃς	ὃς
οὐ μὴ	οὐ	οὐ μὴ	οὐ
20 καθαιρεθῇ,	καταλυθήσεται,	καταλυθῇ.	καταλυθήσεται.

---

[1]Omit O.   [1]Omit D L X 33 700 892 pc lat sy^s sa^pt bo.

H 3.15.2b	Mt. 24.34	Mk. 13.30	Lk. 21.32
	ἀμὴν λέγω	ἀμὴν λέγω	ἀμὴν λέγω
(καί·)	ὑμῖν ὅτι	ὑμῖν ὅτι	ὑμῖν ὅτι
οὐ μὴ	οὐ μὴ	οὐ μὴ	οὐ μὴ
παρέλθῃ	παρέλθῃ	παρέλθῃ	παρέλθῃ
5 ἡ γενεὰ αὕτη,	ἡ γενεὰ αὕτη	ἡ γενεὰ αὕτη	ἡ γενεὰ αὕτη
καὶ	ἕως ἂν	μέχρις οὗ	ἕως ἂν
ἡ καθαίρεσις	πάντα	πάντα	πάντα
ἀρχὴν	ταῦτα	ταῦτα	
λήψεται.	γένηται.	γένηται.	γένηται.

This saying (or these two sayings) and those which follow
in this chapter lack other witnesses among the fathers to their
peculiar forms. While they further demonstrate conflated and
harmonized readings in H, they tell us little in themselves of a
possible source known to other fathers.

That Mt. 24.2 underlies the first saying is proved by the
words ἀμὴν ὑμῖν λέγω and ὧδε in H.[1] Whether Mk. 13.2 must be
presupposed is more problematic. τὰς οἰκοδομὰς ταύτας, the
second οὐ μή, and possibly the use of the aorist subjunctive for
the last verb (καθαιρεθῇ--see Mark's καταλυθῇ) could make a case
for the use of Mk. 13.2. In that case we would have a harmony
involving Matthew and Mark at this point.[2] However the tendency
in the sayings of Jesus in H toward precise parallelism would
explain both the second οὐ μή (parallel to the first) and the
use of the aorist subjunctive in the last verb (see ἀφεθῇ). τὰς
οἰκοδομὰς ταύτας could well be H's own expansion of ταῦτα which
would be ambiguous without proper context or if it stood in a
collection of sayings! Accordingly no recourse to Mark would be
necessary. At least the question must be left open--a harmony of
Matthew and Mark is possible here but by no means certain.

The peculiarities of H's reading are apparently due to his
own changes: (1) ὀρᾶτε, (2) the change of word order in ἀμὴν
ὑμῖν λέγω,[3] (3) in λίθος ἐπὶ λίθον before οὐ--ὧδε, and (4) the
use of καθαιρεῖν. The first three are only stylistic changes.
The last word (καθαιρεῖν) is explained by a preference in H for
this term in reference to the destruction of the temple.[4]

The second saying could be from Mt. 24.34 or Mk. 13.30 or
Lk. 21.32 since all are identical in the wording οὐ μὴ παρέλθῃ
ἡ γενεὰ αὕτη. καὶ ἡ καθαίρεσις ἀρχὴν λήψεται must again be H's
own wording.[5]

---

[1]This disproves the conclusion of Waitz, _Pseudoklementinen_,
p. 297: "Sicher ist das erste hier angeführte Herrnwort in einer
älteren Rezension als bei den Synoptikern erhalten."

[2]Nothing suggests the use of Luke here.

[3]See this same order in H 11.26.2.

[4]Cf. H 3.15.26 and H 2.17.4. So also Strecker, _Judenchri-
stentum_, p. 126, and Waitz, _Pseudoklementinen_, p. 297.

[5]Cf. n. 4.

Therefore these two sayings need presuppose only a joining of Matthew 24.2 and 24.34 although Mark may be involved. The third saying that follows these two (in H 3.15.2c) will be taken up under the Lucan passages.

24. H 3.55.2a

H 3.55.2a	Mt. 22.32b	Mk. 12.27a
οὐκ ἔστιν	οὐκ ἔστιν	οὐκ ἔστιν
θεὸς	⌜ὁ θεὸς⌝[1]	⌜θεὸς⌝[1]
νεκρῶν	νεκρῶν	νεκρῶν
ἀλλὰ ζώντων.	ἀλλὰ ζώντων.	ἀλλὰ ζώντων.

[1] θεος ℵ D W 28 pc; ο θεος θεος Koine θ Φ φ pm.

[1] ο θεος ℵ A C Koine Γ Ψ λ 157 pm; ο θεος θεος θ φ 33 al. txt. B D K L W Δ Φ al.

H follows exactly the reading of Matthew (θεός) according to ℵ D W 28 pc which is also the reading of Mark in B D K L W Δ φ al. Since the use of Mark needs proved in each case, one cannot assume other than the use of Matthew here. The introduction to the saying presupposes also Mt. 22.32a (Mk. 12.26b). Yet it does not make the same point as the synoptic gospels (that God raises the dead) but instead sees the saying as affirming that the Patriarchs did not die! This would suggest that the saying has not been taken directly from the synoptic gospels but from another source such as a sayings source.

25. H 3.52.3c

H 3.52.3c

ζητεῖτε καὶ ⌜εὑρίσκετε,⌝[1]

Mt. 7.7 = Lk. 11.9

αἰτεῖτε καὶ δοθήσεται,
ζητεῖτε καὶ εὑρήσετε,
κρούετε καὶ ἀνοιγήσεται ὑμῖν.

---

[1] εὑρήσετε O.

Aphraates, Hom. 23.48 (Patr. Syr. 1,2.93,23-24 = 96,3)
    "Request and receive;
    for as you see, you will obtain."

(.ܐܠܝܐ܂ ܘܣܒ̈ܘ : ܟܕ ܐܠܓܐ̈ ܐܠ ܐܚܣܝ.)

The striking element in this brief saying is the use of the
imperative (εὑρίσκετε) instead of the future (εὑρήσετε) of
Matthew and Luke.[1] Aphraates also attests the use of an imperative for the second verb of the saying (using ܣܒ̈ܘ 'receive,
take'). But one cannot be sure whether the imperative was
already present in H's source or was a change made by H.[2] Still
it is clearly secondary to the wording of Matthew or Luke.[3]

---

[1] Assuming that P's reading as the lectio difficilior is the
better one while O's εὑρήσετε is more likely a correction back
to the canonical text(s).

[2] Following the saying in H are the words: ὡς μὴ προδήλως
κειμένης τῆς ἀληθείας.

[3] The saying was originally a wisdom saying of the sort known
in Judaism; cf. Pesikta 176a: "When he knocks, the door is
opened for him."

26. H 3.56.1-2

H 3.56.1-2	Mt. 7.9-11	Lk. 11.11-13
τίνα	ἢ τίς ⌜ἔστιν[1]	τίνα ˌδὲ
ὑμῶν	ἐξ ὑμῶν	ἐξ ὑμῶν
	ἄνθρωπος,	⌜τὸν πατέρα
αἰτήσει	ὃν αἰτήσει	αἰτήσει
5 υἱὸς	ὁ υἱὸς αὐτοῦ	ὁ υἱὸς[1]
ἄρτον,	ἄρτον,	ἰχθύν,
μὴ λίθον	μὴ λίθον	μὴ ἀντὶ ἰχθύος ὄφιν
ἐπιδώσει αὐτῷ;	ἐπιδώσει αὐτῷ;	αὐτῷ ἐπιδώσει;
ἢ καὶ ἰχθὺν	[10]ἢ καὶ ἰχθὺν	[12]ἢ καὶ αἰτήσει
10 αἰτήσει,	αἰτήσει,	ᾠόν,
μὴ ὄφιν	μὴ ὄφιν	ἐπιδώσει αὐτῷ
ἐπιδώσει αὐτῷ;	ἐπιδώσει αὐτῷ;	σκορπίον;
[2]εἰ οὖν ὑμεῖς,	[11]εἰ οὖν ὑμεῖς	[13]εἰ οὖν ὑμεῖς
πονηροὶ ὄντες,	πονηροὶ ὄντες	πονηροὶ ὑπάρχοντες
15 οἴδατε	οἴδατε	οἴδατε
⌜δόματα[1] ἀγαθὰ	δόματα ἀγαθὰ	δόματα ἀγαθὰ
διδόναι	διδόναι	διδόναι
τοῖς τέκνοις ὑμῶν	τοῖς τέκνοις ὑμῶν	τοῖς τέκνοις ὑμῶν,
πόσῳ μᾶλλον	πόσῳ μᾶλλον	πόσῳ μᾶλλον
20 ὁ πατὴρ ὑμῶν	ὁ πατὴρ ὑμῶν	ὁ πατὴρ
ὁ οὐράνιος	ὁ ἐν τοῖς οὐρανοῖς	ὁ ⌜ἐξ οὐρανοῦ[2]
δώσει	δώσει	δώσει
ἀγαθὰ	ἀγαθὰ	πνεῦμα ἅγιον
τοῖς αἰτουμένοις	τοῖς αἰτοῦσιν	τοῖς αἰτοῦσιν
25 αὐτὸν	αὐτόν.	αὐτόν.
καὶ τοῖς ποιοῦσιν		
τὸ θέλημα		
αὐτοῦ;		

---

[1]δόγματα O*. [1]Omit B* 565 al it. [1]Omit τόν and ὁ P[45] 1 pc.
[2]ουρανιος P[45] 579 1.

The wording from αἰτήσει (1. 4) - αὐτόν (1. 25) is Matthean. The only question is whether Luke is also involved.[1] τίνα (1. 1),

---

[1]Both Waitz (Pseudoklementinen, p. 306) and Strecker (Juden-christentum, p. 127) assume that it is.

102

υἱός (1. 5) without αὐτοῦ, and ὁ οὐράνιος (1. 21; cf. P[45] of Luke) could be taken as indications of Lucan influence. However the τίνα and υἱός in H seem to be part of a simplified introduction and ὁ οὐράνιος is frequently interchanged with ὁ ἐν τοῖς οὐρανοῖς both in the textual tradition and in the fathers. Therefore only Matthew need be presupposed in this case.[2] The minor differences in H (the beginning [already noted], ὁ οὐράνιος [already noted], the stylistic change to αἰτουμένοις, and the addition of καὶ τοῖς ποιοῦσιν τὸ θέλημα αὐτοῦ) are best taken as H's own changes.

---

[2]At least the case for harmonized texts needs to be made on more certain evidence than this.

27. H 11.29.2, R 6.11.3

H 11.29.2	R 6.11.3	Mt. 23.25-26	Lk. 11.39-40
οὐαὶ	Vae	οὐαὶ	νῦν
ὑμῖν,	vobis,	ὑμῖν	ὑμεῖς
γραμματεῖς	scribae	γραμματεῖς	
καὶ φαρισαῖοι	et Pharisaei	καὶ φαρισαῖοι	οἱ φαρισαῖοι
5 ὑποκριταί,	hypocritae,	ὑποκριταί,	
ὅτι	quia	ὅτι	
καθαρίζετε	mundatis	καθαρίζετε	(1. 11)
		τὸ ἔξωθεν	τὸ ἔξωθεν
τοῦ ποτηρίου	calicis	τοῦ ποτηρίου	τοῦ ποτηρίου
10 καὶ τῆς παρο- ψίδος	et parabsidis	καὶ τῆς παρο- ψίδος	καὶ τοῦ πίνακος
			καθαρίζετε,
τὸ ἔξωθεν,	quod deforis est	(1. 8)	(1. 8)
ἔσωθεν δὲ	intus autem	ἔσωθεν δὲ	τὸ δὲ ἔσωθεν
			ὑμῶν
15 γέμει	plena sunt	γέμουσιν	γέμει
⌜ῥύπους,[1]	sordibus,	ἐξ ἁρπαγῆς	ἁρπαγῆς
		καὶ ⌜ἀκρασίας.[1]	καὶ πονηρίας.
φαρισαῖε	Pharisaee	[26]φαρισαῖε	[40]ἄφρονες,...
τυφλέ,	caece,	τυφλέ,	
20 καθάρισον	munda	καθάρισον	
πρῶτον	prius	πρῶτον	
		τὸ ἐντὸς	
τοῦ ποτηρίου		τοῦ ποτηρίου	
καὶ τῆς παρο- ψίδος		⌜καὶ τῆς παρο- ψίδος⌝[2]	
25 τὸ ἔσωθεν,	quod intus est	(1. 22)	
ἵνα		ἵνα	
γένηται	(1. 31)	γένηται	
καὶ	et	καὶ	
⌜τὰ[2] ἔξω	quod deforis est	τὸ ἐκτὸς	
30 ⌜αὐτῶν[3]		⌜αὐτοῦ[3]	
	erit		
⌜καθαρά.[4]	mundum.	καθαρόν.	

---

[1]P; ῥύπου O Ee.

[2]τό Ee.

[1]αδικιας C
Koine pm f
sy[p]; cf. other
variations.

^{3}αὐτοῦ O Ee.

^{4}καθαρόν Ee.

^{2}Omit D θ it sy^s.

^{3}αυτων $\aleph$ C Koine.

Syr. of H 11.29.2
"Woe to you scribes and Pharisees, hypocrites, because you clean the outside of the cup and the plate, but inside they are full of filth. Blind Pharisee, clean first the inside of the cup and the plate and their outside will be clean."

[Syriac text]

G. Thom. 89
"Jesus said, 'Why do you clean the outside of the cup? Do you not understand that He who created the inside is He who also created the outside?'"

[Coptic text]

Irenaeus, AH 4.31.2 (Harvey 2.202)
Pharisaee, inquit, caece,
emunda quod est intus calicis,
ut fiat et quod foris est, mundum.

Clement, _Paed._ 3.9/48.1 (Stählin 1.264)
οὐαὶ ὑμῖν, ὅτι καθαρίζετε τὸ ἔξω τοῦ ποτηρίου καὶ τῆς
παροψίδος, ἔνδοθεν δὲ γέμουσιν ἀκαθαρσίας.
καθάρισον πρῶτον τὸ ἔνδον τοῦ ποτηρίου,
ἵνα γένηται καὶ τὸ ἔξωθεν καθαρόν.

Clement, _Strom._ 3.4/34.2 (Stählin 2.211)
ἐναντιοῦνται δὲ καὶ τῷ Χριστῷ πρὸς τοὺς φαρισαίους
εἰρήκοτι τὸν αὐτὸν θεὸν
καὶ ἐκτὸς ἡμῶν καὶ τὸν ἔσω ἄνθρωπον πεποιηκέναι.

P. Ox. 840 (Grenfell-Hunt 5.5,31-41)
οὐαί, τυφλοί . . . σὺ ἐλούσω . . . νιψάμε[ν]ος τὸ ἐκτός
. . . ἔνδοθεν δὲ . . . [πεπλ]ήρωται σκορπίων καὶ
[πάσης κα(?)]κίας.

There can be little doubt that H and R are based on Matthew. The use of γραμματεῖς and ὑποκρίται, φαρισαῖε τυφλέ, the omission of Lk. 11.40, and the exhortation clause in essentially Matthean form all confirm this. But some changes from Matthew's wording have also been made.

1. The change of word order in the placing of τὸ ἔξωθεν: but that is hardly significant.

2. γέμει in H. This might point to Lucan influence were it not for the fact that the Syriac ([Syriac]) and R (_plena sunt_) agree in the use of the plural.

3. ῥύπους (P; or ῥύπου OEe) is a change already present in G as confirmed by the Syriac of H (ܠܘܬܐ) and by R (<u>sordibus</u>), presumably to preserve the imagery of the "cup and saucer."

4. Changes in the wording of the final clause--τὸ ἔσωθεν for τὸ ἐντός, τὸ ἔξω or τὰ ἔξω for τὸ ἐκτός, perhaps αὐτῶν for αὐτοῦ, and καθαρά for καθαρόν. These may be explained as stylistic changes: (1) τὸ ἔσωθεν because it had been previously used (1. 13) and τὰ <u>ἔξω</u> because of <u>ἔξωθεν</u> (1. 12), and (2) <u>τὰ</u> ἔξω, αὐτῶν, and καθαρά in a logical change to the plural ("their outsides may be clean"), thus preserving intact the metaphor of cup and saucer.

It should be noted in this case that R (with its final wording of <u>quod intus est, et quod deforis est erit mundum</u>) is further from the canonical text than H. Since R's tendency is to return to the canonical text unless retaining the wording of G, it may be assumed that R probably better preserves G's reading than does H. Still that reading (R = G) presupposes nothing other than the text of Matthew. H's changes in the last part of the saying are either secondary adaptations to the text of Matthew and/or an expansion so as to enhance the parallelism.

106

28. H 19.7.1

H 19.7.1	Mt. 12.34	Lk. 6.45
ἐκ	ἐκ γὰρ	ἐκ γὰρ
περισσεύματος	τοῦ περισσεύματος	περισσεύματος
καρδίας	τῆς καρδίας	καρδίας
στόμα	τὸ στόμα	(1. 6)
5 λαλεῖ	λαλεῖ.	λαλεῖ
		τὸ στόμα
		αὐτοῦ.

Waitz supposes the H reproduces Mt. 12.34[1] while Strecker
thinks it is more based on Lk. 6.45.[2] If one could suggest a
good reason for dropping the articles, then only Matthew is
required. Otherwise a harmony is the best solution in which the
Matthean order but the Lucan anarthrous nouns have been
followed.[3]

---

[1]Pseudoklementinen, p. 299.

[2]Judenchristentum, p. 120.

[3]στόμα was probably made anarthrous to agree with the other
nouns.

29. H 3.53.1

H 3.53.1	Mt. 17.5

οὖτός ἐστίν
⌐μου ὁ υἱὸς¹
ὁ ἀγαπητός,
εἰς ὃν εὐδόκησα,
5 τούτου ἀκούετε.

οὖτός ἐστιν
ὁ υἱός μου
ὁ ἀγαπητός,
ἐν ᾧ εὐδόκησα·
⌐ἀκούετε αὐτοῦ.¹

---

¹ὁ υἱός μου O.

¹αυτου ακουετε C Koine W
ϑ φ pl lat sy^{c,p}.

The form is clearly Matthean rather than Marcan or Lucan since only Matthew has ἐν ᾧ εὐδόκησα in the Transfiguration story (Mark and Luke have no equivalent) while in the Baptism story only Matthew is in the third person as here (Mark and Luke are direct address). The presence of τούτου ἀκούετε points to Mt. 17.5 rather than 3.17. The changes in H are merely stylistic: (1) μου before ὁ υἱός (assuming O to be a correction back toward the canonical order), (2) εἰς ὃν for ἐν ᾧ,¹ and (3) τούτου for αὐτοῦ (for emphasis?). The order αὐτοῦ ἀκούετε is widely enough attested in the manuscripts of Matthew (C Koine W ϑ φ pl lat sy^{c,p}) to assume that it was the order H found in his source.

---

¹Cf. 2 Pet. 1.17: ὁ υἱός μου ὁ ἀγαπητός μου οὖτός ἐστιν, εἰς ὃν ἐγὼ εὐδόκησα.

30. H 19.2.3b

H 19.2.3b	Mt. 12.26	Mk. 3.26	Lk. 11.18
εἰ	καὶ εἰ	καὶ εἰ	εἰ δὲ καὶ
ὁ σατανᾶς	ὁ σατανᾶς	ὁ σατανᾶς	ὁ σατανᾶς
τὸν σατανᾶν	τὸν σατανᾶν		
⌐ἐκβάλλει,[1]	ἐκβάλλει,	ἀνέστη	
5 ἐφ' ἑαυτὸν	ἐφ' ἑαυτὸν	ἐφ' ἑαυτὸν	ἐφ' ἑαυτὸν
ἐμερίσθη·	ἐμερίσθη·	καὶ ἐμερίσθη,	διεμερίσθη,
πῶς οὖν	πῶς οὖν	οὐ δύναται	πῶς
αὐτοῦ	(1. 11)		(1. 11)
⌐στήκη[2]	σταθήσεται	στῆναι	σταθήσεται
10 ἡ βασιλεία;	ἡ βασιλεία		ἡ βασιλεία
	αὐτοῦ;		αὐτοῦ;
		ἀλλὰ	
		τέλος ἔχει.	

---

[1]ἐκβάλλῃ P.

[2]στήκει O.

The text of H is simply Mt. 12.26. αὐτοῦ in another order is a stylistic change. στήκη (P) may represent the tendency in late Greek to use the aorist subjunctive in a futuristic sense.[1]

---

[1]B-D-F § 363.

31. H 3.18.2

H 3.18.2	Mt. 23.2-3

H 3.18.2

ἐπὶ τῆς καθέδρας Μωυσέως
⌜ἐκάθισαν⌝[1]
οἱ γραμματεῖς
καὶ οἱ φαρισαῖοι·
5 ⌜πάντα[2] ὅσα
⌜λέγουσιν[3] ὑμῖν,
ἀκούετε αὐτῶν.

Mt. 23.2-3

ἐπὶ τῆς ⌜Μωυσέως καθέδρας⌝[1]
ἐκάθισαν
οἱ γραμματεῖς
καὶ οἱ φαρισαῖοι.
[3]πάντα οὖν ὅσα ⌜ἐὰν⌝[2]
εἴπωσιν ὑμῖν
⌜ποιήσατε καὶ τηρεῖτε.⌝[3]

---

[1]ἐκάθϊσαν O[1]; ἐκάθησαν O*P.

[2]+ οὖν O.

[3]λέγωσιν P.

[1]21 D ϑ ω pc lat.

[2]Omit 1424 pc.

[3]ακουετε και ποιειτε sy[c].

No other text than Mt. 23.2-3 is required to explain H.
The different order in line 1 is also attested in some manuscripts of Matthew (D ϑ φ pc lat). The omission of οὖν (P) is a
stylistic choice of the author. The dropping of ἐάν is due to
the change of the verb from εἴπωσιν to λέγουσιν. The latter
change may have been intended to contemporize the saying while
the change to ἀκούετε αὐτῶν was perhaps intended to soften the
obligation of listening to the Rabbis. Whether these changes
were in the source or made by the author of H cannot be determined
in the absence of other evidence.

32. H 3.52.1

H 3.52.1	Mt. 15.13
πᾶσα φυτεία	πᾶσα φυτεία
ἣν οὐκ ἐφύτευσεν	ἣν οὐκ ἐφύτευσεν
ὁ πατὴρ	ὁ πατήρ ⌜μου⌝[1]
ὁ οὐράνιος,	ὁ οὐράνιος
5 ἐκριζωθήσεται.	ἐκριζωθήσεται.

[1] Omit ff[1].

H is simply Mt. 15.13 with the omission of μου. This
omission also occurs in one Latin manuscript of Matthew (ff[1]) and
evidently also in the Diatessaron.[1] It may well have already
been absent from H's source. But I fail to detect the reason for
its omission.

_____

[1] So Ephraem, Comm. 12.12 Leloir, Syr. 86: ܠܐ ܕܐ܆ ܘܚܣܐ
[However, ܐ ܒ ܐ can stand for either "the Father" or "my
Father"; cf. TDNT 1.5-6]; Leloir, Arm. 220: "le Pere qui est
aux cieux").
    Cf. G. Thom. 40: ⲡⲉϫⲉ ⲓ̄ⲥ̄ ⲟⲩⲃⲉ ⲛⲉⲗⲟⲟⲗⲉ ⲟⲩⲧⲟϭⲥ
ⲙ̄ⲡⲥⲁ ⲛⲃⲟⲗ ⲙ̄ⲡⲉⲓⲱⲧ... (Jesus said, "A vine was planted apart
from the Father etc."). Quispel 's attempt (VC 12 [1958], 188-
89) to connect the omission of μου in H with a separate tradition
represented in G. Thom. 40 seems to me a little strained.

33. H 3.52.3a

H 3.52.3a	Mt. 11.28
δεῦτε πρὸς μὲ	δεῦτε πρὸς μὲ
πάντες οἱ κοπιῶντες.	πάντες οἱ κοπιῶντες. . .

G. Thom. 90
   "Jesus said, 'Come to me because my yoke is light
   and my lordship is gentle, and you will find rest in your
   yourselves.'"
   (ⲡⲉϫⲉ ⲓⲏⲥ ϫⲉ ⲁⲙⲏⲉⲓⲧⲛ̄ ⲯⲁⲣⲟⲉⲓ ϫⲉ ⲟⲩⲭⲣⲏⲥⲧⲟⲥ ⲡⲉ
      ⲡⲁⲛⲁⲣⲃ·
   ⲁⲩⲱ ⲧⲁⲙⲛ̄ⲧⲭⲟⲉⲓⲥ ⲟⲩⲣⲙ̄ⲣⲁⲯ ⲧⲉ ⲁⲩⲱ ⲧⲉⲧⲛⲁϧⲉ ⲁⲩⲁⲛⲁⲩⲡⲁⲥⲓⲥ
      ⲛⲏⲧⲛ̄.)

H agrees exactly with the wording of Mt. 11.28a. The
Gospel of Thomas, on the other hand, lacks an equivalent to
πάντες οἱ κοπιῶντες.

112

34. H 3.55.4

H 3.55.4

Mt. 6.6

σὺ δὲ ὅταν προσεύχῃ
εἴσελθε εἰς τὸ ταμιεῖόν σου
καὶ κλείσας τὴν θύραν σου

(1. 7)

πρόσευξαι

5

τῷ πατρί σου

ἐν τῷ κρυπτῷ

⌈τῷ⌉[1] ἐν τῷ κρυπτῷ·

εὔχεσθε (εἰπών)·

καὶ ὁ πατὴρ

καὶ ὁ πατὴρ

ὑμῶν

σου

10 ὁ βλέπων

ὁ βλέπων

τὰ κρυπτὰ

ἐν τῷ κρυπτῷ

ἀποδώσει

ἀποδώσει

ὑμῖν.

σοι.

---

[1]Omit D al latt sy^{s,c} bo^{pt}.

H 14.1.2
ἐν κρυφαίῳ τόπῳ πορευθέντες εὐχόμεθα.

R 8.1.1
ad locum quendam secretiorem secessimus orationis gratia.

H 3.55.4 is based on Mt. 6.6 with some of its own changes.
They are:
1. εὔχεσθαι for προσεύχεσθαι. H reveals a preference for
εὔχεσθαι (e.g., 3.19.3; 3.29.4; 8.24.2; 9.23.3; 11.20.3-5; 12.
32.1) and εὐχή (3.23.3; 11.20.5) although προσεύχεσθαι is
occasionally used (10.26.1).
2. Second person plural for the singular. In general in
the Sermon on the Mount Matthew seems to use the plural for the
obviously community instructions and the singular for the specific example in which one person and his acts are in focus. H
appears to have made this saying in a community instruction if
we judge by this criterion. As a result ἐν τῷ κρυπτῷ in H perhaps refers to the community's meeting "in secret" in place of
the individual's going εἰς τὸ ταμιεῖον αὐτοῦ as in Matthew.
3. τὰ κρυπτά for ἐν τῷ κρυπτῷ (1. 11). This is a tenden-
tious or dogmatic change which fits well with the concern in H
(= KP) with the "secret things." The books of the sect are not

to be revealed to outsiders (see the Ep. Pet.). True γνῶσις is
the knowledge of τὸ μυστήριον τῶν γραφῶν (2.40.4) or τῶν βιβλῶν
(3.4.1), i.e., ability to distinguish the true from the false
pericopes as the True Prophet had taught them. They are those
who εἰδότες τὰ μυστήριον (3.28.2; 9.14.3). For Jesus had explained τὸ μυστήρια privately to his disciples (19.20.1-3). In
fact ἡ κλεὶς τῆς βασιλείας τῶν οὐρανῶν is ἡ γνῶσις τῶν ἀπορρήτων
(18.15.7). Thus τὰ κρυπτά are the "mysteries" or "secrets" of
God which he has revealed to his elect (cf. 18.6-16).

114

35. H 8.4.2

H 8.4.2	Mt. 22.14*
πολλοὶ (φησίν)	πολλοὶ γάρ
	εἰσιν
κλητοί,	κλητοί,
ὀλίγοι δὲ	ὀλίγοι δὲ
5 ἐκλεκτοί.	ἐκλεκτοί.

---

*Cf. Mt. 20.16 C D Koine W ϑ
λ φ latt sy bo[pt].

    Although the saying is known also in Judaism of the period,[1]
H is simply Matthew's text with two omissions: (1) γάρ which was
not required with the saying when it is removed from a context
where connected with other sayings as in Matthew, and (2) εἰσιν
which makes the first phrase more exactly parallel with the
second phrase.

---

   [1] 4 Ezra 8.3: "Many have been created, but few shall be
saved."

36. H 19.2.4a

H 19.2.4a	Mt. 13.39
ὁ δὲ	ὁ δὲ ἐχϑρος
τὸ κακὸν σπέρμα	(1. 4)
σπείρας	ὁ σπείρας
	αὐτά
5 ἐστὶν	ἐστιν
ὁ διάβολος.	ὁ διάβολος.

Only Matthew has the Parable of the Tares in which the saying is found. H has supplied τὸ κακὸν σπέρμα from the previous verse in Matthew which was necessary to define the αὐτά of Mt. 13.39 when the saying was removed from its context. Otherwise H has dropped the ἐχϑρός.

37. H 19.2.5a

H 19.2.5a	Mt. 6.13*	Did. 8.2
ῥῦσαι ἡμᾶς ἀπὸ τοῦ πονηροῦ.	ἀλλὰ ῥῦσαι ἡμᾶς ἀπὸ τοῦ πονηροῦ.	ἀλλὰ ῥῦσαι ἡμᾶς ἀπὸ τοῦ πονηροῦ.

*Cf. Lk. 11.4 ℵ¹ A C
D Koine W ϑ λ p͟m it
sy^c,P bo^pt.

Matthew, a text of Luke, or even liturgical tradition could all account for the saying in H. The fact that H 19.2 contains other sayings from Matthew and Luke, a conflated Matthean passage, and an agrapha points to the Saying's source as H's source for all these sayings in H 19.2. The dropping of ἀλλά is to be expected when the saying was removed from its context within the Lord's Prayer.

B. MARK

38. H 2.51.2, 3.50.1, 18.20.3

H 2.51.2 = 3.50.1 = 18.20.3	Mt. 22.29	Mk. 12.24
		οὐ
διὰ τοῦτο		διὰ τοῦτο
πλανᾶσθε,	πλανᾶσθε	πλανᾶσθε
μὴ εἰδότες	μὴ εἰδότες	μὴ ⌐εἰδότες⌐[1]
5 τὰ ἀληθῆ		
τῶν γραφῶν·	τὰς γραφὰς	τὰς γραφὰς
οὗ εἵνεκεν		
ἀγνοεῖτε		
καὶ	μηδὲ	μηδὲ
10 τὴν δύναμιν	τὴν δύναμιν	τὴν δύναμιν
τοῦ θεοῦ.	τοῦ θεοῦ.	τοῦ θεοῦ.

[1] γινωσκοντες D it.

This saying occurs three times in H (2.51.2; 3.50.1; 18.20. 3), always in identical wording and always connected with the saying γίνεσθε τραπεζῖται δόκιμοι (see Saying No. 55 below) in the context of true versus false pericopes in the OT. The saying seems to offer the clearest evidence for the use of the Gospel of Mark in H since διὰ τοῦτο is found in the saying in Mk. 12.24 but not in Mt. 22.29.[1] However διὰ τοῦτο, it must be admitted, is not very good evidence for the use of Mark in the absence of other evidence.

The changes from τὰς γραφάς to τὰ ἀληθῆ τῶν γραφῶν and the addition of οὗ εἵνεκεν ἀγνοεῖτε καί in H are clearly dogmatic changes to adapt the saying to the theory of "true and false pericopes" in scripture found in the Pseudo-Clementines.[2] Both Waitz and Strecker attribute the saying and the theory of the false pericopes to the source KP.[3]

---

[1] So also Strecker, Judenchristentum, p. 121.

[2] Cf. ibid., pp. 162-87.

[3] Cf. Waitz, Pseudoklementinen, p. 281; Strecker, Judenchristentum, p. 167.

39. H 3.57.1c, 16.7.8, R 2.44.2b

H 3.57.1c	H 16.7.8	R 2.44.2b	Dt. 6.4	Mk. 12.29
ἄκουε,	˙ακουε,	audi,	ἄκουε,	ἄκουε,
Ἰσραήλ,	Ἰσραήλ,	Israhel,	Ἰσραήλ,	Ἰσραήλ,
κύριος	κύριος	dominus	κύριος	κύριος
ὁ θεὸς	ὁ θεὸς	deus	ὁ θεὸς	ὁ θεὸς
5 ⌐ὑμῶν¹	⌐ὑμῶν¹	tuus	⌐ἡμῶν¹	⌐ἡμῶν¹
κύριος	κύριος	⌐deus¹	κύριος	κύριος
εἷς ἐστιν.	⌐εἷς²ἐστιν.	unus est.	εἷς ἐστιν.	εἷς ἐστιν.

¹σου O.	¹ἡμῶν P*.	¹dominus Σ	¹υμων l m	¹υμων i; σου
	²Omit P*.	ϑˣ φᵗ (vg).	q*; σου c	aur c (vg).
			bo eth lat	
			pal.	

In H 3.57.1 the words are cited as a saying of Jesus (ἔφη) and in H 16.7.8 as an OT scripture within a series of OT citations. It is impossible to decide if H 3.57.1 is quoting Mk. 12.29 or Dt. 6.4 LXX since their wording is identical.[1] If the former, it would be another example of the use of Mark in H; if the latter, it would be another case of OT scriptures cited as sayings of Jesus (see the chapter on "Sayings Based on the OT").

Neither does H's use of ὑμῶν offer much help since a few witnesses of Mark and a few minuscules of Deuteronomy LXX read ὑμῶν.[2] ὑμῶν might also be H's own change.

R's use of tuus and of deus in place of κύριος in the second instance may be due to the influence of the Vulgate.[3]

---

[1]Both Waitz (Pseudoklementinen, p. 306) and Strecker (Judenchristentum, p. 119) consider both without choosing one against the other.

[2]For ὑμῶν in Mark Tischendorf (Novum Testamentum Graece, 8th ed. [1869], p. 352) gives as witnesses: five minuscules (al⁵) which are not listed, c [but according to Jülicher, Itala II (1940), p. 115, it should be i], vgᵉᵈ, cop, aeth. For Dt. 6.4 ὑμῶν is read by l m q*.

[3]Some Vulgate manuscripts of Dt. 6.4 read deus while some of Mk. 12.29 read tuus.

C. LUKE

40. H 8.7.4, R 4.5.4

H 8.7.4	R 4.5.4	Lk. 6.46
τί με	quid autem	τί ⌐δέ¹ με
λέγεις·	dicitis mihi:	⌐καλεῖτε·²
κύριε, κύριε,	domine, domine,	κύριε, κύριε,
καὶ οὐ ποιεῖς	et non facitis	καὶ οὐ ποιεῖτε
5 ἃ λέγω;	quae dico?	ἃ λέγω;

[1] Omit $p^{75(vid)}$ D 543 pc sy^p.

[2] λεγετε D d.

Irenaeus, AH 4.60.1 = 5.8.2 (Harvey 2.287, 341)
    Quid mihi dicitis, Domine, Domine,
    et non facitis quae dico (vobis)?

Clement, Strom. 4.7/43.3 = 7.18/110.1 = Quis div. sal. 29.6
(Stählin 2.267; 3.78, 179)
    τί με λέγετε· κύριε κύριε
    καὶ οὐ ποιεῖτε ἃ λέγω;

The source is Lk. 6.46 but in a form known to some of the
fathers, i.e., with λέγετε instead of καλεῖτε. The use of the
singular (λέγεις - ποιεῖς) however is unique to H. It may be an
adaptation to the introductory phrase in H: τούτου γὰρ ἕνεκεν
ὁ Ἰησοῦς ἡμῶν πρός τινα πυκνότερον κύριον αὐτὸν λέγοντα, μηδὲν
δὲ ποιοῦντα ὧν αὐτὸς προσέτασσεν ἔφη. But the introduction may
be on the other hand an ad hoc one for the saying with the singular form. Or even a combination of these two explanations is
possible: the author changed the plural to the singular and
added the introduction to give it a quasi-historical vividness.[1]

    R, on the other hand, reverts to the plural of the canonical
text although his introduction seems to betray the singular form:
"sed salus in eo est ut voluntatem eius, cuius amorem et diser-
derium deo largiente conceperis, facias, ne dicatur ad te ille
sermo eius quem dixit."

----

[1] Contrast H 3.55.4 where H changed Matthew's (6.6) singular
to the plural (see Saying No. 34).

41. H 11.20.4, R 6.5.5

H 11.20.4	R 6.5.5	Lk. 23.34	Ac. 7.60
πάτερ,		⸀πάτερ,	κύριε,
ἄφες		ἄφες	μὴ στήσῃς
αὐτοῖς		αὐτοῖς,	αὐτοῖς
τὰς ἁμαρτίας			ταύτην
αὐτῶν,			τὴν ἁμαρτίαν.
οὐ γὰρ		οὐ γὰρ	
οἴδασιν		οἴδασιν	
ἃ		τί	
ποιοῦσιν.		ποιοῦσιν.[1]	

[1] See the discussion which follows for the listing of witnesses.

Syr. of H 11.20.4
"My Father, forgive them this sin; for they know not what they do."
(ܐܒܝ ܫܒܘܩ ܠܗܘܢ ܣܟܠܘܬܐ ܗܕܐ ܠܐ ܓܝܪ ܝܕܥܝܢ ܡܢܐ ܥܒܕܝܢ.)

Hegesippus in Eusebius, HE 2.23.16
παρακαλῶ, κύριε θεὲ πάτερ, ἄφες αὐτοῖς·
οὐ γὰρ οἴδασιν τί ποιοῦσιν.

Irenaeus, AH 3.19.5 (Harvey 2.99)
Pater dimitte (or remitte) eis,
non enim sciunt quid faciunt.

Origen, Hom. in Lev. 2.1 (Baehrens 290)
Quod et Dominus confirmat in evangeliis, cum dicit:
"Pater, remitte illis; non enim sciunt, quid faciunt."

Didascalia 6/2.16.1 (Lagarde 20,4-6; cf. Connolly 52 & note)
"As it is written in the Gospel,
'My brothers (or, My Father),
they know not what they do, neither what they speak;
but if possible, forgive them.'"
(ܐܝܟ ܕܟܬܝܒ ܒܐܘܢܓܠܝܘܢ. ܐܚܝ. ܠܐ ܝܕܥܝܢ ܠܐ ܡܢܐ ܕܥܒܕܝܢ
ܐܦܠܐ ܡܢܐ ܕܡܡܠܠܝܢ. ܐܠܐ ܐܢ ܡܡܟܢܐ ܫܒܘܩ ܠܗܘܢ.)

Didascalia 25/6.14.4 (Lagarde 105,27-29; cf. Connolly 212)
"And again our Lord said concerning them, 'My Father,
they know not what they have done nor what they speak;
if possible, forgive them.'"
(ܘܬܘܒ ܥܠܝܗܘܢ ܐܡܪ ܡܪܢ. ܐܒܝ ܠܐ ܝܕܥܝܢ ܠܐ ܡܢܐ ܕܥܒܕܘ.
ܘܠܐ ܡܢܐ ܕܡܡܠܠܝܢ. ܐܢ ܡܡܟܢܐ ܫܒܘܩ ܠܗܘܢ.)

Ap. Const. 2.16.1 (Funk 61)
(ὡς γέγραπται ἐν τῷ Εὐαγγελίῳ· [2.16.1])
"Πάτερ, ἄφες αὐτοῖς,
οὐ γὰρ οἴδασιν, ὃ ποιοῦσιν."

Ephraem, De octo cog. (Opera omnia IIgr. 321D)
καὶ ἔλεγε (Jesus),
"Πάτερ, ἄφες αὐτοῖς τὴν ἁμαρτίαν ταύτην,
οὐ γὰρ οἴδασι τι ποιοῦσιν."

Ephraem, In transfig. Dom. (Opera omnia IIgr. 48C)
Πάτερ συγχώρησον αὐτοῖς.

In considering the question, Where did this saying come
from?, one naturally turns his attention to Lk. 23.34a. But
already there is a serious textual problem. The saying is not
found in P^{75} $\aleph^a$ B D* W ϑ 0124 1241 it^{a,d} sy^s sa bo^{pt}; it is
found in $\aleph$ *,c A C D^b Koine L Γ Δ λ ω it$^{aur,b,c,e,f,ff^2,l,r^1}$
vg sy^{c,p} bo^{pt}. It is also found in Tatian's Diatessaron,[1] Hegesippus,[2] Irenaeus, Origen, (the Didascalia), the Apostolic
Constitutions, Ephraem, and other later fathers.[3] The major

---

[1] a, e (arm/syr), f, n, p, t. However there are two different forms of the saying involved which will be discussed below
in the text.

[2] But as the dying cry of James the Just!

[3] However, it should be noted that some of the fathers
offered as witnesses for the saying in The Greek New Testament,
ed. Kurt Aland et al. (American Bible Society, etc., 1966), p.
311, do not attest the saying: namely, Marcion, Justin, and
Clement (of Alexandria). Presumably Marcion has been adduced on
the weight of Harnack's note (Marcion, 236*) in which he thought
that the saying stood in Marcion's "Gospel" on the basis of its
occurrence in Ephraem, Comm. 21.3 (Moesinger 256; Leloir, Arm.,
375-76). It is true that the opponents against whom Ephraem is
polemicizing in the context are Marcionites but one can hardly
presume from that that Ephraem was using the Marcionite Bible for
his quotation of the saying. The Diatessaron is the more likely
text. Otherwise the saying is not found in those fathers who
cite the Marcionite Bible at that location. In fact Tertullian,
AM 4.42 (CSEL 47. 562) indicates its absence from Marcion:
"vestitum plane eius a militibus divisum partim, partim sorti
concessum Marcion abstulit . . ." Also Epiphanius, Pan. 42.11.15
(Holl 2.152) cites the Marcionite text at Lk. 23.33-34 as follows:
καὶ ἐλθόντες εἰς τόπον λεγόμενον Κρανίου τόπος ἐσταύρωσαν αὐτὸν
καὶ διεμερίσαντο τὰ ἱμάτια αὐτοῦ καὶ ἐσκοτίσθη ὁ ἥλιος. Although
Epiphanius disagrees with Tertullian, neither knows of the forgiveness saying in Marcion. Perhaps Marcion's omission of the
passage was influential on some of the later manuscript tradition.
    In the case of Justin he does cite Lk. 23.34b or parallels
(Apol. 35.8, Dial 97.3) but never Lk. 23.34a.
    With reference to Clement of Alexandria one does find the

arguments adduced against the originality of the saying in Luke are:[4]

1. That the absence of a whole saying from Codex Vaticanus and Codex Beza must indicate a later interpolation.

2. That the saying "breaks into" the Marcan narrative (cf. Mk. 15.24).

3. That there is no good explanation for the omission of the saying if considered original.

But none of these arguments is really convincing.

1. We must get away from mechanical textual decisions, from a sort of tyranny of textual rules that says when B and D agree in omitting something, it must not be original.[5] For it well could be. In this case there are also some very strong counter witnesses.

2. Luke frequently "breaks into" the Marcan connection when it serves his purposes to do so. (Cf. the story of a trial before Herod in Lk. 23.6-12 and Pilate's declaration of Jesus' innocence in vv. 13-16, all coming between Mk. 15.5 and 6.) Further why should it be assumed that Luke could not "break in" at this point with such a saying but a later interpolator could?

3. On the contrary there is a very good reason why the saying may have been omitted and was not quoted by some of the early fathers. That reason is an anti-Jewish bias! For the

---

words οὐκ εἰδότες ἃ ποιοῦσιν (Strom. 1.9/45.6 [Stählin 2.30]) but they are in another context and have nothing to do with our saying.

[4]Cf. Adolf von Harnack, Studien, I.91-98. Here Harnack gives his classic defense of the originality of the passage as Lucan. (The original article appeared in the Sitzungsberichte der Preussischen Akademie in 1901.) But he later attributed the saying to Marcion. (Cf. reference in n. 3.) But, as noted, that is very unlikely.

[5]Cf. the remarks of B. H. Streeter on both Lk. 22.43-44 and 23.34a in The Four Gospels, pp. 137-39.

[6]Whether or not the saying in Luke, if original, was intended to refer to the Roman soldiers or to the Jews, it is clear that it was often understood in later Christian writers as referring to the Jews. Cf., e.g., Ps.-Justin, Quaestiones et Responsiones ad Orthodoxos, Q. 108 (Otto, CAC, 3rd ed., 5.172-76). [This writing is attributed by Harnack (Studien, I.96-98) to Diodorus of Tarsus (d. before 394) but by others (cf. Altaner, Patrology, pp. 397-98) to Theodoret of Cyrus (d. ca. 466) or unknown (cf. Quasten, Patrology, I.206-07).] Cf. also Ephraem, De octo cog. (Opera omnia IIgr. 321D).

saying seems to stand in strong contrast to the attitude that
"the Jews killed Christ" and are under God's punishment for it.[7]

Hence we may in fact be dealing with a saying which was
found in the original Lucan text of the gospel.

Regarding its form H (in Greek) has the addition of τὰς
ἁμαρτίας αὐτῶν after ἄφες αὐτοῖς. The Syriac of H reads the
singular |ܐ ܠܚܛܝܐ 'this sin,' as does R 6.5.5 (peccatum).
This latter is more likely the earlier form in G.[8] It is also
attested in some of the Diatessaron versions: 1,[9] p,[10] and
Ephraem.[11] Quispel thinks that the reading was originally in the
Diatessaron of Tatian.[12] If so, it could be a harmonized reading
of Lk. 23.34 and Ac. 7.60; but also τὴν ἁμαρτίαν ταύτην may be a
natural enough addition (without the influence of Ac. 7.60) so as
to specify that the intent of Jesus' prayer was for forgiveness
for the sin of crucifying him. The dropping of the phrase from
the other versions of the Diatessaron would then be explained as
due to readjustment toward the canonical (Lucan) form of the
saying. Thus H 11.20.4 could attest the Diatessaron or a common
source behind each or one used by H which had an influence on

---

    Cf. Justin, Dial. 17 and 136; G. Peter; Melito of Sardis,
Hom. pascal 73-100; Tertullian, Apol. 21.3-4, 18-20 (CSEL 69.53
and 57-58), AM 3.6.2 (CSEL 47.383), AJ 8.18 (CSEL 70.285-86):
Didascalia 21/5.14.8-9 (Funk 274, 276; Connolly 184), 21/5.19.4-5
(Funk 290; Connolly 189-90 [there it is Herod who commands the
crucifixion of Jesus']); Eusebius, HE 2.5.6, etc. Cf. on Codex
Beza: E. J. Epp, HTR 55 (1962), 56.

[8]Even H introduces the saying with the singular: αὐτὸς γὰρ
ὁ διδάσκαλος προσηλωθεὶς ηὔχετο τῷ πατρὶ τοῖς αὐτὸν ἀναιροῦσιν
ἀφεθῆναι τὸ ἁμάρτημα εἰπών.

[9]Bergsma 257: "vader verghef dese mesdaet."

[10]Messina 353: "perdona il loro peccato."

[11]De octo cog. (Opera omnia IIgr. 321D): τὴν ἁμαρτίαν
ταύτην. However the phrase is not found in either the Armenian
or Syriac versions of Ephraem's Comm. (10.14; 21.3,18 have only
the last half of the saying).
    The additional phrase is also attested in the Greek version
of the later A. Pil. 10.5 (Tischendorf, Ev. Apoc., p. 307: μὴ
στήσῃς αὐτοῖς τὴν ἁμαρτίαν ταύτην, οὐ γὰρ οἴδασιν τί
ποιοῦσιν) but the Lucan form of the saying without the additional
phrase is found in the Armenian (Conybeare 103) and Coptic
(Revillout 94) versions. The saying is missing altogether in the
Syriac version (Ephraem II Rahmani 20[b]).

[12]VC 13 (1959), 100.

Tatian. Since there is so little in H to suggest a direct
relationship of H and Δ and since we now know that a common
harmonized Sayings' source was used by Justin and H, the most
logical suggestion is that this saying was in the Sayings' source
(with the phrase τὴν ἁμαρτίαν ταύτην) and that Tatian was
influenced by this reading when he composed the Diatessaron. The
secondary change in H to τὰς ἁμαρτίας αὐτῶν can be explained as
an adaptation of the saying to paranetic use[13] or simply a later
scribal change.

---

[13]Cf. the continuation of the context in H 11.20.5.

42. H 17.5.4

H 17.5.4	Lk. 18.6-8
εἰ οὖν	ἀκούσατε τί
ὁ κριτὴς	ὁ κριτὴς
τῆς ἀδικίας	τῆς ἀδικίας
ἐποίησεν οὕτως	λέγει·
5 διὰ τὸ ἑκάστοτε	
ἀξιωθῆναι,	
πόσῳ μᾶλλον	
ὁ πατὴρ	[7] ὁ δὲ θεὸς
ποιήσει	οὐ μὴ ⌐ποιήσῃ[1]
10 τὴν ἐκδίκησιν	τὴν ἐκδίκησιν
	τῶν ἐκλεκτῶν αὐτοῦ
τῶν βοώντων	τῶν βοώντων
πρὸς αὐτὸν	⌐αὐτῷ[2]
ἡμέρας καὶ νυκτός;	ἡμέρας καὶ νυκτός,
15 ἢ διὰ τὸ	καὶ
μακροθυμεῖν	μακροθυμεῖ
αὐτὸν	
ἐπ᾽ αὐτοῖς	ἐπ᾽ αὐτοῖς;
δοκεῖτε ὅτι	
20 οὐ ποιήσει;	
ναὶ λέγω ὑμῖν,	[8] λέγω ὑμῖν ὅτι
ποιήσει,	ποιήσει
	τὴν ἐκδίκησιν αὐτῶν
καὶ ἐν τάχει.	ἐν τάχει.

---

[1] ποιησει A E F L Ψ λ pm.

[2] προς αυτον A Koine W Δ Θ λ
φ pl; αυτων D.

The Parable of the Unjust Judge is known only from Luke. H's wording is clearly based on Lk. 18.6-8. Two of H's differences from Luke are also attested in some manuscripts of Lk. 18.7: (1) ποιήσει instead of ποιήσῃ (A E F L Ψ λ pm) and (2) πρὸς αὐτόν instead of αὐτῷ (A Koine W Δ Θ λ φ pl).

Otherwise H has made its own changes from the Lucan wording:

1. The connection of Lk. 18.6 to 7 has been made more obvious in H by an εἰ . . . , πόσῳ μᾶλλον . . . construction.

2. The reason for the unjust judge's action is given (διὰ τὸ ἑκάστοτε ἀξιωθῆναι), a comment considered necessary when the sayings are cited without the actual parable preceding them. Of course a knowledge of the parable is presupposed.

3. ὁ πατήρ has replaced Luke's ὁ θεός and τῶν ἐκλεκτῶν αὐτοῦ has been omitted. If the sayings are intended to represent the Marcionite viewpoint, then ὁ πατήρ would hardly replace ὁ θεός before ποιήσει τὴν ἐκδίκησιν. But if it is intended as an anti-Marcionite statement, then the omission of τῶν ἐκλεκτῶν αὐτοῦ seems strange.[1] I leave the question open.[2]

4. The ending of Lk. 18.7b has been reformulated so as to refer both to God's goodness and his justice. This better adapts it to the context in which Simon and Peter are debating this issue.

5. Apart from the minor additions of ναί and καί in H and the dropping of ὅτι, H drops the final τὴν ἐκδίκησιν αὐτῶν. This can be explained as a paralleling to the use of ἐποίησεν standing alone in lines 4 and 20.

---

[1]Marcion apparently retained the phrase: cf. Tertullian, AM 4.36 (CSEL 47.543): "sed [et] subiunxit facturum deum vindictam electorum suorum."

[2]Waitz (Pseudoklementinen, pp. 306-07) wanted to see H as a more original form of the text than Luke. But I find his reasons very weak and better taken as evidence of the opposite--H is secondary to Luke. He sees in H 17.5.4 the text of the Marcionite Gospel but does not consider the problem of ὁ πατήρ as the subject of ποιήσει τὴν ἐκδίκησιν.

43. H 19.2.3c

H 19.2.3c	Lk. 10.18

καὶ ὅτι ἑώρακεν
τὸν πονηρὸν
"ὡς ἀστραπὴν
πεσόντα
5 ἐκ τοῦ οὐρανοῦ"

ἐθεώρουν
τὸν σατανᾶν
⌐ὡς ἀστραπὴν

ἐκ τοῦ οὐρανοῦ
πεσόντα.[1]

ἐδήλωσεν.

---

[1]3-5 1 2 6 B; 1 2 6 3-5 p[75]
472.

H 11.35.5
. . . ἵνα μὴ ἡ κακία . . . ὕστερον
ὡς ἀστραπὴν ἐξ οὐρανοῦ ἐπὶ γῆς πεσοῦσα
καθ᾽ ὑμῶν ἐκπέμψῃ κήρυκα, . . .

H 19.2.3c is identical in its wording to Lk. 10.18, even in
word order if the text of Luke in p[75] is read. 11.35.5 is
probably a paraphrase of the saying as known in 19.2.3c.

44. H 3.71.3

H 3.71.3	Lk. 10.7	1 Tim. 5.18	Mt. 10.10
ἄξιός ἐστιν ὁ ἐργάτης τοῦ μισθοῦ αὐτοῦ.	ἄξιος γὰρ ὁ ἐργάτης τοῦ μισθοῦ αὐτοῦ.	ἄξιος ὁ ἐργάτης τοῦ μισθοῦ αὐτοῦ.	ἄξιος γὰρ ὁ ἐργάτης τῆς ⌜τροφῆς⌝[1] αὐτοῦ.

[1]τοῦ μισθου K
565 892 <u>al</u> it.

Since we know of H's use of Luke, it is the simplest solution to assume Luke as the source here although a use of a text of Matthew that read του μισθου (so K 565 892 <u>al</u> it) is also possible. H has simply added ἐστιν for stylistic reasons.

45. H 3.15.2c

H 3.15.2c	Lk. 19.43-44
ἐλεύσονται γὰρ	ἥξουσιν
	ἡμέραι ἐπὶ σέ
καὶ καθιοῦσιν	
ἐνταῦθα	
5	καὶ παρεμβαλοῦσιν
	οἱ ἐχθροί σου
καὶ περιχαρακώσουσιν	χάρακά σοι
	καὶ περικυκλώσουσίν σε
	καὶ συνέξουσίν σε πάντοθεν,
10 καὶ τὰ τέκνα ὑμῶν	44καὶ (+ l. 13)
ἐνταῦθα	
⌜κατασφάξουσιν.¹	
	ἐδαφιοῦσίν σε
	καὶ τὰ τέκνα σου
	ἐν σοί.

---

¹κατασφάξωσιν P.

The wording of H 3.15.2c finds its closest parallel in
Lk. 19.43-44. In common they speak of:

1. a "coming": ἐλεύσονται   ἥξουσιν ἡμέραι
   ἐπὶ σέ

2. the erection περιχαρακώσουσιν   παρεμβαλοῦσιν οἱ
   of palisades   ἐχθροί σου χάρακά
   around them: σοι καὶ περικυκλώ-
                                    σουσίν σε

3. the slaying τὰ τέκνα ὑμῶν   ἐδαφιοῦσίν σε καὶ
   of their   ἐνταῦθα   τὰ τέκνα σου ἐν σοί.
   children: κατασφάξουσιν.

At the same time except for καὶ τὰ τέκνα, none of the
wording is the same.¹ If Lk. 19.43-44 has provided the impetus
for H, one must speak of very faulty memory or a very free
rewriting.²

---

¹Cf. κατασφάξατε in Lk. 19.27.

²Waitz (Pseudoklementinen, pp. 159-60) wanted to use this
saying in H to help date the KP source (shortly after 135 C.E.)
by arguing that it described the events of the Destruction of
Jerusalem in 135 C.E. as recently witnessed events. The saying

in H is followed by the words: ὁμῶς καὶ τὰ ἑξῆς εἴρηκεν σαφεῖ
φωνῇ ἅτινα αὐτοῖς ὀφθαλμοῖς ἰδεῖν ἔχομεν. τὰ ἑξῆς Waitz
believed referred to the subsequently prophecied Destruction of
Jerusalem of which the KP author's readers were contemporaries
and could thus confirm the prophecies of the True Prophet of
that recent event by eyewitnesses. But see the objections of C.
Schmidt, Studien zu den Pseudo-Clementinen (TU 46,1; 1929), pp.
293-96.

D. JOHN

46. H 19.22.6

H 19.22.6	Jn. 9.2-3
[. . .] εν[1]	τίς ἥμαρτεν,
οὗτος ἢ	οὗτος ἢ
οἱ γονεῖς αὐτοῦ,	οἱ γονεῖς αὐτοῦ,
τυφλὸς ἐγεννήθη,	ἵνα τυφλὸς γεννηθῇ,
5 ἀπεκρίνατο·	[3]ἀπεκρίθη ʼΙησοῦς·
οὔτε οὗτός	οὔτε οὗτος
τι ἥμαρτεν	ἥμαρτεν
οὔτε οἱ γονεῖς αὐτοῦ,	οὔτε οἱ γονεῖς αὐτοῦ,
ἀλλʼ ἵνα	ἀλλʼ ἵνα
10 διʼ αὐτοῦ	(1. 14)
φανερωθῇ	φανερωθῇ
ἡ δύναμις	τὰ ἔργα
τοῦ θεοῦ.	τοῦ θεοῦ
	ἐν αὐτῷ.

---

[1]The whole sentence is:
ὅθεν καὶ [ὁ διδάσκ]αλος ἡμῶν
περὶ τοῦ ἐκ γενετῆς πηροῦ καὶ
ἀναβλέψαντος παρʼ αὐτοῦ
ἐξετα[ζόμενος, εἰ ὅτι
ἥμαρτ]εν etc. The missing
letters have been filled in
according to Rehm.

The only question is whether H is based on the Gospel of
John or presupposes John's source. Although Dodd[1] saw all of Jn.
9.3 from his source, Bultmann[2] and Fortna[3] argue that v. 3b is
from the Evangelist himself. For ἀλλʼ ἵνα is Johannine (cf. 1.8,
31; 11.52; 13.18; 14,31; 15.25; 1 Jn. 2.19) as is the theme of the
"manifesting of God's works" (cf. 3.21; 10.32; etc.). H must
therefore be post-Johannine and based on his text.

---

[1]Historical Tradition in the Fourth Gospel (1963), pp.
107-08.

[2]Das Evangelium des Johannes (1964), p. 251. (Hereafter =
Johannes.)

[3]The Gospel of Signs (1970), p. 71.

132

The changes in H from the text of John are: (1) the
addition of τι (1. 7) which simply adds emphasis to the statement of the innocence of the blind man and his parents; (2) the
change from τὰ ἔργα τοῦ θεοῦ to ἡ δύναμις τοῦ θεοῦ because ἡ
δύναμις τοῦ θεοῦ is a more relevant category for H;[4] and (3) the
change from ἐν αὐτῷ to δι᾿ αὐτοῦ which better fits with ἡ
δύναμις.

---

[4]Cf. of Simon Magus: θέλει νομίζεσθαι τις ἀνωτάτη δύναμις
καὶ αὐτοῦ τοῦ τὸν κόσμον κτίσαντος θεοῦ (2.22.3). Cf. Peter's
refutation of Simon's "theology" in 18.12.1. Cf. also 2.51.2 =
3.50.1 = 18.20.3.

47. H 3.52.3b

H 3.52.3b	Jn. 10.27
τὰ ἐμὰ πρόβατα	τὰ πρόβατα τὰ ἐμὰ
⌐ἀκούει¹	(1. 4)
τῆς ἐμῆς φωνῆς.	τῆς φωνῆς μου
	⌐ἀκούουσιν.¹

---

¹ἀκούουσι O.   ¹ακουει P⁷⁵ A D Koine Δ Ψ
λ p̲m̲.

Lacking any good reason to suspect that H goes back to
John's source rather than the Gospel of John itself, this must
stand as another example of the use of John in H. The reading
of ἀκούει may have been that of the text of John used (as in P⁷⁵
A D Koine Δ Ψ λ p̲m̲). The change of order in the pronouns and of
μου to ἐμῆς is easily explained by H's preference for precise
parallelism. The changed order of ἀκούει is a minor stylistic
change or represents the text of John read by H.

48. H 11.26.2, R 6.9.2

	H 11.26.2 s	R 6.9.2	Ju, A. 61.4	Jn. 3.5	Mt. 18.3
	ἀμὴν	Amen		ἀμὴν ἀμὴν	ἀμὴν
	Γὑμῖν λέγω,[1]	dico vobis,		λέγω σοι,	λέγω ὑμῖν,
	ἐὰν μὴ	nisi	ἂν μὴ	ἐὰν μὴ	ἐαν μη
		quis denuo			
5	ἀναγεννηθῆτε	renatus fuerit,	ἀναγεννηθῆτε	τις Γγεννηθῇ[1]	στραφῆτε
	Γὕδατι	ex aqua		ἐξ ὕδατος	καὶ γένησθε
	ζῶντι,[2]	viva,		καὶ πνεύματος,	ὡς τα παιδία,
	Γεἰς ὄνομα				
	πατρός,				
10	υἱοῦ,				
	ἁγίου πνεύματος,[3]				
	οὐ μὴ	non	οὐ μὴ	οὐ δύναται	οὐ μη
	εἰσέλθητε	introibit	εἰσέλθητε	Γεἰσελθεῖν[2]	εἰσέλθητε
	εἰς τὴν βασιλείαν,	in regna	εἰς τὴν βασιλείαν,	εἰς τὴν βασιλείαν,	εἰς την βασιλειαν
15	τῶν οὐρανῶν.	caelorum.	τῶν οὐρανῶν.	Γτοῦ θεοῦ.[3]	τῶν οὐρανῶν.

Jn. 3.5 notes:

[1] ἀναγεννηθη lat (renatus).
[2] ιδειν ℵ* M (cf. v. 3).
[3] των ουρανων ℵ* e m.

H 11.26.2 notes:

[1] 21 E.
[2] PO; δι' ὕδατος καὶ πνεύματος E; ⲗ Sy.
[3] Omit e; + articles E.

Irenaeus, Frag. 33 (Harvey 2.498)
καθὼς καὶ ὁ Κύριος ἔφη·
ἐὰν μή τις ἀναγεννηθῇ δι᾽ ὕδατος καὶ πνεύματος,
οὐ μὴ εἰσελεύσεται εἰς τὴν βασιλείαν τῶν οὐρανῶν.

Tertullian, De bap. 13 (CSEL 20.213)
Nisi quis renatus fuerit ex aqua et spiritu,
non intrabit in regnum coelorum.

Docetists in Hippolytus, Phil. 8.10.8 (Wendland 3.230)
τοῦτό ἐστι, φησίν [the Docetist], ὃ λέγει ὁ σωτήρ·
ἐὰν μή τις γεννηθῇ ἐξ ὕδατος καὶ πνεύματος,
οὐκ εἰσελεύσεται εἰς τὴν βασιλείαν τῶν οὐρανῶν·
ὅτι τὸ γεγεννημένον ἐκ τῆς σαρκὸς σάρξ ἐστιν.

Apostolic Constitutions 6.15 (Funk 337, 339)
λέγει γὰρ ὁ κύριος·
Ἐὰν μή τις βαπτισθῇ ἐξ ὕδατος καὶ πνεύματος,
οὐ μὴ εἰσελθῇ εἰς τὴν βασιλείαν τῶν οὐρανῶν.

Cf. H 7.8.1; 9.19.4; R 3.67.4.

This saying is included within this chapter only because it
will be recognized most readily by most for its resemblance to
Jn. 3.5. But even a quick look at the saying in H indicates that
its wording stands closer to Justin than to the Gospel of John.
Likewise the context for the saying is similar in H and Justin:
in H it is within a context of defending the necessity of Christian baptism and in Justin of describing Christian baptism and
its purpose while the Gospel of John has (twice--vv. 3 and 5)
used the saying to introduce the "Revelation Discourse" of John
3:6ff.[1] But even so, it is a "baptismal saying" that has been
taken up by the Gospel of John.[2] In addition the form of the
Justinian saying is not dependent on the Gospel of John but
represents an independent and even older form of the saying than

---

[1]R. Bultmann, Johannes, pp. 92-93, 95, n. 1, and passim.
Cf. also the reconstruction of the "Revelation Discourse" of John
3 in H. Becker, Die Reden des Johannesevangeliums und der Stil
der gnostischen Offenbarungsrede (1956), pp. 94-96, 129.

[2]Cf. Köster, "History and Cult," JThCh 1 (1965), 118-19; cf.
also Bultmann, Johannes, p. 98, n. 2. However Bultmann suggests
that ὕδατος καί of John 3.5 should be seen as the addition of the
"ecclesiastical redactor" in introducing an explicit reference
to baptism while the author of the Gospel of John is concerned
about τὸ πνεῦμα. I think on the contrary that the argument
indicates that the saying itself read ὕδατος and that the
Evangelist added καὶ πνεύματος so as to adopt it to his discourse
material about τὸ πνεῦμα.

that in the Gospel of John.[3] When one adds to this that the
language of "rebirth" is common enough in early Christian
literature in reference to baptism,[4] it becomes fairly certain
that this saying had its Sitz im Leben in the baptismal liturgy
of the early church.[5]

From the simplest form of the saying--that found in Justin
--there developed in the formula elaborations of the act of
baptism itself, presumably in accordance with local praxis, e.g.,
ὕδατι ζῶντι 'in running water,'[6] and the use of the trinitarian
formula.[7] The other major factor in the history of this saying
was the influence of the Johannine form which accounts for the
addition of ἐξ/δι' ὕδατος καὶ πνεύματος/ex aqua et spiritu in
the Irenaeus fragment, Tertullian, the Docetists in Hippolytus,
and the Apostolic Constitutions; the use of the third person
instead of the second person in the same authors and in R 6.9.2;
and the addition of denuo in R 6.9.2 (= Jn. 3.3; cf. ἄνωθεν in
Macarius). At the same time all these sources retain the wording
of not (οὐ μή/οὐκ/non) entering the kingdom τῶν οὐρανῶν/caelorum

---

[3]Bellinzoni, Sayings, pp. 134-38.

[4]Cf. Tit. 3.5; 1 Pet. 1.3,23; Justin, Apol. 61.3; 66.4;
Dial. 138.2; A. Thom. 132 (Lipsius 239). On the background of
this terminology, see the references in Bultmann, Johannes, p.
982, and J. Ysebaert, Greek Baptismal Terminology (1962).

[5]So Bellinzoni, Sayings, pp. 136-38.
The striking similarity of the wording of Mt. 18.3 may be
due to the fact that the baptismal saying and Mt. 18.3 are both
rooted in a form which Windisch has called "laws (toroth) of
entry or admission." Cf. his article, "Die Sprüche vom Eingehen
in das Reich Gottes," ZNW 27 (1928), 163-92.

[6]Even though the Syriac text of H 11.26.2 reads ܡ ܟ
'of water,' the reference to ܬܐܠ ܘ܂ܣ 'life-giving water' in
11.26.4 and the double witness of H and R confirm the reading
of "running water." Presumably this condition was not accept-
able to the Syriac translator. But it is a praxis known also
to Did. 7.1 and P. Ox. 840, R 43 (Grenfell-Hunt 5.6).

[7]The formula stands in the baptismal contexts of both Did.
7 and Justin, Apol. 61, even though not part of the saying itself
in Justin. (On Mt. 28.19 see Köster, Syn. Überlieferung, pp.
190-92.) In H there is a further question of whether the trinitarian formula belongs to the saying in its early form or was a
later addition. Strecker (Judenchristentum, pp. 128 and 194,
n. 1) sees it as the addition of the Homilist. The absence of
the formula from R 6.9.2 argues for this since the Recognitionist
is certainly not opposed to the formula (cf. R 1.63.3; 1.69.5;
3.67.4; 7.29.).

against the Johannine wording of not being able (οὐ δύναται) to enter (or see) the kingdom τοῦ θεοῦ .[8]   In short we have a good example of dual influence on the citation of this saying of Jesus: (1) that of the form known from the baptismal liturgy of the church, and (2) that of the form known from a "canonical gospel."

The form of the saying in H can therefore be accounted for in terms of the baptismal liturgy of the church without any reference to the Gospel of John.   The only question is the intro-ductory formula ἀμὴν ὑμῖν λέγω.   But even here one can hardly prove the influence of the Johannine text.   It is just as likely that the Johannine text presupposes this formulation itself and has characteristically doubled the ἀμήν as well as changed the ὑμῖν to σοι to fit into the context of the discussion with Nico-demus.   Perhaps also the formulations in the baptismal liturgies themselves varied.[9]

In the case of R we clearly see the secondary influence of the Johannine text in the wording nisi quis denuo renatus fuerit. But otherwise it also attests the older form of Justin and H.

Conclusion

The main problem in dealing with the sayings in this chapter is that most of them lack other witnesses to H's readings.   This makes it very difficult to assess whether they belong to the harmonized source or not.   A priori those which cite Matthew or Luke and come from the sections in which harmonized sayings are found could easily belong to the source.   But an obvious uncer-tainty must remain in individual cases.

Another way of considering the problem is to ask if a given saying in H fails to show harmonistic characteristics when it could, i.e., when there are parallel texts to the one cited in one of the other synoptic gospels.   For a saying which has synoptic parallels and did not show harmonistic characteristics in H would seem to indicate that it did not belong to the harmonized source.   But this really does not help us very much

---

[8]However a few witnesses of Jn. 3.5 read των ουρανων: א* e m.

[9]It may even be argued that the Gospel of John has known the saying in a form closer to H than to Justin, i.e., with the introductory ἀμὴν λέγω ὑμῖν and with (ἐξ) ὕδατος ζῶντος.   The latter word would permit the shift to καὶ πνεύματος in John.

138

in the sayings in this chapter. For first, there are those
sayings which are found only in one gospel: nos. 19, 20, 31-36
are found only in Matthew, no. 39 only in Mark, nos. 40-43 (cf.
45) only in Luke, and nos. 46 and 47 (cf. 48) only in John.
Second, there are those sayings which have the same wording in
different gospels: no. 23 (the second saying H 3.15.26) has the
same wording in Matthew, Mark, and Luke; no. 24 has the same
wording in some manuscripts of Matthew as in Mark; no. 25 has
the same wording in Matthew and in Luke; and no. 38 has the same
reading in Matthew and some texts of Luke. Third, there are
those sayings which might well show harmonistic traits but were
not included in the previous chapter only because the presence
of harmonistic features was not clear enough, i.e., their reading
in H could be explained from one gospel. These included nos.
26 and 28. Fourth, the remaining sayings (nos. 21, 22, 23a, 27,
29, 30, and 44) had parallel texts in another synoptic gospel
than that followed by H. But this often means only that the
wording of the saying which has parallels in two (or three)
synoptic gospels was very close and that where they differed one
would obviously have to choose the wording of one instead of the
other. Thus, for example, in no. 21 the wording of Mt. 11.25
and Lk. 10.21 is identical except that Matthew read ἔκρυψας and
Luke ἀπέκυψας. The fact that H has ἔκρυψας can hardly mean that
H must have used Matthew directly and could not have used a
harmony. A harmony would have had to choose one or the other.
While the other cases are not quite as simple as this one, they
nevertheless have the possibility of this same explanation.

Turning to a survey of the sayings, the <u>Matthean</u> texts
occupy most of this group. No. 19 and probably no. 20 indicate
that H has taken them not from Matthew itself but from the source
shared with Justin.[1] No. 22 indicates a common source with
Clement. Otherwise the Matthean sayings lack other witnesses
to H's peculiar variations.[2] This prevents our relating them to
the harmonized source except on the problematic grounds of source

---

[1] Only here and in no. 48 are there parallels in Justin to
the sayings in this chapter.

[2] No. 25 with a possible parallel in Aphraates is uncertain
and slight evidence; no. 37 with the prayer formula found also in
Didache does not help since only Matthew, which has been cited
in the previous verse in H (19.2.4a = no. 36), need be presupposed.

analysis of H.[3] Most of them could fit into the source but it is
difficult to tell in any individual case.

It should also be noted that there is some uncertainty in
the classification of some of these sayings. No. 19 reflects
either the influence of Jm. 5.12 or his tradition, nos. 23 and
24 the possibility of Marcan influence (but questionable), no. 25
could as well be Lk. 11.9 as Mt. 7.7 since the wording of Mt.
7.7 and Lk. 11.9 is the same, and nos. 26-28 have the possibility
of Lucan influence (also uncertain).

The Marcan influence remains doubtful. It seems clearest
in no. 38 but even there the evidence is not very strong. No. 39
has a parallel only in Mark of the synoptic gospels but could be
from Dt. 6.4. Bellinzoni argues for Marcan influence in Justin
but adds that Justin never cites a text found only in Mark.[4] Of
course there are not many such texts. But whether or not
Bellinzoni has succeeded in making a good case for Marcan influence in Justin, the presence of Marcan influence in H is
slight and questionable.

The Lucan texts present the same problem as the Matthean:
they could belong to the harmonized source but it is impossible
to tell. However some evidence is offered for nos. 40 and 41
which have witnesses in other fathers to peculiar readings in H.
No. 45, on the other hand, is loose paraphrase at best of Lk.
19.43-44. This style is closer to nos. 17 and 18. Whether it
could be based on the source or not I leave open.

The Johannine texts present a special problem. Bellinzoni
concluded (I think rightly) that there is no direct use of the
Gospel of John in Justin. But no. 46 in H must certainly be
based on Jn. 9.2-3 and no. 47 is probably based on Jn. 10.27.
However Waitz argued that both should be attributed to the
Homilist. In the case of no. 46 (H 19.22.6) there is no problem.
But no. 47 (H 3.52.3b) occurs in the same grouping (H 3.50-56)
that contains sayings from the source common to H and Justin.
Of course the Homilist (as Waitz argued) could still have been

[3]Nos. 19, 20, 24-26, 29, 32-34 come from H 3.50-56 which
includes harmonized readings; no. 27 from H 11.29.2 (cf. nos. 10
and 16 from H 11); and nos. 30, 36, 37 from H 19.2 as does no.
1--a saying with a certainly common source for H and Justin.

[4]Sayings, p. 140.

at work here. Since this is the only case of a Johannine saying (omitting no. 57 as I will argue in chapter 5) among the sayings which may belong to the harmonized source, I think it best to follow Waitz's suggestion. Otherwise one has the difficult task of explaining why, if John has been used, does he not show up more in H or in Justin. No. 48, as I argued, is not from John but from the baptismal tradition of the church as is the case in Justin's citation of the saying.[5]

Finally, it may be noted that I find no good evidence for these sayings being based on a pre-synoptic source or sources as Waitz argued in some cases. Rather they are all post-synoptic. Only no. 48 (the baptismal saying) goes back to a form behind the canonical gospels, and that because of its use in the baptismal liturgy.

---

[5]This does not mean that it was not in the harmonized source. That source included noncanonical sayings (see chapter 5) and could easily be the source of this saying for both Justin and H.

CHAPTER IV

SAYINGS BASED ON THE OLD TESTAMENT

The following chapter takes up those sayings which cite an
Old Testament text as a saying of Jesus.

49. H 3.56.4, R 1.37.2

H 3.56.4	R 1.37.2	Hos. 6,6
	(quia)	διότι
ὁ θεὸς	deus	
ἔλεος	misericordiam	ἔλεος
θέλει	vult	θέλω
5 καὶ οὐ	et non	καὶ οὐ
θυσίας,	sacrificium.	θυσίαν
ἐπίγνωσιν		⌜καὶ⌝[1] ἐπίγνωσιν
αὐτοῦ		θεοῦ
καὶ οὐχ		ἢ
10 ὁλοκαυτώματα.		ὁλοκαυτώματα.

---

[1]Omit 46[1] 87[1]-239.

Mt. 9.13 and 12.7 protray Jesus quoting Hos. 6.6a (ἔλεος
θέλω καὶ οὐ θυσίαν). But H cites all of Hos. 6.6 as a saying of
Jesus (ἔφη). Therefore this is an example of an OT scripture
being made into a saying of Jesus, perhaps with the Matthean
example having provided the impetus.

The change to the third person with the addition of ὁ θεὸς
as the named subject was necessary both for the context of H 3.
56 and because Jesus is not a divine being in H (at least in G)
to speak in God's place as "I . . ." The change of θυσίαν to
θυσίας serves two purposes: (1) it emphasizes the doctrine in H
that God is against the sacrificial cult,[1] and (2) it enhances
the parallelism with ὁλοκαυτώματα. The latter explanation also
explains the change of ἢ to καὶ οὐχ (cf. καὶ οὐ in l. 5).

R has apparently dropped the last half of the saying
(rather than the Homilist or a later scribe having added it)
because as a saying of Jesus he wanted it to conform to the
Matthean text. He further changed H's θυσίας back to the
singular.[2]

---

[1]Cf. Strecker, Judenchristentum, pp. 179-84.

[2]The Syriac of R has the plural (ܚܒ̈ܬܐ). Assuming that
the pointing of the Syriac is correct, this indicates that
Rufinus made the change back to the singular in his translation
while the Recognitionist had been the one who dropped the latter
half of the saying (as its omission in the Syriac shows).

143

50. H 8.21.5, 10.5.1, 17.7.1

H 8.21.5	H 10.5.1	Dt. 6.13 = 10.20	Mt. 4.10	Lk. 4.8
γέγραπται·			γέγραπται γάρ·	γέγραπται·
κύριον	κύριον	κύριον	κύριον	⌐κύριον
τὸν θεόν σου	τὸν θεόν	τὸν θεόν σου	τὸν θεόν σου	τὸν θεόν σου
φοβηθήσῃ	φοβηθήσῃ	⌐φοβηθήσῃ[1]	προσκυνήσεις[1]	προσκυνήσεις[1]
5 καὶ αὐτῷ	καὶ αὐτῷ	καὶ αὐτῷ[2]	καὶ αὐτῷ	καὶ αὐτῷ
λατρεύσεις	(1. 8)	λατρεύσεις.	(1. 8)	(1. 8)
μόνῳ.	μόνῳ		μόνῳ	μόνῳ
	λατρεύσεις.		λατρεύσεις.	λατρεύσεις.

Lk. 4.8: [1] 1-4 A Koine θ al r.

[1] προσκυνήσεις
 A o.
[2] + μονω A
 Fa,mg N b-gia?j
 nprstvwyz Arm.
 ed. Bo Sa Eth Lat.

R 2.44.2a
 dominum deum tuum adorabis et ipsi soli servies.

R 4.34.4
 scriptum est; dominum deum tuum adorabis et illi soli servies.

R 5.13.3
 dominum deum tuum ⌐timebis[1] et ipsi soli servies.
 [adorabis Δbc δ Πac; txt. w Δf.]

144

H 17.7.1	Ju, A. 16.6	Mt. 22.38,37
ἀφ' ὧν ἐντολῶν	(cf. 1. 4)	(cf. 1. 4)
αὕτη		αὕτη ἐστιν
πρώτη καὶ		ἡ μεγάλη
μεγάλη	μεγίστη ἐντολή	καὶ πρώτη ἐντολή.
5 τυγχάνει,	ἐστι·	(1. 2)
τὸ φοβηθῆναι	(1. 8)	[37]ἀγαπήσεις
κύριον τὸν θεὸν	⌐Κύριον τὸν θεόν σου	κύριον τὸν θεόν σου
	προσκυνήσεις	
καὶ αὐτῷ μόνῳ	καὶ αὐτῷ μόνῳ	
10 λατρεύειν.	λατρεύσεις*	
	ἐξ ὅλης	ἐν ὅλῃ
	τῆς καρδίας σου	τῇ καρδίᾳ σου
		καὶ ἐν ὅλῃ
		τῇ ψυχῇ σου
15	καὶ ἐξ ὅλης	καὶ ἐν ὅλῃ
	τῆς ἰσχύος σου,	τῇ διανοίᾳ[1] σου.
	κύριον τὸν θεὸν	
	τὸν ποιήσαντά σε.	

[1]ισχυι c sy[s,c];
ισχυι . . . διανοια
ϑ φ al (e) sy[p]
(cf. M̄k. 12.30; Lk.
10.25; Dt. 6.5).

*Lines 7-10 = Dial. 103.6; 125.4 (+ γέγραπται).

Of the citations of this text in H and R, H 8.21.5, 17.7.1
(see infra), R 4.34.4, and probably 5.13.3 are cited as sayings
of Jesus; R 2.44.2 as the OT scripture; and H 10.5.1 as that
which the Christian is to reply to the Tempter (hence the
omission of σου).

H 8.21.5 and 10.15.1 (and 17.7.1) reflect the influence of
Dt. 6.13 (or 10.20) in the use of φοβηθήσῃ while Matthew and
Luke read προσκυνήσεις. The use of μόνῳ can reflect either
Deuteronomy according to many manuscripts (see columns) or
Matthew or Luke. Thus only Deuteronomy is required to explain
the readings in H. But H 8.21.5 is cited in reference to the
Temptation story with Jesus' reply, γέγραπται etc. This again
suggests that sayings of Jesus which cite the OT passage in H
are given according to their OT (LXX) wording.

That the use of φοβηθήσῃ goes back to G is supported by the fact that, although R 2.44.2 and 4.34.4 substitute adorabis (= προσκυνήσεις) for φοβηθήσῃ to harmonize with the gospel text,[1] R 5.13.3 still preserves (in some manuscripts) timebis and that immediately following a clear saying of Jesus (Lk. 6.36 and Mt. 5.45).

H 17.7.1 deserves special attention because it combines the wording of Mt. 22.38 (αὕτη ἐστιν ἡ μεγάλη καὶ πρώτη ἐντολή) with the "Fear God" commandment; or put another way it substitutes the "Fear God" commandment for the "Love God" commandment of Mt. 22. 27 (and synoptic parallels). Justin seems to have done the same thing in Apol. 16.16: μεγίστη ἐντολή ἐστι· etc. (but with προσκυνήσεις), + Mk. 12.30 (ἐξ ὅλης τῆς καρδίας σου etc.), + the phrase κύριον τὸν θεὸν τὸν ποιήσαντά σε.[2] Elsewhere (Dial. 93.2) Justin also cites the "Love God" form. That both places in Justin reflect harmonization of the synoptic texts is well demonstrated by Bellinzoni.[2] H 17.7.1 agrees with Justin in the combination of Mt. 22.38 and the "Fear (or worship) God" commandment but differs in the use of φοβηθήσῃ against Justin's use of προσκυνήσεις. Can we assume a direct relationship of H and Justin?[3] This choices seem to be:

1. That the combination in H and Justin is coincidental.

2. That H and Justin reflect some common tradition, perhaps catechetical.

3. That H and Justin are directly related, i.e., go back to a common source.

Coincidence is a poor choice unless all other explanations fail. Against the choice of a common catechetical tradition

---

[1]This is an inconsistent change in R 2.44.2 since R purports to cite the OT and not Jesus. However I think the knowledge of the gospel text(s) is sufficient to explain R's change. Waitz (Pseudoklementinen, pp. 286-87) wanted to explain R 2.44.2 as providing that προσκυνήσεις already stood in G at this point and that it therefore went back to Justin's Syn. adv. Marc. This evidence is much too weak to prove this. Of greater interest in regard to the relationship with Justin is H 17.7.1 discussed below in the text.

[2]Cf. Bellinzoni, Sayings, pp. 37-43.

[3]Waitz (Pseudoklementinen, pp. 300-01) sees the hard of the anti-Marcionite redactor even though he admits that H 17.7 does not reflect any anti-Marcionite polemic. Strecker (Judenchristentum, p. 133) does not think of H as dependent on Justin and so speaks of "ein unkanonisches Zitat."

is the lack of its showing up elsewhere in early Christian texts in this combination. The presupposition of a common source would fit well with the other sayings common to H and Justin but faces the problem of H's φοβηθήσῃ versus Justin's προσκυνήσεις. One has two major possibilities: (1) Justin's texts (for he reads προσκυνήσεις also in <u>Dial</u>. 103.6 and 125.4) have been changed by later scribes to the synoptic wording or H originally read προσκυνήσεις but was changed by the author of G or H to φοβηθήσῃ to agree with the OT text. This latter would agree with the suggestion made in the previous saying that the sayings of Jesus which cite an OT text are then given according to their OT (LXX) wording.

51. H 3.53.3, R 1.36.2

H 3.53.3	R 1.36.2	Ac. 3.22-23	Dt. 18.15-16,19
ἐγώ εἰμι			
περὶ οὗ			
Μωυσῆς			
προεφήτευσεν			
5 εἰπών·			
"Προφήτην	Prophetam	προφήτην	προφήτην
⌐ἐγερεῖ¹	vobis	ὑμῖν	(1. 14)
ὑμῖν	suscitabit	ἀναστήσει	(1. 14)
κύριος ὁ θεὸς	dominus deus	κύριος ὁ θεὸς¹	(1. 15)
10 ἡμῶν	vester		(1. 16)
ἐκ τῶν ἀδελφῶν		ἐκ τῶν ἀδελφῶν	ἐκ τῶν ἀδελφῶν
⌐ὑμῶν²		ὑμῶν	σου
ὥσπερ καὶ ἐμέ·	sicut me,	ὡς ἐμέ·	ὡς ἐμὲ
			ἀναστήσει σοι
15			κύριος ὁ θεός
			σου,
αὐτοῦ ἀκούετε	ipsum audite	αὐτοῦ ἀκούσεσθε	αὐτοῦ ἀκούσεσθε
κατὰ πάντα.	secundum omnia	κατὰ πάντα	¹⁶κατὰ πάντα,..
	quae dixerit	ὅσα ἂν ⌐λαλήσῃ²	
20	vobis.	πρὸς ὑμᾶς.	
		²³ἔσται δὲ	
		πᾶσα ψυχὴ	
ὃς ἂν ⌐δὲ³	quicumque enim	ἥτις ἐὰν	¹⁹... ὃς ἐὰν
μὴ ἀκούσῃ	non audierit	μὴ ἀκούσῃ	μὴ ἀκούσῃ
			ὅσα ἐὰν λαλήσῃ
25 τοῦ προφήτου	prophetam	τοῦ προφήτου	ὁ προφήτης¹
ἐκείνου	illum,	ἐκείνου	
			ἐπὶ τῷ ὀνόματι
			μου,
⌐ἀποθανεῖται.⁴	exterminabitur	ἐξολεθρευθήσε-	ἐγὼ ἐκδικήσω
		ται	
	anima eius		
30	de populo suo.	ἐκ τοῦ λαοῦ.	ἐξ αὐτοῦ.

---

¹ᵖcorr; ἐγειρεῖ P;
ἐγείρῃ O.
²ἡμῶν O.
³καί O.
⁴ἀποθανῆται P.

¹+ ημων ℵ* C E
Koine pm; υμων
A D al.
²λαλησει C pc.

¹+ εκεινος B.

The saying in H has made the OT text into a saying of Jesus
while R retains it as the words of Moses. The question involved
is that of the text used. Both H and R, although with differences from each other, come closer to the wording of Ac. 3.22-23
than to Dt. 18.15-19LXX. Agreeing with Acts against Deuteronomy
are the following:

1. Word order of lines 6-16 (H and R).

2. Use of ὑμῖν/vobis (lines 7f.) versus σοι in Deut., and
ὑμῶν (1. 12) in H versus σου in Deut.[1]

3. The immediate joining of the wording of Dt. 18.16a to
18.19b (H and R).

4. Quae dixerit vobis (lines 19-20) of R = ὅσα ἂν λαλήσῃ
(or λαλήσει) πρὸς ὑμᾶς in Acts.

5. τοῦ προφήτου ἐκείνου as direct object of ἀκούσῃ (H and
R).

6. A verb of destruction or expulsion (1. 28) in H
(ἀποθανεῖται), R (exterminabitur), and Acts (ἐξολεθρευθήσεται)
versus ἐγὼ ἐκδικήσω ἐξ αὐτοῦ of Deut.[2]

Only in 1. 22 (H: ὃς ἄν; R: quicumque enim) do H and R
come closer to Deuteronomy (ὃς ἐάν) than to Acts (ἔσται δὲ πᾶσα
ψυχὴ ἥτις ἐάν).

That H and R are derived in common from G seems obvious
enough in light of their agreements. Their disagreements are of
a nature that they can be explained without rejecting their common derivation from G.[3] Hence the choice is between G's using
Acts as its source or another source (such as a "testimony
book"?)[4] which cited Dt. 18.15-19 in a form almost identical to
that in Ac. 3.22-23. I would lean toward the latter in the light
of the one agreement of H and R (1. 22) with Deuteronomy against

---

[1]One should probably add ἡμῶν (1. 10) in H, vester in R,
both of which find some textual support in Acts (ἡμων C E Koine;
υμων A D al) versus σου in Deuteronomy.

[2]However R and Acts probably borrow from Lev. 23.29 in the
final clause. But H does not appear to do so. This probably
means: (1) that R has been corrected according to Acts, and (2)
that H is not dependent on Acts but reflects a text of Dt. 18
like that known to Acts.

[3]E.g., whether H added the identification formula (lines 1-
5) or R dropped it, no other source is required. The same can
be said of R's dropping ἐκ τῶν ἀδελφῶν ὑμῶν, H's dropping (?) of
the words in lines 19-20, and H's shortening of the final threat
to a simple ἀποθανεῖται.

[4]Cf. C. H. Dodd, According to the Scriptures (1953),

Acts. A direct use of the Book of Acts is therefore unproved.[5]

---

pp. 28-60, and especially pp. 53-57.

[5]Waitz (Pseudoklementinen, p. 323) fails to note the similarity with Acts at all. Strecker (Judenchristentum, p. 122) on the other hand affirms: "Nicht Dt. 18,15ff., sondern Act 3,22f. ist frei zitiert."

Conclusion

The main conclusion of this chapter is that the sayings of Jesus which cite an OT text are given according to their OT (LXX) form.[1] This is clearly the case in no. 49. Also in no. 50. the three occurrences of that saying are cited according to the wording of Deuteronomy (with φοβηθήσῃ) instead of Matthew or Luke (with προσκυνήσεις). Once (in H 17.7.1) this probably meant changing the wording of the common source (see Justin) from προσκυνήσεις to φοβηθήσῃ. In other words the author (probably G) consistently carried out the above principle. No. 51 leads to the same conclusion if my argument is correct that H follows an OT text very similar to that found in Ac. 3.22-23 instead of citing from Acts itself.

It is also very possible that no. 39 (Dt. 6.4 = Mk. 12.29) belongs to this chapter instead of under a saying citing Mark.[2]

---

[1]A reverse situation occurs in H 18.15.4 in which Ps. 77(78). 2 is cited according to the wording found in Mt. 13.35, and is introduced by τῷ καὶ τὸν 'Ησαίαν εἰπεῖν.

[2]A complete study of the OT quotations in H would be very useful to relate its findings to the question of sources and layers in H along with those of this study. I have made my own survey of the OT quotations in H but find it to be another thesis to attempt to analyze and present them carefully. However I am convinced that Waitz's attempt to distinguish those OT quotations which find agreements with Justin's citations (therefore they would belong to the anti-Maricionite source according to Waitz) from those which do not find agreements with Justin simply does not hold up. For usually the agreements of H and Justin are simple cases of both following the LXX. Only twice did I find agreements of H and Justin against the major witnesses of the LXX. In the first H 3.49.1 and Justin (Apol. 32.2) read οὐδέ in Gen. 49.10 against the majority of witnesses which read καί (A B D F M a-c_z Eth Lat^V). But several LXX witnesses also read οὐδέ (k m Arm Bo Lat Sa). Hence H and Justin simply read the same LXX text. Elsewhere Justin also reads καί (Dial. 52.2; 120.8; Apol. 54.11). In the second case H 16.6.9, 16.7.3, and Justin (Dial. 55.1) read σου in Dt. 10.17 instead of the LXX's ὑμῶν. But Justin (Dial. 16.1) also reads ὑμῶν. Although no other witnesses could be found to the reading σου, the evidence is much too slight to assume a common source for the OT quotations in H and Justin.

CHAPTER V

AGRAPHA

The following chapter is a discussion of those sayings in H which do not have parallels in the canonical gospels, at least with the wording which they have in H.

52. H 7.4.3

H 7.4.3	Ju, D. 93.2
ἅπερ	ἅπερ
ἕκαστος	
ἑαυτῷ	⌈ἑαυτῷ⌉[1]
βούλεται	βούλεται
5 καλά,	ἀγαθά,
τὰ αὐτὰ	
βουλευέσθω	(1. 9)
καὶ τῷ πλησίον.	κἀκείνῳ
	βουλήσεται·

[1]αὐτῷ A.

H 11.4.4
πάντα ὅσα ἑαυτῷ τις θέλει καλά,
ὡσαύτως ἄλλῳ χρήζοντι παρεχέτω.

H 12.32.4
ὃ θέλει ἑαυτῷ, θέλει καὶ τῷ πλησίον.

Mt. 7.12
πάντα οὖν ὅσα ἐὰν θέλητε ἵνα ποιῶσιν ὑμῖν οἱ ἄνθρωποι,
οὕτως καὶ ὑμεῖς ποιεῖτε αὐτοῖς.

Lk. 6.31
καὶ καθὼς θέλετε ἵνα ποιῶσιν ὑμῖν οἱ ἄνθρωποι,
ποιεῖτε αὐτοῖς ὁμοίως.

The wording of H and Justin shows such remarkable agreement that, even though neither cites the words as a saying of Jesus, a common source is very likely.[1] For they agree in a form of the saying that uses βούλεσθαι instead of the canonical θέλειν and ποιεῖν.[2] Nor are the differences between H and Justin of great significance. The fact that Justin adjoins his words as an explanation of "loving one's neighbor" to καὶ ὁ τὸν πλησίον ὡς ἑαυτὸν ἀγαπῶν easily explains two of the differences: (1) ἕκαστος has been dropped in Justin because ὁ . . . ἀγαπῶν of the

---

[1]Bellinzoni does not take up these words as a saying of Jesus in Justin. But cf. Resch, Agrapha, No. 131, p. 174.

[2]But H 11.4.4 and 12.32.4 use θέλειν. Waitz (Pseudoklementinen, pp. 288-89) sees this as evidence of the different layers within H.

previous clause is now the subject and ἕκαστος become redundant;
and (2) κἀκείνῳ is sufficient for καὶ τῷ πλησίον since τὸν
πλήσιον has just been mentioned in the previous clause. The use
of καλά (H) or ἀγαθά (Justin) could be a personal preference by
one of the other authors. τὰ αὐτά in H is an insignificant addition by H or omission by Justin. In short, a common source for
this saying in H and Justin is once again indicated.[3]

---

[3]Strecker (Judenchristentum, p. 132 and n. 1) thinks that
H and Justin have formulated the words independently of each
other. But this fails to take seriously enough the agreement in
wording and order which outweigh the differences.

53. H 16.21.4

ἔσονται γάρ, ὡς ὁ κύριος εἶπεν,
ψευδαπόστολοι, ψευδεῖς προφῆται, αἱρέσεις, φιλαρχίαι.

Justin, Dial. 35.3
εἶπε (Jesus) γάρ· ἔσονται σχίσματα καὶ αἱρέσεις.
(Cf. v. 3a; ψευδοπροφῆτων; v. 4: ψευδόχριστοι καὶ
ψευδαπόστολοι.)

Didascalia 6.5/23 (Lagarde 99,9; cf. Connolly 197-98)
"There will be heresies and schisms."

(. ܠܗܘܝܢ ܕܝ̈ܢ ܗܪܣܝ̈ܣ)

Didymus, De trin. 3.22 (MPG 39.920)
ἔσονται ἐν ὑμῖν αἱρέσεις καὶ σχίσματα.

Lactantius, Div. instit. 4.30 (MPL 6.540)
quod plurimae sectae et haereses haberent existere.

Cf. H 2.17.4
οὕτως δή, ὡς ὁ ἀληθὴς ἡμῖν προφήτης εἴρηκεν, πρῶτον
ψευδὲς δεῖ ἐλθεῖν εὐαγγέλιον ὑπὸ πλάνου τινὸς καὶ εἶθ'
οὕτως μετὰ καθαίρεσιν τοῦ ἁγίου τόπου εὐαγγέλιον ἀληθὲς
κρύφα διαπεμφθῆναι εἰς ἐπανόρθωσιν τῶν ἐσομένων αἱρέσεων·

Cf. R 4.34.5
[The devil] festinat continuo emittere in hunc mundum
pseudoprophetas et pseudoapostolos falsosque doctores.

The saying ἔσονται σχίσματα καὶ αἱρέσεις (or ἔσονται
αἱρέσεις καὶ σχίσματα) is cited by Justin, the Didascalia, and
Didymus as a saying of Jesus.[1] H attests the ἔσονται and
αἱρέσεις of the saying. In addition, it is noteworthy that
Justin in Dial. 35.1-4 has four anti-heretical sayings of Jesus
strung together: (1) a possibly harmonized form of Mt. 24.5 and
7.15 which H may also have known,[2] (2) this present saying, (3)
Mt. 7.15 (without the introduction of 24.5), a saying against
ψευδοπροφῆται, and (4) Mt. 24.11,24 against ψευδόχριστοι and
ψευδαπόστολοι (which has been exchanged for the ψευδοπροφῆται
of Mt. 24.24).[3] Three of the elements in H are readily explained

---

[1]Lactantius refers to Paul's words in 1 Cor. 11.18-19. On
the question of the relationship of "the saying of Jesus" in
Justin and 1 Cor. 11.18-19, see Bellinzoni, Sayings, pp. 101-02.

[2]See H 11.35.6 (no. 10, pp. 56-58).

[3]Cf. Bellinzoni's discussion, Sayings, pp. 100-06.

as a condensed form of this same listing: ψευδαπόστολοι, ψευδεῖς προφῆται, and αἱρέσεις. φιλαρχίαι could easily be H's own substitution for σχίσματα. Thus H would not only attest a common knowledge of the saying known to Justin, the Didascalia, and Didymus, but more importantly, would attest a knowledge of the anti-heretical grouping of sayings found in Justin.[4] Bellinzoni suggests that the source used by Justin at this point was an early Christian vade mecum against heresies,[5] which was perhaps also known to the Apostolic Constitution.[6]

H 2.17.4 is unique to H and may be H's own invention to describe his concept of the end time schema. The use of καθαίρεσιν is probably H's preferred word for the destruction of the Temple.[7]

R 4.34.5 seems to be R's own paraphrasing and not an actual quotation.

---

[4]Waitz (Pseudoklementinen, p. 314) does not recognize this possibility at all; Strecker (Judenchristentum, p. 135) notes the saying common to H, Justin, the Didascalia, Didymus (and Lactantius ?), but says "ob der Verfasser nur den Mt-Text (Mt. 24.11, 24) wiedergeben will oder aber auf eine Lesart des durch Justin. etc. bezeugten unkanonischen Logions ἔσονται σχίσματα καὶ αἱρέσεις zurückgreift, lässt sich nicht entscheiden." But Mt. 24.11,24 does not account for αἱρέσεις nor does Strecker reckon with the possibility of Justin's grouping of the four sayings being reflected in H's listing.

[5]Sayings, p. 106.

[6]Ap. Const. 6.13 (Funk 1.355) also combines Mt. 7.15-16 and 24.11,24: Ἐλεύσονται πρὸς ὑμᾶς ἄνθρωποι ἐν ἐνδύμασι προβάτων, ἔσωθεν δέ εἰσιν λύκοι ἅρπαγες· ἀπὸ τῶν καρπῶν αὐτῶν ἐπιγνώσεσθε αὐτούς, προσέχετε ἀπ᾽ αὐτῶν· ἀναστήσονται γὰρ ψευδόχριστοι καὶ ψευδοπροφῆται καὶ πλανήσουσι πολλούς.

[7]Cf. H 3.15.2 (no. 23, pp. 133ff.). Cf. also Strecker, Judenchristentum, p. 126.

54. H 19.20.1

H 19.20.1	Clem., Str. 5.10/63.7*	Isa. 24.16
τὰ μυστήρια	μυστήριον	τὸ μυστήριόν
	ἐμὸν	μου
ἐμοι	ἐμοὶ	ἐμοὶ
καὶ τοῖς υἱοῖς	καὶ τοῖς υἱοῖς	καὶ τοῖς ἐμοῖς.
5 τοῦ οἴκου μου	τοῦ οἴκου μου.	
φυλάξατε.		

---

*Stählin 2.368.

Theodoret, In Ps. 65.16 (MPG 80.1369)
    Τὰ μυστήριά μου ἐμοί, καὶ τοῖς ἐμοῖς.

John Chrysostum, In Ep. 1 ad Cor., Hom. 7.2 (MPG 61.56)
    Τὸ μυστήριόν μου ἐμοὶ καὶ τοῖς ἐμοῖς.

John of Damascus, De sacris par. θ.1 (MPG 96.9)
    Τὸ μυστήριον ἐμοὶ καὶ τοῖς ἐμοῖς.

The saying in H and Clement has most likely developed out of
a text of Isa. 24.16 as read by some of the LXX witnesses: το
μυστηριον μου εμοι και τοις εμοις (L'-233-456 403' 538).[1]
    The testimony of the other fathers listed attests only their
text of Isa. 24.16.[2] But H and Clement depart from this text in
adding τοῦ οἴκου μου and in citing it as a saying of Jesus. In
fact, Clement refers to his source as "a certain gospel"
(παρήγγειλεν ὁ κύριος ἐν τινι εὐαγγέλιον). Thus it can be
assumed that H shared a common source with Clement for this saying, a source which could be referred to as an εὐαγγέλιον.

---

[1]The following witnesses double the το μυστηριον μου εμοι;
22-48-231-36-96-233 538); others omit και τοις εμοις: V-οπΩ
(anon.) σ' θ'.
    MT reads: "I pine away, I pine away. Woe is me!" (RSV)
(רָזִי־לִי רָזִי־לִי אוֹי לִי). The translation of the LXX witnesses
noted above is due to an incorrect interpretation of רָזִי.
Instead of understanding it from רזה of classical Hebrew ("to
grow lean"), it has been translated as if from the later Persian
loanword used in Daniel-- רָז ("secret"). Cf. Schoeps, Die
Tempelerstörung des Jahres 70 in der jüdischen Religionsgeschichte (Coni. Neot. 6; 1942), pp. 84-85.

[2]However, in Theodoret, In Psa. 65, the words immediately
follow the citation of Mt. 7.6.

The differences in H from Clement can be explained as H's own changes (the change to the plural τὰ μυστήρια,[3] the dropping of ἐμόν, and the addition of φυλάξατε), made in order to adapt the saying to the special use of H: "Guard the mysteries (= the secret teachings of the True Prophet) which belong to me (the True Prophet) and to the sons of my house (= the members of the sect)."[4]

---

[3]Whether the use of the plural in Theodoret is coincidental with H or not I cannot tell. Also I do not know if Ev. Thom. 62 is related or not. It reads: "Jesus said, 'I tell my mysteries to those [. . .] mystery/mysteries.'" (ⲡⲉϫⲉ [ⲏ︦ⲥ︦ ϫⲉ ⲉⲓ̈ϫⲱ ⲛ̄ⲛⲁⲙⲩ-ⲥⲧⲏⲣⲓⲟⲛ ⲛ̄ⲛ[. . .]ⲙⲩⲥⲧⲏⲣⲓⲟⲛ).

[4]Cf. especially the Ep. Peter to James for this theme in H.

158

55. H 2.51.1, 3.50.2a, 18.20.4

γίνεσθε τραπεζῖται δόκιμοι.

This saying is so widely attested in the fathers (Resch lists 69 occurrences)[1] that no attempt will be made here to list or cite them. But a few observations will be made concerning the nature of the early citations of the saying. Although the words γίνεσθε δόκιμοι τραπεζῖται are often cited by themselves as in H, they are also frequently joined to the words found in 1 Thes. 5.21-22: πάντα δὲ δοκιμάζετε, τὸ καλὸν κατέχετε· ἀπὸ παντὸς εἴδους πονηροῦ ἀπέχεσθε.[2] The saying is cited as:

1. A Saying of Jesus or Christ or the Savior or the Lord:
   a. quod ait (Christus) (Origen, 3 [the numbers refer to the listings in Resch]).
   b. τὴν ἐντολὴν 'Ιησοῦ (Origen, 27).
   c. Salvatoris verba dicentis (Jerome, 30).
   d. Salvator Mariae respondet (Pistis Sophia, 15).
   e. secundum praeceptum Domini (Cassianus, 24).
2. Scripture:
   a. ἡ γραφή . . . παραινεῖ (Clement Alex., 1).
   b. κατὰ τὴν γραφήν (Origen, 2).
3. From a Gospel (or the Gospels):
   a. ἔφη ἐν τῷ εὐαγγελίῳ (Apelles in Epiphanius, 23).
   b. τὰ ῥήματα ἐν εὐαγγελίοις (Caesarius, 11).
   c. secundum illam Evangelicam parabolam (Cassianus, 25; cf. 64).

4. A Word of Paul (Cyril of Alex., 34-36; cf. Dionysius Alex. [wrongly termed "Rom." by Resch] in Eusebius, 37).

The application of the saying is also quite varied. It is applied to whatever one is asked to discern: true from false doctrine, moral good from evil, evil spirits, etc.

Concerning the origin of the saying it may be noted that, besides the evidence of H, Apelles (according to Epiphanius) knew the saying as ἐν τῷ εὐαγγελίῳ, while both Clement and Origen knew it in the combined form (with the Pauline words of 1 Thes. 5) as γραφή. But the "scripture" or "Gospel" involved

---

[1]Agrapha, 2nd ed., no. 87, pp. 112-28.

[2]Cf. Clement, 1; Origen, 2-3; and other examples in nos. 4-9. [The numbers refer to Resch's listing.]

is never identified. Various words of the canonical gospels and of Paul can be adduced that have a "ring" of these words,[3] but apart from 1 Thes. 5.21-22 there is no direct attestation of the words before the second century.

In the case of H the saying is always (three times) joined with the H form of Mk. 12.24 (cf. Mt. 22.29)[4] in the context of a charge to discern the true from the false pericopes of scripture. If we could assume that the two sayings were drawn from the same source, then the possibility of the saying γίνεσθε δόκιμοι τραπεζῖται being found in the (harmonized) sayings collection would be increased.[5] But, as it is, we can only conjecture the possibility. Nothing, as far as I see, really speaks against it.

---

[3] Cf. Resch, Agrapha, pp. 127-28.

[4] Cf. Saying no. 38, p. 116.

[5] Justin's citations include non-synoptic sayings of Jesus which were probably not drawn from a separate (Jewish-Christian) gospel (cf. Bellinzoni, Sayings, pp. 131-38).

56. H 12.29.1

H 12.29.1	Aphr., Dem. 5.1*	Manichaean Ps.**	Mt. 18.7	Lk. 17.1
τὰ ἀγαθὰ		ⲡⲁⲧⲟⲑⲟⲛ		
ἐλθεῖν δεῖ,		ⲥϭⲛ̄ⲏⲉⲧ ⲇⲉⲓ		
μακάριος δὲ		ⲛⲉⲓ̈ⲉⲧⲩ̄		
(φησίν)				
5 δι᾽ οὗ		ⲙ̄ⲡⲉⲧⲩ̄ⲛⲏⲩ		ἀνένδεκτόν ἐστιν
ἔρχεται·		ϭⲓⲧⲟⲟ[ⲧⲩ] ⲡⲉ,		τοῦ
ὁμοίως καὶ				τὰ σκάνδαλα
τὰ κακὰ		ⲧⲣⲉⲩ ⲟⲛ		μὴ ἐλθεῖν
ἀνάγκη		ϧⲁⲛⲧ̄	ἀνάγκη γὰρ	οὐαὶ δὲ
10 ἐλθεῖν,		ϣⲩⲱⲡⲉ	ἐλθεῖν	
			τὰ σκάνδαλα,	
οὐαὶ δὲ¹		ⲟⲩⲁⲓ̈	πλὴν οὐαὶ	
			τῷ ἀνθρώπῳ	
15 δι᾽ οὗ		ⲙ̄ⲡⲉⲧⲩ̄ⲛⲏⲩ	δι᾽ οὗ	δι᾽ οὗ
			⌜τὸ σκάνδαλον¹	
ἔρχεται.		ⲛ̄ⲧⲉⲩⲗϥ[ⲓⲥ]ϥ̣.	ἔρχεται.	ἔρχεται.

¹ + τῷ ἀνθρώπῳ E.

¹τα σκανδαλα ⲱ al
syᶜ,ᵖ; omit θ syᶜ

*(Graffin 1.185,8-11)
  "The good is ready to come ('to be'),
  and blessed is he through whom it comes;
  and the evil is ready to come ('to be'),
  and woe (is he) through whom it comes."

**(Allberry 39,27f.)
  "The good is ready to come,
  blessed is he through whom it comes;
  the evil also must[1] come ('be'),
  woe (to him) because of whom it comes."

[[1]Allberry translates, "is near," taking ϧⲁⲛⲧ as the
qualitative of ϧⲱⲛⲧ. However, I would suggest that it
is related to AA[2] ϧⲁⲛ-, meaning "necessity" (?) and
which translates δεῖ in Jn. 3.7 (A[2]).]

R 3.49.4
  Necesse est enim saeculo huic venire scandala;
  vae tamen illi per quem veniunt. (Cf. R 3.65.2.)

H cites a form of the saying, known in the East by
Aphraates and the Manichaean Psalms which forms a complete
parallelism (of good and evil, blessing and woe) in contrast to
the synoptic form which speaks only of τὰ σκάνδαλα and an οὐαί.
The question may be raised, Is the parallel form a derivation
from the synoptic form or does it represent an earlier tradition
than that in Q? Quispel has argued for the latter on the
grounds that the parallel form should be considered prior as it
would have been at home to Aramaic speakers, but strange to
"Greek ears."[1] But such a "natural tendency" toward parallelism
(in this case "antithetical parallelism") could as easily have
brought about an expansion of the Q saying into the parallel
form, especially among some Jewish Christians.
  As to the source of the saying in H, Aphraates, and the

---

[1]VC 11 (1957), 199; cf. also pp. 195-99, and 13 (1959),
101-02.
  While the Semitic tendency would be to repeat the same
words, the Greek tendency would be to alter the wording. This
might help explain the wording of the Manichaean Psalm which
uses different words for "the necessity" (ⲥϧⲛⲏⲧ and ϧⲁⲛⲧ, as
does H with δεῖ and ἀνάγκη), "the coming" (ⲁⲉⲓ and ⲁϣⲱⲡⲉ),
and "him through whom it comes" (ⲙ̄ⲡⲉⲧϥ̄ⲛ̄ⲏⲩ ϧⲓⲧⲟⲟ[ⲧϥ] and
ⲁⲡⲉⲧϥ̄ⲛ̄ⲏⲩ ⲛ̄ⲧⲉϥⲗⲁ[ⲓⲥ]ⲉ). It is the Syriac of Aphraates that
offers the most complete parallelism in wording! On this
difference of parallelism, cf. E. Norden, Die Antike Kunstprosa,
5th ed., p. 509, n. 1.

Manichaean Psalms,[2] it may be noted that Aphraates introduces
the saying as "scripture" (ܟܬܒܐ ܒܕ ܟܬܝܒ) and H as the
words of the True Prophet (ὁ τῆς ἀληθείας προφήτης ἔφη).   If one
adds that the saying in H reveals harmonistic characteristics
(ἀνάγκη ἐλθεῖν = Matthew, οὐαὶ δὲ δι' οὗ ἔρχεται [without τῷ
ἀνθρώπῳ and τὸ σκάνδαλον] = Luke), then the possibility that H
has taken the saying from the harmonized sayings source becomes
a distinct possibility.

R has simply dropped the first half of the saying to conform with the synoptic form.

---

[2]Quispel's conjecture that it belongs to a Jewish Christian
gospel simply lacks any confirmation. Aphraates' citation might
suggest Tatian's Diatessaron. But Quispel's appeal to Δ p 4.18
to find in the Diatessaron additional evidence for the form of
the saying known to H, Aphraates, and the Manichaean Psalms
fails because "mali" translates hair = σκάνδαλον (cf. Messina
305, n. 3) and not τὸ κακόν. The appeal to Δ 1 113 also proves
nothing more than Lucan influence (or less likely a text of
Matthew which omits τὸ σκάνδαλον as in ϑ sy^s).

57. H 3.52.2

H 3.52.2	Mt. 7.14	Jn. 10.7	Jn. 10.9
		ἀμὴν ἀμὴν	
		λέγω ὑμῖν ὅτι	
ἐγώ εἰμι		ἐγώ εἰμι	ἐγώ εἰμι
ἡ πύλη	ἡ πύλη	⌜ἡ θύρα⌝¹	ἡ θύρα·
5 τῆς ζωῆς·		τῶν προβάτων.	
ὁ δι' ἐμοῦ	ἡ		δι' ἐμοῦ
εἰσερχόμενος	ἀπάγουσα		ἐάν τις εἰσέλθῃ
			σωθήσεται,
εἰσέρχεται			καὶ εἰσελεύσεται
10 εἰς τὴν ζωῆν.	εἰς τὴν ζωῆν.		
			καὶ ἐξελεύσεται
			καὶ νομὴν
			εὑρήσει.

¹ο ποιμην P⁷⁵ sa.

Hegesippus in Eusebius, HE 2.23.8,12 (Schwartz 2,1.168)
ἐπυνθάνοντο αὐτοῦ τίς ἡ θύρα τοῦ 'Ιησοῦ;
¹²ἀπάγγειλον ἡμῖν τίς ἡ θύρα τοῦ 'Ιησοῦ.

Naassenes in Hippolytus, Phil. 5.8.20 (Wendland 3.93)
διὰ τοῦτο, φησί [ὁ Ναάσσηνος], λέγει ὁ 'Ιησοῦς·
ἐγώ εἰμι ἡ πύλη ἡ ἀληθινή.

This saying is unique in its wording to H. That Jn. 10.7.9
underlies it is tenuous at best.[1] The relationship is more
formal than direct; i.e., the use of ἐγώ εἰμι and the language
of "door" or "gate"[2] and of "entering through it." But Mt. 7.13-
14, without the ἐγώ εἰμι, has the same elements as well as the
expression "entering into life." Still a harmony of Mt. 7.13-14
and Jn. 10.7.9 can hardly be proved.[3]

_____

[1]Against John as its source, see Credner, Beiträge 1.326;
Hilgenfeld, Krit. Untersuchungen, pp. 344-45; Waitz, Pseudoklementinen, p. 287.

[2]Cf., besides those examples listed in the columns, the
examples in Resch, Aussercan. Paralleltexte, 3.126-27. These
can hardly have all had a single source even "inspiring" them.

[3]Strecker (Judenchristentum, p. 127) wants to maintain such,
but with the formula: "Joh 10,9 + Mt 7,14 + ?"!

The commonness of such language ("door," "life," and "entering") make it the best course to leave the source of this saying as unknown.

58. H 3.55.2b

ὁ πονηρός ἐστιν ὁ πειράζων.

Lacking other attestation to H's wording one cannot determine H's source. The fact that ὁ πειράζων occurs in Mt. 4.3 and 1 Thes. 3.5 does not really help us either. Therefore we can only list the saying in H as otherwise unknown.

166

59. H 19.2.4b

H 19.2.4b	Eph. 4.27	1 Tim. 5.14
μὴ	μηδὲ	μηδεμίαν
⌐δότε¹	δίδοτε	διδόναι
πρόφασιν	τόπον	ἀφορμὴν
τῷ πονηρῷ.	τῷ διαβόλῳ.	τῷ ἀντικειμένῳ.

---

¹δῶτε O.

The similarity of thought but difference in language suggests a common moral exhortation,[1] but not a common written source. Only in H is it made into a saying of Jesus within a group of other sayings. But a direct dependence on either Ephesians or 1 Timothy can hardly be assumed.[2]

---

[1] Cf. in Judaism Pesiq 177b: ". . . in order not to give an opportunity to Satan" (‎לשׂטן פתחון פה לתת שׁלא כדי).

[2] Waitz (Pseudoklementinen, p. 307) describes it as "ein unkanonisches Herrnwort, das an Eph. 4.27 erinnert." Strecker (Judenchristentum, p. 135), with some uncertainty, suggests that Eph. 4.27 is being quoted, but with a "Gedächtnisirrtum." Neither of them notes the similarity of 1 Tim. 5.14.

167

60. H 3.50.2b

καὶ τῷ εἰπεῖν· "Διὰ τί οὐ νοεῖτε τὸ εὔλογον τῶν γραφῶν;"

Although the words are cited as a saying of Jesus, the fact
that they do not occur in the same context in H 2.51 or 18.20 nor
are they cited by any other early Christian writer to my knowledge argues against their coming from H's source or sources of
sayings of Jesus. Rather they appear to be the ad hoc creation
of the writer to fit his immediate context and argument on the
false pericopes of scripture.[1]

---

[1]So also Strecker, Judenchristentum, p. 134. One may add
that εὔλογος and εὐλόγως are frequently used terms in H (see
Chawner's index ad loc).

Conclusion

Some of the Agrapha in H appear to belong to the common
source with Justin, i.e., nos. 52 and 53. This is not at all
surprising when one considers that Justin certainly included
some non-synoptic or Agrapha in his quotations.[1] Still a source
such as a Jewish-Christian gospel cannot be proved either for
Justin or H.[2]

Nos. 54 (known to Clement) and 55 (known to numerous
fathers) might well be included in the common source.

No. 56, known to Aphraates and the Manichaean Psalms, is
difficult to assess because one does not know to which layer in
H it belongs.[3]

In no. 57 it is difficult to tell if the saying is directly
related to Mt. 7.14 and/or Jn. 10.7,9 or is a separate Agrapha.
If the latter, as I suggest, then we have no other witness to
this saying.

Nos. 58 and 59 are unique to H, although there are similar
exhortations to no. 59 in Eph. 4.27 and 1 Tim. 5.14. This need
mean only a common tradition of moral instruction.

No. 60 is most likely the creation of H.

---

[1]Cf. Bellinzoni, Sayings, pp. 131-38.

[2]Waitz's theory of an Ebionite Gospel underlying KP will be
taken up in the concluding chapter.

[3]Waitz with some uncertainty ascribed it to the Praxeis
Petrou.

CHAPTER VI

CONCLUSIONS

Critique of Waitz

Because it was Waitz who most clearly and thoroughly
attempted to distinguish the sources of the Pseudo-Clementines
and to relate the sayings of Jesus to them, and because subsequent works have either built upon Waitz's hypotheses or
opposed him, it is appropriate to reconsider his hypotheses of
sources in the Pseudo-Clementines as they relate to the sayings.
Those of greatest relevance to this thesis are his hypotheses
that the KP source used the Ebionite Gospel (EE) = the Gospel of
the Twelve Apostles (E 12) for its gospel material, and that the
anti-Marcionite redaction of KP (= A-M) used Justin's Syn. adv.
Marc. as a source.

The KP hypothesis is based in part on his source analysis.
It is beyond the scope of this thesis to enter into the source
analysis debate as such or to offer a new analysis of the
sources of the Pseudo-Clementines. Rather I wish to suggest,
based on the findings of the thesis, some new points of departure
and considerations that must be taken into account in future
analyses of the sources and layers of H and R.

The "KP use of EE" hypothesis.--Waitz's listing of those
sayings in H and R which he considered to be from KP can be found
most easily in an article subsequent to his book.[1] There he
gives the characteristics of this group of sayings as follows:[2]

1. The citations, although sometimes freely quoted as
though from memory, are nevertheless based on a written Vorlage
and not on oral tradition. In repeated citations of the same
saying they most often agree verbatim. KP thus presupposes one
or more gospel writings.

---

[1]"Das Evangelium der zwölf Apostel," ZNW 13 (1912), 338-48;
14 (1913), 38-64, especially pp. 50-56.

[2]Ibid., pp. 56-61.

2.   The quotations are never derived from John.

3.   Where KP and Justin cite the same saying, KP's readings usually have differences from Justin's readings.

4.   The quotations never cite sayings which are found only in Matthew nor those which occur in Matthew and Mark and/or Luke together.

5.   The quotations only seldom agree verbatim with the canonical text(s). They also use uncanonical sayings.

6.   The quotations clearly betray a Jewish-Christian and indeed a syncretistic Jewish-Christian stamp.

7.   The quotations are often introduced as if the (12) Apostles are the speakers (see the use of ἡμεῖς and ἡμῶν), + other characteristics similar to those of EE.

Most of these observations seem basically sound, at least for a large portion of the sayings in H and especially for those which Waitz attributes to KP. My main objection is to point no. 3 regarding sayings with parallels in Justin. First, Waitz simply makes this point by attributing those sayings in which he sees agreement with Justin to A-M instead of to KP. But once (H 17.7.1) there is no anti-Marcionite polemic in the context at all to indicate an anti-Marcionite source. Often the sayings with precise agreements with Justin occur in the same grouping as those he attributes to KP. Second, even these sayings, which Waitz attributed to KP because he thought they did not agree with the Justinian citation, do in fact often reflect a common source for H and Justin:

a.   H 3.19.3 (= my no. 2)--I have argued that H and Justin do in fact presuppose a common source as does Didache in this case.

b.   R 3.41.4 etc. (= Mt. 6.33)--Lacking confirmation in H it must be doubted if these citations in R belong to KP or even go back to G.

c.   H 3.18.3, R 2.30.1, 2.46.3-4 (cf. Mt. 23.13 and Lk. 11.52)--These texts are at best loose paraphrases and can hardly qualify as actual citations of sayings of Jesus.

d.   H 11.35.4, 19.2.3 (cf. Mt. 4.3 and Lk. 4.2)[3]--This is more of a reference to the Temptation story than an actual quotation of a saying of Jesus.

---

[3]The last three (d-f) are not attributed by Waitz to KP but to a related source which used the same Gospel as KP.

e. H 11.35.6 (= my no. 10)--Here there is a real difference
in wording in H and Justin. However, this may be offset by the
fact that H 16.21.4 (= my no. 53) seemed to show that H knew the
anti-heretical grouping of sayings which Justin has in Dial. 35
and which includes this saying in H 11.35.6. Otherwise, H 11.
35.6 may belong to a later layer of H or may have been reworded
(by H?) to bring it closer to the canonical text.

f. H 8.7.4, R 4.5.4 (= my no. 40)--This is an unfair comparison because H 8.7.4 cites Lk. 6.46 (and that in a form known
to other fathers), while Justin (Apol. 16.9-10) cites Mt. 7.21 +
a saying related to Mt. 10.40 = Lk. 10.16.[4]

In sum, these examples, for the reasons noted, simply do
not confirm Waitz's contention of a distinction between KP and
A-M sayings based on the supposition that the former show signif-
icant differences from Justin and the latter close agreement with
Justin. Already it must be said that his distinction between
KP and A-M is precarious.

Next Waitz wanted to identify the sayings he listed under
KP as belonging to the same source (EE = E 12) that Epiphanius
supposedly used in his discussion of the Ebionites (Pan. 30).[5]

Without entering into the question of the nature of
Epiphanius' "gospel source" in Pan. 30 (Waitz thinks he had an
actual copy of EE in hand), Waitz's identification of the sayings
in KP and those in Epiphanius, Pan. 30, must be seriously
questioned.

(1) Most of the citations in each have no parallel in the
other. Where they do, a direct relation or identification of
the two is very questionable. There are two such cases:

(a) Epiphanius, Pan. 30.13 (no. 8 in Waitz's list) and H 3.
53.1 (= my no. 29). Pan. 30.13 is based on Mt. 3.17 and reads:
οὗτός ἐστιν ὁ υἱός μου ὁ ἀγαπητός, ἐφ᾽ ὃν ηὐδόκησα. H 3.53.1,
based on Mt. 17.5, reads: οὗτός ἐστίν μου ὁ υἱος ὁ ἀγαπητὸς
εἰς ὃν εὐδόκησα, τούτου ἀκούετε. Mt. 3.17 and 17.5 have ἐν ᾧ
εὐδόκησα. Nothing really speaks for the same source for Pan.
30.13 and H 3.53.1 (outside the Gospel of Matthew). For where
they differ from Matthew, they fail to agree with each other!

---

[4]Cf. Bellinzoni, Sayings, pp. 20-22, 67.

[5]The gospel citations are listed by Waitz in the above
mentioned article, pp. 342-43.

(b) Epiphanius, <u>Pan</u>. 30.16 (no. 9 in Waitz's list) and H
3.15.2 (= my no. 11). <u>Pan</u>. 30.16 reads: ἦλθον καταλῦσαι τὰς
θυσίας, καὶ ἐὰν μὴ παύσησθε τοῦ θυεῖν, οὐ παύσεται ἀφ' ὑμῶν ἡ
ὀργή; H 3.15.2 reads οὐκ ἦλθον καταλῦσαι τὸν νόμον (and follows
with Mt. 5.18 influenced by Mt. 24.35 = Mk. 13.31). Waitz
argued that EE read οὐκ ἦλθον καταλῦσαι τὸν νόμον (so H), ἀλλ'
ἦλθον καταλῦσαι τὰς θυσίας (so <u>Pan</u>.). That is clever but hardly
constitutes convincing evidence of a common source. The issue
is not whether both <u>Pan</u>. 30 and H (cf. R 1.64.1) reflect similar
attitudes or viewpoints (let that be granted), but whether there
is a common, written source! There is simply no convincing
evidence for the latter.

Other elements of similar ideas, use of the synoptics,
authority of the 12 Apostles, etc., can well be explained as the
common property of related Jewish-Christian groups (and others
as well), but hardly requires an identical gospel source for
each. One element that Waitz has overlooked is that EE in
Epiphanius includes clearly narrative material.[6] As has been
observed in the thesis, the introductions to the sayings often
betray not our synoptics, but represent quite different introductions, perhaps even very <u>ad hoc</u> introductions. This latter
picture is much better understood on the basis of a source of
collected sayings of Jesus than of a "gospel" which combined
sayings within narrative accounts as apparently EE did.

<u>The A-M hypothesis</u>.--The difficulty in dealing with this
part of Waitz's hypothesis is that it is so much dependent on
the source analysis itself, i.e., a KP layer which supposedly
does not reflect anti-Marcionite elements versus sections that
reflect an anti-Marcionite polemic. On this issue I would
simply note that (1) some scholars since Waitz have denied any
anti-Marcionite polemic or source at all in H,[7] and (2) even

---

[6]This is not to say that there are not narrative references
and allusions in H. But that these should be joined with the
direct citations of sayings is what I dispute.

[7]Schmidt, <u>Studien zu Pseudo-Clementinen</u> (TU 46,1; 1929),
p. 296[1]; Cullmann, <u>Le problème littéraire et historique du roman
Pseudo-Clémentin</u> (1930), pp. 93-94; Bousset, "Rezension zu
Waitz: Die Pseudoklementinen" in <u>Göttingische gelehrte Anzeigen</u>
(1905). Cf. Waitz's reply to Schmidt and Bousset in ZNW 28
(1929), 245-47, and to Cullmann in ZKG 50 (1931), 188-89. I
think this total rejection of anti-Mariconite polemic in H is
unjustified and would agree with Waitz's refutation.

those who follow Waitz in a KP source and in anti-Marcionite
elements in H do not accept his idea of A-M as a reworking of
KP.[8] For my part I would note that the characteristics of the
sayings which Waitz attributed to A-M are the same as those in
KP except that Waitz thought the sayings in KP had no direct
relation with Justin, while those in A-M did.[9] But, as was noted
above, this distinction does not hold. Therefore I find no firm
basis for distinguishing the citations of KP and A-M!

Suggestions

This leads me to the suggestion that if KP included sayings
of Jesus,[10] it is really impossible to distinguish its quotations
from those of G. For the author of G seems to have been quite
sympathetic to the viewpoints of KP. We can then further suggest that it was the author of G who is primarily responsible
for the sayings of Jesus in H, perhaps finding some (a very few?)
already in his KP source (as Ep. Pet. shows) and others in his A-M
source. But nothing prevents, as far as I can see, the solution
that the author of G expanded his sources with the inclusion of
sayings of Jesus which he took primarily from a harmonized sayings source that was based on Matthew and Luke (with some Marcan
influence?) and which was used by Justin and known to other
fathers of the early church.[11] As to the origin of this source
one cannot, on the basis of the H citations, go beyond the

---

[8]Schoeps (Theologie, pp. 55, 313-14) sees A-M as based on
the use of Justin's lost Syn. adv. Marc., as Waitz had argued,
but that the author of KP is himself the one who used it as
well as other sources for his work at the end of the second
century. Strecker (Pseudoklementinen, pp. 255 ff.) dates KP
around 200; he sees the A-M source in R 2.47-60 par. and other
places in H and R as a source employed by the author of G
(along with KP and other sources).

[9]Pseudoklementinen, pp. 362-63.

[10]If we follow Waitz and Strecker in the existence of a
Jewish-Christian source (KP) which was probably anti-Pauline in
character and to which Ep. Pet. belongs, the one certain case of
a quotation from KP is that of Ep..Pet. 2.5 = H 3.51.3 (my no.
11). But that only tells us that KP used Matthew and conflated
Mt. 5.18 and Mt. 24.35 (= Mk. 13.31).

[11]This solution solves the dilemma of harmonized sayings
which agree with Justin in both KP sections and A-M sections.
Otherwise, one has to suppose that KP, A-M, and perhaps G all
used the harmonized source. But that only compounds the problems and one must question the likelihood of it.

suggestion that Bellinzoni has already made, that perhaps Justin himself composed it for use in his school at Rome. Interestingly, Waitz places the author of G in Rome about 220-230 for the composition of his work![12]

Still the problem of saying just what sayings belong to this layer and what do not simply cannot be solved with any kind of certainty. One could logically place in it all those with agreements in Justin (nos. 1-7, 8-10?, 19, 20, 52, and 53). Probably most of the other harmonized sayings also belong (excepting 17 and 18?). A good portion of the Matthean, Lucan, and Agrapha could also belong, but one cannot attain any certainty here because:

1. they could also go back to KP or an A-M source and may not presuppose a harmonized source at all;

2. G may have used other sources than the sayings source, i.e., Matthew and/or Luke directly, and perhaps others (?); and

3. they could in some cases be from H.

The fact that many of the citations revealed stylistic improvements, changes to enhance the parallism, and dogmatic changes does not help us much. For it tells us no more than that the hand of G has probably been at work. But it does not provide us with any clear criteria for distinguishing the hand of the Homilist in the quotations from that of G (or his sources).[13] The attribution of certain sayings (by Waitz) to a Praxeis Petrou source or to H lack confirmation beyond purely source critical considerations, i.e., they are not really based on criteria concerning the characteristics of the sayings themselves. The exception could be that the Johannine citations come from H if G did not use the Gospel of John. But that affects only two sayings (nos. 46 and 47). Even here it is possible that G did use John in addition to the sayings source.

---

[12]Pseudoklementinen, p. 366.

[13]Of course, one can know that sayings common to H and R (especially if they agree in departures from the canonical texts) go back to G. But sayings in H and not in R do not necessarily mean that they belong to the Homilist. For R has omitted parts of G. The problem is in trying to say how a saying from the Homilist would differ from one in G. It presumedly would not show common harmonistic features with Justin. But would it always agree closely with the wording of the canonical texts? Even if so, that sheds little light since G could also cite a text in close agreement with the canonical text(s).

Hence we can speak of the hand of the Homilist in the sayings of Jesus only very infrequently.[14]

What does this study of the sayings in H tell us about the history of gospel material in the early church? Primarily, it confirms the existence and influence of a harmonized sayings collection[15] which was used by Justin and H (= G) and probably known to others (Did. 1.3, 2 Clement, perhaps Clement and Origen and others).[16] The evidence of H, of course, expands the evidence of sayings to be included in the collection, but individual citations from H are always open to question as to whether they really belong to this source or not.

It is likely that Tatian in his creation of the Diatessaron was influenced by his teacher Justin who had used (composed?) a harmonized sayings source. The occasions where sayings in H shared peculiar readings with Δ are probably best explained not be a dependence of H on the Δ, but by the influence of the sayings source on Tatian's composition. Tatian, however, expanded on the idea of a harmony of sayings into a harmony of the Gospels (including John) with their narratives included.

Still the influence of the sayings collection probably continued for some time. It may even have exercised an influence on the textual tradition. We saw numerous occasions in which readings of H departed from the Nestle text, but were found in the manuscript tradition. The problem is whether any individual reading represents simply the gospel text that H or one of its sources read or represents the influence that the harmonized source may have had on the manuscript tradition, especially in those cases where the reading is a harmonistic reading.

---

[14]Such a case would be the addition of the trinitarian formula in H 11.26.2 (my no. 48).

[15]Whether there was more than one cannot be said from the evidence of H. Bellinzoni distinguished catechetical material (especially based on the Sermon on the Mount material) and an anti-heretical grouping. But nothing really prevents these from belonging to a single sayings collection which grouped sayings into various categories. I fail to discover in H any logical way to separate the sayings on the basis of genres.

[16]The gospel material in Clement, Origen and other early Christian writers needs to be researched anew in this light.

APPENDIX: THE INTRODUCTORY FORMULAE

This appendix deals with the way in which the sayings of Jesus are introduced in H and R. There are a few cases of sayings taken up in the thesis which are not cited as a direct saying of Jesus in H and therefore are not included in the listing below. On the other hand, the use of the "I remember" (μέμνημαι) formula in H 20.9.2, although it does not introduce a direct saying of Jesus, is listed along with three other occurrences of this formula in H which do introduce direct sayings of Jesus. A few sayings are listed more than once (e.g., H 19.2.3b is listed under εἴρηκεν, no. 7, and memory formulae no. 5).

H

Past Tense

1. ἔφη: 3.15.2a, 3.54.2, 3.55.1,2ab,3,4, 3.56.1,3,4, 3.57.1ac, 8.7.4, 8.21.5, 11.35.6, 12.29.1, 18.3.4, 19.2.4a.

2. εἶπεν: Ep. Pet. 2.5, H 3.18.3, 11.33.2, 16.21.4, 18.17.3, 18.20.4, 19.7.1, 19.20.1.

    a. Participle: 8.4.1, 17.4.2, 18.15.1; + another verb: 3.53.2, 11.20.4, 11.26.2, 11.33.1.

    b. Infinitive: 3.50.1,2b, 3.51.2,3, 3.64.1; + another verb: 19.2.5b.

3. ἔλεγεν: 2.51.1, 3.52.2, 3.53.3, 11.29.2, 17.4.3.

4. εἴρηκεν: Ep. Pet. 2.6, H 2.17.4, 19.2.4c,

    a. Participle: 19.2.3b; cf. 19.2.5a.

5. ἀπεκρίνατο: 19.22.6.

Present Tense

1. λέγει: 3.52.1, 8.6.4, 18.3.4, 18.4.2, 18.20.3.

    a. Participle + another verb: 2.51.2, 3.52,3a, 17.5.1,3.

    b. Infinitive: 3.18.2, 18.1.3.

Verbless

1. καί: 3.15.2bc.

2. ἀλλὰ καί: 8.4.2.

3. καὶ πάλιν: 3.52.3b, 3.57.1b, 19.2.4b.

4. καὶ ἄλλοτε: 3.52.3c.

    5. καὶ ἀλλαχοῦ που: 18.17.4.

    6. καὶ ἀλλαχῆ που: 18.20.3.

    7. καὶ ἄλλῃ που: 19.2.3b.

    8. καὶ ἄλλοθι: 19.2.4a.

    9. Cf. που: 3.50.1.

Memory Formulae

    1. μέμνημαί που αὐτόν . . . εἰπεῖν: 3.50.1.

    2. μέμνημαι γὰρ αὐτοῦ εἰπόντος: 8.4.1.

    3. μεμνήμεθα τοῦ κυρίου ἡμῶν καὶ διδασκάλου ὡς ἐντελλό-
μενος εἶπεν ἡμῖν: 19.20.1.

    4. καὶ γὰρ καὶ τοῦτο μέμνημαι εἰρηκότος αὐτοῦ τοῦ
διδασκάλου: 20.9.2.

    5. Cf. καὶ ἄλλη που οἶδα αὐτὸν εἰρηκότα: 19.2.3b.

R

Indefinite

    1.. ait: 1.65.2, 2.28.2, 2.29.5 (+ indicit), 3.5.4, 3.13.8,
4.5.5 (+ indicabat), 6.14.2,3.

    2. inquit: 2.30.3, 3.20.3, 5.9.4.

Past

    1. dixit: 2.26.6, 2.27.5, 3.30.4, 4.4.3, 4.5.4.

        a. dicebat: 6.4.3,6, 6.5.5 (+ orabat), 6.11.3.

        b. dixerit: 2.27.2; infinitive: 2.32.2, 4.4.2.

        c. est dictum: 8.4.2; infinitive: 3.5.6.

    2. praecepit: 2.30.2.

    3. respondit: 4.34.4 (+ confirmans).

    4. addidit: 7.37.3.

    5. est testatus: 6.9.2.

Present

    1. dicit: 2.29.4 (+ iubet), 2.47.3, 7.37.3 (+ dedit).

        a. Participle: 3.4.5 (+ docuit), 3.41.4, 5.2.4 (+ pro-
misit), 5.13.1 (+ docet).

Memory Formula

    1. memini enim dixisse eum: 4.4.2.

    While the terms ἡ γραφή (scriptura), αἱ γραφαί, and
γέγραπται (scriptum est) are frequently used to introduce OT
passages, they are never used to introduce sayings of Jesus or
any NT text in H or R. Moreover, the term εὐαγγέλιον is never
used to introduce a saying of Jesus in H or R. This fact along
with the dominant use of the past tense and the presence of the

"memory formulae" might be taken as evidence that the earliest
layer of the sayings of Jesus in H along with their introductory
words go back to an early stage of gospel tradition in which one
quoted them as "the words of the Lord" and not as "scripture" or
as a <u>written</u> "gospel."[1] However, this conclusion is beset by
certain difficulties.

1. The memory formulae of H and R[2] are not identical with
the early ones found in Ac. 20.35 and 1 Clem. 13.1 and 46.7
which combine a form of μιμνήσεσθαι with τῶν λόγων ἡμῶν κυρίου
'Ιησοῦ. This would suggest that the memory formulae in H and R
are a later adaptation of the early form and serve different
function: to introduce the words of Jesus as quotations by
Peter (in most cases) who is <u>remembering</u> what his teacher had
said! Thus they serve the novelistic setting.

2. That the words are consciously taken from a written
source is betrayed by the expressions ἀλλαχοῦ που, ἀλλαχῆ που,
ἄλλῃ που, ἄλλοθι, and που.

3. I see no clear criteria for determining to which stage
of the redaction the introductory words belong.

Therefore the introductory formulae cannot provide us with
an argument that the earliest layer of sayings of Jesus in H
belong to the primitive period of gospel tradition, i.e., early
second century.

---

[1]Cf. Köster, <u>Syn. Überlieferung</u>, pp. 4-12.

[2]The memory formula in R does not introduce a Saying of
Jesus which H cites. So there is no common saying introduced
by the memory formula in both H and R.

BIBLIOGRAPHY

Primary Sources

Corpus Scriptorum Ecclesiasticorum Latinorum. Vindobonae, 1866
    -1971 (and continuing). (= CSEL)

Die Griechischen Christlichen Schriftsteller der ersten drei
    Jahrhunderte. Leipzig and Berlin, 1897-1971 (and continu-
    ing). (= GCS)

Migne, J. P. Patrologia Graeca. Paris, 1857-66. (= MPG)

_____. Patrologia Latina. Paris, 1844-65. (= MPL)

Acta Apostolorum Apocrypha:

    Conybeare, F. C. "Acta Pilati," Studia Biblica et Eccle-
        siastica 4. Oxford, 1896. (Armenian - English)

    Ephraem II Rahmani, Ignatius. Apocryphi Hypomnemata Domini
        Nostri seu Acta Pilati. Monte Libano, 1908. (Syriac)

    Revillout, E. Les Apocryphes Coptes II: Les Acta Pilati.
        Patrologia Orientalis 9.2, ed. R. Graffin and F. Nau.
        Paris, 1913. (Coptic)

    Tischendorf, Constantius. Evangelia Apocrypha. 2nd ed.
        Leipzig, 1876. (Greek)

Adamantius:

    Bakhuyzen, W. H. von Sande. Origenes. Doubtful and
        Spurious Works. GCS 4. Leipzig, 1901.

Aphraates:

    Graffin, R. Patrologia Syriaca. Vols. 1 and 2. Paris,
        1894-1907.

Apocrypha of the NT:

    Hennecke, Edgar. Neutestamentliche Apokryphen. 2nd ed.
        Tübingen, 1924.

    _____, and W. Schneemelcher. New Testament
        Apocrypha. Eng. tr. ed. by R. M. Wilson. 2 vols.
        Philadelphia, 1963-65.

    Klostermann, Erich. Apocrypha II, Evangelien. 3d ed.
        Kleine Texte 8. Berlin, 1929.

182

Apocrypha of the OT:

>   Charles, R. H. The Apocrypha and Pseudepigrapha of the Old
>   Testament. 2 vols. Oxford, 1913.

Apologists:

>   Goodspeed, E. J. Die ältesten Apologeten. Göttingen, 1914.

>   Otto, J. C. T. Corpus Apologetarum Christianorum. 3rd ed.
>   5 vols. in 2. Jena, 1876-79.

Apostolic Constitutions (see Didascalia Apostolorum)

Apostolic Fathers:

>   Bihlmeyer, K. Die apostolischen Väter. Tübingen, 1924.

>   Lake, Kirsopp. The Apostolic Fathers. 2 vols. The Loeb
>   Classical Library. Cambridge, Mass., 1948-52.

Augustine:

>   Zycha, I. Sancti Aureli Augustini [Opera]. CSEL 25
>   (Aug. I). Vindobonae, 1891.

Clement of Alexandria:

>   Stählin, Otto. Clemens Alexandrinus, 3 vols. GCS 12,2;
>   15; 17. Leipzig, 1936, 1939, 1905.

Cyril of Alexandria: MPG.

Didascalia Apostolorum:

>   Connolly, R. H. Didascalia Apostolorum. Oxford, 1929.
>   (English)

>   Funk, F. X. Didascalia et Constitutiones Apostolorum.
>   2 vols. in 1. Paderborn, 1906. (Greek and Latin)

>   Lagarde, P. de. Didascalia Apostolorum Syriace. Göttingen,
>   1911. (Syriac)

Didymus: MPG.

Ephraem of Syria:

>   Leloir, Louis. Commentaire de l'évangile concordat; texte
>   syriaque. Dublin, 1963. (Syriac - Latin)
>   [= Leloir, Syr.]

>   _____. Commentaire de l'évangile concordat; version
>   arménienne. 2 vols. Louvain, 1953-54. (Armenian -
>   French) [= Leloir, Arm.]

>   Opera omnia quae exstant Graece, Syriace, Latine. 6 vols.
>   Rome, 1732-46. (Greek and Syriac - Latin)

Epiphanius:

>   Holl, K. Epiphanius. 3 vols. GCS 25, 31, 37. Leipzig,
>   1915, 1922, 1933.

183

Eusebius: MPG.

    Heikel, I. A. Eusebius Werke: Die Demonstratio Evangelica.
        GCS 23 (Eus. 6). Leipzig, 1913.

    Klostermann, E. Eusebius Werke: Gegen Marcell, etc.
        GCS (Eus. 4). Leipzig, 1906.

    Schwartz, E. Eusebius Werke: Die Kirchengeschichte. GCS
        9,1-3 (Eus. 2,1-3). Leipzig, 1903, 1908, 1909.

Gospel of Thomas:

    Guillaumont, A. et al. The Gospel according to Thomas.
        Leiden, 1959. (Coptic - English)

Gregory Nyssa: MPG.

Hilary: MPL.

Hippolytus:

    Bonwetsch, G. N. and H Achelis. Hippolytus Werke:
        Exegetische und Homiletische Schriften. GCS 1 (Hip.
        1,2). Leipzig, 1897.

    Wendland, P. Hippolytus Werke: Refutatio omnium haere-
        sium (= Philosumena). GCS 26 (Hip. 3). Leipzig,
        1916.

Irenaeus:

    Harvey, W. W. Libros quinque adversus haereses. 2 vols.
        1857.

Jerome: MPL.

John Chrysostom: MPG.

John of Damascus: MPG.

Justin Martyr (see Apologists)

Lactantius: MPL.

Macarius: MPG.

Manichaean Psalms:

    Allberry, C. R. C. A Manichaean Psalm-Book. Part 2.
        Stuttgart, 1938. (Coptic - English)

Methodius:

    Bonwetsch, G. N. Methodius. GCS 27. Leipzig, 1917.

New Testament and Gospels in Greek:

    Aland, Kurt. Synopsis Quattuor Evangeliorum. 2nd ed.
        Stuttgart, 1964.

184

Nestle, Eberhard. Novum Testamentum Graece. 25th ed. Stuttgart, 1963.

Tischendorf, Constantin von. Novum Testamentum Graece. 8th ed. 2 vols. Leipzig, 1877.

New Testament in Other Versions:

it: Jülicher, Adolf. Itala: Das Neue Testament in alt-lateinischer Überlieferung. 4 vols. Berlin, 1938-63.

sy^C: Burkitt, F. C. Evangelion da-Mepharreshe. 2 vols. Cambridge, 1904.

sy^P: Pusey, P. E. Tetraeuangelium Sanctum. Oxonii, 1901.

sy^S: Bensly, R. L. et al. The Four Gospels in Syriac Transcribed from the Sinaitic Pamlimpsest. Cambridge, 1894.

Lewis, A. S. The Old Syriac Gospels. London, 1910.

Origen:

Baehrens, W. A. Origenes Werke: Homilien zum Hexateuch in Rufins Übersetzung. GCS 29, 30 (Or. 6, 7). Leipzig, 1920, 1921.

Klostermann, E. Origenes Werke: Matthäuserklärung III. Fragmente und Indices. GCS 41,1 and 2 (Or. 12,1 and 2). Leipzig, 1941, 1955.

Lommatzsch, C. H. E. Opera Omnia. 25 vols. Berlin, 1831-48.

Rauer, M. Origenes Werke: Die Homilien zu Lukas. GCS 35 (Or. 9). Leipzig, 1930.

Papyri:

Grenfell, B. P. and A. S. Hunt. The Oxyrhynchus Papyri. Vols. 5 and 10. London, 1908, 1914.

Pseudo-Clementines:

Dressel, A. R. M. Clementinorum Epitomae Duae. 2nd ed. Leipzig, 1873.

_____. Clementis Romani quae feruntur Homiliae viginti nunc primum integrae. Göttingen, 1853.

Frankenberg, Wilhelm. Die syrischen Clementinen mit griechischem Paralleltext. Texte und Untersuchungen 48,3. Leipzig, 1937.

Lagarde, P. A. de. Clementis Romani Recognitiones Syriace. Leipzig, 1861.

Rehm, Bernhard. Die Pseudoklementinen I: Homilien. 2nd ed. by F. Paschke. GCS 42. Berlin, 1969.

_____. Die Pseudoklementinen II: Rekognitionen. GCS 51. Berlin, 1965.

Roberts, A. and J. Donaldson (eds.). The Pseudoclementina. The Ante-Nicene Fathers 8. Buffalo, 1886.

Schwegler, Albert. Clementis Romani Homiliae. Stuttgart, 1847.

Siouville, A. Les homélies clémentines. Paris, 1933.

Septuagint:

Brooke, A. E. and N. McLean. The Old Testament in Greek. Vol. 1: The Octateuch. Cambridge, 1917.

Rahlfs, A. Septuaginta. 2 vols. Stuttgart, 1935.

_____, and J. Ziegler, et al. Septuaginta Societatis Scientiarum Gottingensis auctoritate. Stuttgart, 1926-71 (and continuing).

Tatian's Diatessaron:

a: Ciasca, A. Evangeliorum Harmoniae Arabice. Rome, 1888. (Latin tr.)

Marmardji, A. S. Diatessaron de Tatien. Beyrouth, 1935. (Arabic - French)

e: See Ephraem of Syria.

f: Ranke, E. Codex Fuldensis. Marburg, 1868. (Latin)

g: Kraeling, C. H. A Greek Fragment of Tatian's Diatessaron from Dura. London, 1935. (Greek - English)

i (t and v): Todesco, V. et al. Il Diatessaron in volgare Italiano. Vatican, 1938. (Old Italian)

n (l and s): Bergsma, J. De levens van Jezus in het Middelnederlandsch. Groningen, 1895-98. (Old Dutch)

Bruin, C. C. de. Het Luikse Diatessaron. Leiden, 1970. (Dutch - English)

p: Messina, G. Diatessaron Persiano. Rome, 1951. (Persian - Italian)

Tertullian:

Kroymann, A. Q. S. F. Tertulliani Opera. CSEL 47 (Ter. 3). Vindobonae, 1906.

Reifferscheid, A. and G. Wissowa. Q. S. F. Tertulliani Opera. CSEL 20 (Ter. 1). Vindobonae, 1890.

Theodoret: MPG.

186

Secondary Sources

Altaner, Berthold. Patrology. Tr. by H. C. Graef. New York, 1958.

Becker, Heinz. Die Reden des Johannesevangeliums und der Stil der gnostischen Offenbarungsrede. Göttingen, 1956.

Bellinzoni, Arthur J., Jr. The Sayings of Jesus in the Writings of Justin Martyr. Leiden, 1967.

Blass, F. and A. Debrunner. A Greek Grammar of the New Testament and Other Early Christian Literature. 9th-10th eds. Tr. and ed. by R. W. Funk. Chicago, 1961.

Bornkamm, Günther et al. Tradition and Interpretation in Matthew. Tr. by P. Scott. Philadelphia, 1963.

Böhlig, Alexander. Mysterion und Wahrheit; gesammelte Beiträge zur Spätantiken Religionsgeschichte. Leiden, 1968.

Bousset, Wilhelm. Kyrios Christos. 5th ed. Tr. J. E. Steely. Nashville, 1970.

_____. "Rezension zu Waitz: Die Pseudoklementinen," Göttingische gelehrte Anzeigen (1905).

Bultmann, Rudolf. Das Evangelium des Johannes. Göttingen, 1964.

_____. Die Geschichte der synoptischen Tradition. 5th ed. Göttingen, 1961.

_____. History of the Synoptic Tradition. 2nd ed. Tr. by J. Marsh. New York, 1968.

Chawner, William. Index of Noteworthy Words and Phrases Found in the Clementine Writings Commonly Called the Homilies of Clement. London, 1893.

Conzelmann, Hans. The Theology of St. Luke. Tr. by G. Buswell. New York, 1961.

Credner, K. A. Beiträge zur Einleitung in die biblischen Schriften. 2 vols. Halle, 1832-38.

Cullmann, Oscar. Le problème littéraire et historique du roman Pseudo-Clémentin; étude sur le rapport entre le gnosticisme et le judéo-christianisme. Paris, 1930.

Dibelius, Martin. Der Brief des Jakobus. 11th ed. by H. Greeven. Göttingen, 1957.

_____. Die Formgeschichte des Evangeliums. 3rd ed. by G. Bornkamm. Tübingen, 1959.

_____. From Tradition to Gospel. Tr. by B. L.
Woolf. New York, n.d.

Dodd, C. H. According to the Scriptures; the sub-structure of
New Testament Theology. New York, 1953.

_____. Historical Tradition in the Fourth Gospel.
Cambridge, 1963.

Epp, Eldon Jay. "The 'Ignorance Motif' in Acts and Anti-Judaic
Tendencies in Codex Bezae," HTR 55 (1962), 51-62.

Fortna, Robert T. The Gospel of Signs. Cambridge, 1970.

Frankenberg, Wilhelm. "Zum syrischen Text der Clementinen,"
Zeitschrift der deutschen morgenländischen Gesellschaft 91
(1937), 577-604.

Grundmann, W. "Matth. xi. 27 und die Johanneischen 'Der Vater -
Der Sohn' - Stellen," NTS 12 (1965-66), 42-49.

Harnack, Adolf von. Marcion: Das Evangelium vom fremden Gott.
2nd ed. TU 45,2. Leipzig, 1924.

_____. New Testament Studies. II: The Sayings of
Jesus: the Second Source of St. Matthew and St. Luke. Tr.
by J. R. Wilkinson. New York, 1908.

_____. Studien zur Geschichte des Neuen Testaments
und der Alten Kirche. Vol. 1. Berlin, 1931.

Heintze, Werner. Der Klemensroman und seine griechischen
Quellen. TU 40,2. Leipzig, 1914.

Hilgenfeld, Adolf. Die clementinischen Recognitionen und
Homilien, nach ihrem Ursprung und Inhalt. Jena, 1848.

_____. Kritische Untersuchungen über die Evangelien
Justins, der clementinischen Homilien und Marcions. Halle,
1850.

Jeremias, Joachim. Unbekannte Jesusworte. 2nd ed. Gütersloh,
1951.

Köster, Helmut. "Die ausserkanonischen Herrenworte als Produkte
der christlichen Gemeinde," ZNW 48 (1957), 220-37.

_____. "Gnomai Diaphoroi: The Origin and Nature of
Diversification in the History of Early Christianity," HTR
58 (1965), 279-318.

_____. "History and Cult in the Gospel of John and in
Ignatius of Antioch," JThCh 1 (1965), 111-23.

_____. "One Jesus and Four Primitive Gospels," HTR 61
(1968), 203-47.

_____. Synoptische Überlieferung bei den Apostolischen
Vätern. TU 65. Berlin, 1957.

Layton, Bentley. "The Sources, Date and Transmission of Didache
1.3b-2.1," HTR 61 (1968), 343-83.

Lehmann, J. C. Die Clementinischen Schriften. Gotha, 1869.

Massaux, Édouard. Influence de l'Évangile de saint Matthieu sur la littérature chrétienne avant saint Irénée. Louvain, 1950.

Nes, H. M. van. Het Nieuwe Testament in de Clementinen. Amsterdam, 1887.

The New Testament in the Apostolic Fathers by a Committee of the Oxford Society of Historical Theology. Oxford, 1905.

Norden, Eduard. Die Antike Kunstprosa. 5th ed. 2 vols. Darmstadt, 1958.

Perrin, Norman. Rediscovering the Teaching of Jesus. New York, 1967.

Peters, Curt. Das Diatessaron Tatians. Rome, 1939.

Plummer, Alfred. A Critical and Exegetical Commentary on the Gospel according to St. Luke. New York, 1896.

Preuschen, Erwin. Antilegomena. 2nd ed. Giessen, 1905.

Quasten, Johannes. Patrology. 3 vols. Westminster, Maryland, 1951-60.

Quispel, G. "Discussion of Judaic Christianity," VC 22 (1968), 81-93.

_____. "L'Évangile selon Thomas et les Clementines," VC 12 (1958), 181-96.

_____. "L'Évangile selon Thomas et le Diatessaron," VC 13 (1959), 87-117.

_____. "L'Évangile selon Thomas et le 'Texte Occidental' du nouveau Testament," VC 14 (1960), 204-15.

_____. "The Gospel of Thomas and the New Testament," VC 11 (1957), 189-207.

_____. "The Syrian Thomas and the Syrian Macarius," VC 18 (1964), 226-35.

Rehm, Bernhard. "Clemens Romans II," Reallexikon für Antike und Christentum 3 (1957), 197-206.

_____. "Zur Entstehung der pseudoclementinischen Schriften," ZNW 37 (1938), 77-184.

Resch, Alfred. Agrapha: Aussercanonische Schriftfragmente. 2nd ed. Darmstadt, 1967.

_____. Aussercanonische Paralleltexte zu den Evangelien. 3 vols. TU 10,1-3. Leipzig, 1893-97.

Ropes, J. H. Die Sprüche Jesu. Leipzig, 1896.

Sanday, William. The Gospels in the Second Century. London, 1876.

Schmidt, Carl. Studien zu den Pseudo-Clementinen. TU 46,1.
     Leipzig, 1929.

Schmidtke, Alfred. Neue Fragmente und Untersuchungen zu den
     judenchristlichen Evangelien. TU 37,1. Leipzig, 1911.

Schoeps, H. J. Aus frühchristlicher Zeit, religionsgeschicht-
     liche Untersuchungen. Tübingen, 1950.

_____. "Iranisches in den Pseudoklementinen," ZNW 51
     (1960), 1-10.

_____. Die Tempelzerstörung des Jahres 70 in der jüdi-
     schen Religionsgeschichte. Coniectanea Neotestamentica 6.
     Uppsala, 1942.

_____. Theologie und Geschichte des Judenchristentums.
     Tübingen, 1949.

Schwartz, E. "Unzeitgemässe Beobachtungen zu den Clementinen,"
     ZNW 31 (1932), 151-99.

Semisch, Karl. Die apostolischen Denkwürdigkeit des Märtyrers
     Justinus. Hamburg, 1848.

Siouville, A. "Introduction aux Homélies clémentines," Revue de
     l'Histoire des Religions 100 (1929), 142-204.

Strack, Hermann L. and Paul Billerbeck. Kommentar zum Neuen
     Testament aus Talmud und Midrasch. 2nd ed. 6 vols.
     München, 1956-61.

Strecker, Georg. Das Judenchristentum in den Pseudoklementinen.
     TU 70. Berlin, 1958.

Streeter, B. H. The Four Gospels. London, 1924.

Suggs, M. J. "The Use of Patristic Evidence in the Search for a
     Primitive New Testament Text," NTS 4 (1957-58), 139-47.

_____. Wisdom, Christology, and Law in Matthew's Gospel.
     Cambridge, Mass., 1970.

Thomas, J. B. "Les Ébionites baptistes," RHE 30 (1934),
     257-96.

_____. Le mouvement baptiste en Palestine et Syrie.
     Gembloux, 1935.

Uhlhorn, Gerhard. Die Homilien und Recognitionen des Clemens
     Romanus, nach ihrem Ursprung und Inhalt dargestellt.
     Göttingen, 1854.

Waitz, Hans. "Das Evangelium der zwölf Apostel," ZNW 13 (1912),
     338-48; 14 (1913), 38-64, 117-32.

_____. "Die Lösung des pseudoclementinischen Problems?"
     ZKG 59 (1940), 304-41.

_____. "Neues zur Text- und Literarkritik der Pseudo-
     klementinen?" ZKG 52 (1933), 305-18.

190

_____. "Pseudoklementinische Probleme," ZKG 50 (1931), 186-94.

_____. Die Pseudoklementinen, Homilien und Rekognitionen. TU 25,4. Leipzig, 1904.

_____. "Die Pseudoklementinen und ihre Quellenschriften," ZNW 28 (1929), 241-72.

Windisch, Hans. "Die Sprüche vom Eingehen in das Reich Gottes," ZNW 27 (1928), 163-92.

Winter, Paul. "Matthew xi 27 and Luke x 22 from the First to the Fifth Century. Reflections on the Development of the Text," NovT 1 (1956-57), 112-49.

Wright, Leon E. Alterations of the Words of Jesus as Quoted in the Literature of the Second Century. Cambridge, Mass., 1952.

Ysebaert, J. Greek Baptismal Terminology. Nijmegen, 1962.

INDEX

(The numbers in the right hand columns refer to the numbers
of the sayings in the thesis and not to page numbers.)

191

History of Research

In the history of research on the sayings of Jesus or the
gospel material in the Pseudo-Clementine Homilies (= H) in the
eighteenth and nineteenth centuries attention was focused on two
main points: (1) How does one explain the material which
deviates from the canonical wording or has no parallel in the
canonical gospels? and (2) How does one explain the relationship
of H and Justin when they cite material with the same deviations
from the canonical text? In the case of the first question a
Jewish-Christian gospel was often proposed, while others spoke
more vaguely of the non-canonical sources such as apocryphal
traditions, oral traditions, or a post-synoptic uncanonical
gospel. There was also debate as to whether the canonical
gospels had been used directly or not and which of them had been
used (with the most agreement that Matthew and Luke had been
used). In the case of the second question concerning the relation of H and Justin both Credner and Hilgenfeld saw the common
use of a Jewish-Christian gospel, while W. Sanday suggested the
possibility of the common use of a gospel harmony, thus calling
attention to the fact that sayings common to H and Justin often
reveal harmonistic features. Unfortunately, no one else really
picked up this point and developed it further in the case of H.

In the twentieth century Hans Waitz was the first to
attempt to distinguish clearly the sources and layers of H and
to try to decide which sayings belonged to each and what were
the characteristics of each. His most important results for our
purposes were: (1) the identification of a Kerygmata Petrou
source (= KP) which, he believed, took its gospel material from
the Gospel of the Ebionites (known to Epiphanius in Pan. 30),
and (2) his argument that the KP source had undergone an anti-
Marcionite reworking, using Justin's (lost) Syntagma adversus
Marcionem (= A-M) as a source. Thus he accounted for the gospel
material common to H and Justin and deviating from the reading
of the canonical texts.

H. J. Schoeps basically followed Waitz's lead, adding one
additional conjecture: KP had used not the Gospel of the
Ebionites directly, but the (lost) "commentary" of Symmachus,
presumedly a commentary on the Ebionite Gospel. Georg Strecker,
on the other hand, sees in the gospel material of H the use of
all four gospels and uncanonical material (with no attempt to
identify its source), explains harmonistic material by assuming
that it has been quoted from memory (as if that explained it),
and sees no direct relationship between H and Justin.

The Sayings in H

My research has led me to analyze the sayings of Jesus in H
under the following headings: (1) harmonistic and conflated
sayings, (2) sayings based on a canonical gospel, (3) sayings
based on the Old Testament, and (4) Agrapha.

The study of the harmonistic texts revealed that there are
harmonistic readings common to H and Justin (known to other
fathers as well). But these do not seem best explained by a
hypothesis of H's using Justin (as Waitz thought); rather the
relationship is most often one for which a common source for H
and Justin is the best explanation. The nature of the source,
to judge from this group of sayings, is a harmony of sayings of
Jesus based at least on Matthew and Luke with some evidence of
Marcan influence at times. But the sayings with harmonistic
characteristics belong both to Waitz's KP and A-M layers, thus
calling in question his hypotheses regarding the KP and A-M
layers.

The chapter on sayings based on one canonical gospel found
examples from all four canonical gospels. Most were from
Matthew and Luke, one perhaps showed Marcan influence in a saying with a Matthean parallel, and two were from the Gospel of
John. The Johannine sayings do not prove a use of the Gospel of
John for the harmonized source since they reflect no harmonistic
features and could be attributed to the redaction of the Homilist
(so Waitz). But do the synoptic sayings indicate a direct use
of the synoptic gospels or could they also have come from the
harmonistic source? Nothing would prevent most of them from
coming from the harmonistic source. A few things point in favor
of it: (1) a few had parallels with Justin in readings that
deviated from the canonical texts, (2) a few of them also seemed
to reflect wording from parallel sayings in another synoptic

gospel, although it was not as clear as those listed in the previous chapter, and (3) the introductions to some of the sayings indicated that one had created his own introduction to the saying rather than taken it from its context in the synoptic gospels.

The chapter on sayings based on the Old Testament showed three or four such sayings. The wording of the sayings is given in H according to their OT (LXX) wording. Even in cases in which there is a citation of the OT text in the gospels, it is cited in H according to its OT wording instead of that in the gospels. One of the sayings cited Dt. 18.15ff. in a form very close to that found in Acts 3.

The chapter on Agrapha found eight such sayings in H, two of which were known to Justin and one to Clement. Another found a parallel in Aphraates and the Manichaean Psalms. That some of them (all of them?) could have belonged to the harmonized sayings source used by Justin seems probable enough. The identification of another source (such as a Jewish-Christian gospel) can neither be established nor is it required.

Conclusions

The problem of relating the sayings of Jesus in H to the various sources or layers of H is one that could not be fully dealt with since it presupposes detailed source analysis of H that goes beyond the scope of this thesis. However, it can be argued that on the basis of the results of this thesis Waitz's theory of a KP source which used the Gospel of the Ebionites and its anti-Marcionite reworking (= A-M) which used Justin's Syn. adv. Marc. must be seriously doubted. For the sayings in H (or KP) have no real parallels with those in the Gospel of the Ebionites (= EE) found in Epiphanius (Pan. 30) and differ from EE in containing only sayings, while EE also contained narrative material. Further, it was concluded that Waitz could not successfully distinguish between the characteristics of the sayings he attributed to KP from those he attributed to A-M. Nor should the relationship of harmonistic sayings and other sayings which deviated from the canonical text(s) in H and Justin be explained by H's use of Justin, but by a common source.

A large portion of the sayings in H could easily belong to a single harmonized sayings source known to Justin (composed by him?) and other fathers. But whether it was the author of a

198

source called the Kerygmata Petrou or the author of the Grundschrift (the writing underlying the Pseudo-Clementine Homilies
and Recognitions) who made use of this source was not finally
decided in this study. I would lean toward the author of the
Grundschrift (whom Waitz put in Rome around 220-230 for the composition of his work).

The significance of this study for the history of gospel
tradition in the early church is that it further confirms the
use of a harmonized sayings source for Justin (as Bellinzoni has
already demonstrated) and probably other early fathers (2 Clement, perhaps the Didache 1.3-2.1, Clement of Alexandria, Origen,
and possibly others), and it adds additional material to the
content of such a source. Finally, it once again shows the
freedom with which an author of the late second or early third
centuries, in this case with a Jewish-Christian outlook, could
adapt the sayings of Jesus to his own purposes.